POSTCARD HISTORY SERIES

Bozeman and the Gallatin Valley

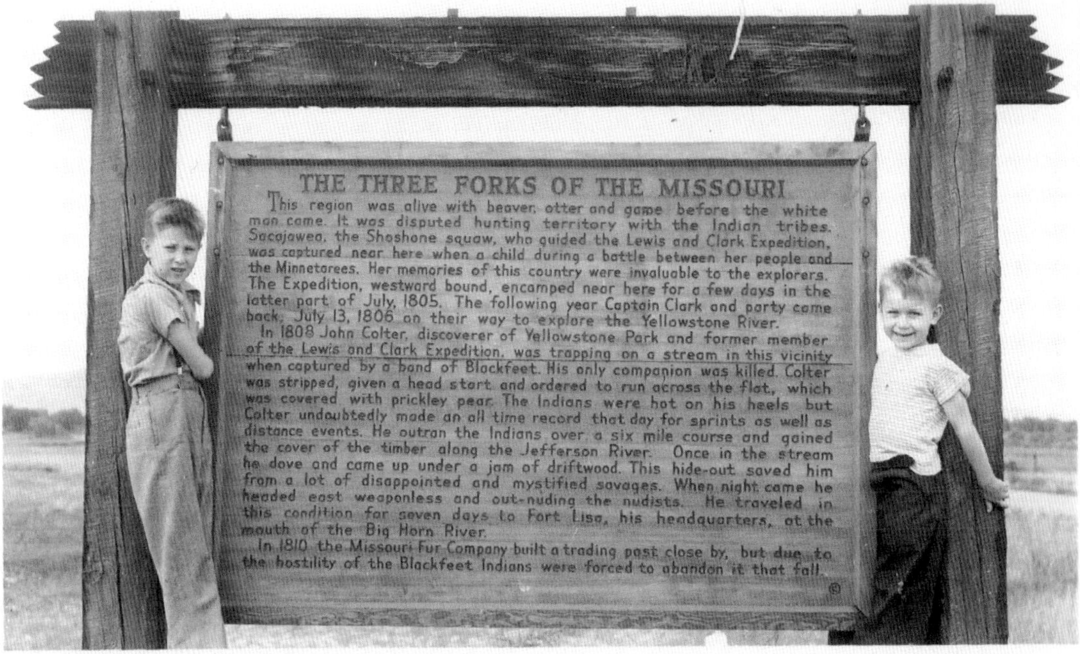

THREE FORKS OF THE MISSOURI ROAD SIGN. Two unidentified lads showcase a Montana road sign, seen in this *c.* 1945 real-photo postcard. This sign was located along Highway 10 near Three Forks in northwest Gallatin County. These historic signs decorated Montana highways before the advent of the freeway system, and Bob Fletcher, a Montana Department of Highways employee, wrote the roadside histories. (Courtesy of Steve and Robin Hamilton.)

ON THE FRONT COVER. "The Five Best in Bozeman"—that is how the caption on this *c.* 1920 real-photo postcard describes these five cowboys at the Bozeman Roundup. From left to right are Coleman, Coates, Tegland, Canutt, and Lucas. The Bozeman Roundup, which included a parade, rodeo, and Wild West show, was held in Bozeman from 1919 to 1926. (Courtesy of the author.)

ON THE BACK COVER. Five cowgirls stop for a smile and a picture, as shown on this *c.* 1920 real-photo postcard image taken at the Bozeman Roundup. From left to right are Rose Smith, Donna Glover, Bonnie McCarroll, Mabel Strickland, and Fox Hastings. All five of these cowgirls were highly regarded on the early-day women's rodeo circuit. (Photograph by Ralph R. Doubleday, traveling rodeo photographer; courtesy of the author.)

POSTCARD HISTORY SERIES

Bozeman and the Gallatin Valley

Tom Mulvaney

ARCADIA
PUBLISHING

ISBN 978-0-7385-7084-6

Published by Arcadia Publishing
Charleston, South Carolina

Printed in the United States of America

Library of Congress Control Number: 2009924708

For all general information contact Arcadia Publishing at:
Telephone 843-853-2070
Fax 843-853-0044
E-mail sales@arcadiapublishing.com
For customer service and orders:
Toll-Free 1-888-313-2665

Visit us on the Internet at www.arcadiapublishing.com

Dedicated to two longtime "Bobcats" who have had a positive influence on the lives of many people (including mine): former Montana State University track and cross-country coach Rob Stark and former Montana State University alumni director and sportscaster Dan Rieder.

Contents

ACKNOWLEDGMENTS

Thanks to John Russell, Ann Butterfield, Rachel Phillips, Kay McAllister, and Harriet DeWitt at the Pioneer Museum in Bozeman for their superb historical expertise and friendly assistance; Lory Morrow, Becca Kohl, Barbara Pepper-Rotness, Brian Shovers, and the rest of the library and photograph archive staff of the Montana Historical Society; Sandy Hart of the Broken Hart Ranch south of Gallatin Gateway; Carol Pinkerton Chambers of Three Forks, whose family was among the earliest settlers in the Gallatin Valley in the 1860s, for her information on the dude ranches and businesses in the Gallatin Canyon; Terri Sullivan, who worked for her father at the AMC Photo Studio store in downtown Bozeman, for sharing her Main Street knowledge; Mike Yawitz, writer for the *Bozeman Chronicle*; Debra Youngberg and Renee Koenig of the Belgrade Chamber of Commerce and Greta Deichmann of the Gallatin County Clerk and Recorder Office for offering their support and information to this project.

Thanks to my Bozeman and Gallatin Valley collecting friends R. Dale Beland; Costas, Giles, and Sally Cokelet; Jack and Susan Davis; Doug and Suzanne Dwyer; Jacki Erickson; Bob and Annette Evans; Steve and Robin Hamilton; Ken and Pat Hamlin; Ron Iverson; Debbie Moro; and Ron Tobias for sharing their knowledge and their postcard images to make this a better book.

Special thanks to the following: Ron Iverson, a historical trailblazer who wrote the first comprehensive history of Belgrade in 1965, *The Princess of the Prairie*; Steve Hamilton, who made his expansive personal library available to me for researching images; Ken Hamlin, who shared much information along with choice cards from his collection; and, especially, my longtime friends Jack and Susan Davis, who were instrumental in promoting the historical importance of postcards, photographs, and paper memorabilia in Montana over the past two decades. Their paper store, located on Peach Street in Bozeman, was legendary as one of the finest shops of its type in the entire West during the 1990s. Susan donated her comprehensive Gallatin Valley postcard collection to the Bozeman Pioneer Museum, now there for all to view.

Thanks also goes to Nels Sanddal of Bozeman, a friend and classmate from our school days. Nels calmly talked me down when I found myself trapped on a cliff face. If not for Nels, I may not have been around to write this book. Thanks to Ove Braskerud, who traded me many great Gallatin Valley cards over three decades; John Poultney and the rest of the staff from Arcadia Publishing for their expertise and technical assistance; and, finally, my wife, Jill, and my mother, Betty Mulvaney, for their unconditional backing. Unless otherwise noted, all images appear courtesy of the author.

Introduction

Many fine books have been written about Bozeman and the Gallatin Valley, some strongly history oriented and some featuring photographic illustrations as the highlighting feature of the book. Phyllis Smith, Grace Bates, and Merrill Burlingame wrote three books that I found particularly good from a history standpoint. Three books I found to be wonderfully illustrated were the two-volume Gallatin collections published by the *Bozeman Chronicle* and the Arcadia-published book on Bozeman by Denise Glaser Malloy and the Pioneer Museum. The titles and publishing details of these books are listed in the bibliography at the back of this book. The book you are now reading will hopefully fit in the latter type and does have an interesting distinction: all of the images—yes, every one of them—come from a picture postcard. Some of the postcard illustrations in this book will be found in other publications, but most of them have never been published before in book or magazine form. This is a look at Bozeman and the Gallatin Valley as you have never seen her.

Some Postcard Collecting Basics

For the reader who is new to the world of postcards, a brief overview is in order. Postcard collectors collect mainly for the image shown on the postcard. The old stamp on the back of a mailed card can be fun, a cancellation marking on the back is collectible if it was marked from a scarce post office, and the message written on the back can often be entertaining, but a postcard collector collects based on the picture or image shown on the front of the card, not what is on the back.

Most collectors collect geographically. Often this means collecting views from one's hometown or area. Some collectors may look for cards from within a county, or from a specific area of a state. Only a few serious geographical collectors try to collect an entire state, as the number of cards that qualify is immense, even for less populated states like Montana, and the cost to pursue such a wide category with any degree of seriousness requires some deep pockets.

The cards shown in this book, for the most part, represent cards that fit the geographical area of Bozeman and the Gallatin Valley, as the book's title implies. Some of the cards in chapter one, Business and Advertising, overlap between the two broad types. That is okay. An advertising card from Bozeman, for example, will be both topical (it has an advertising theme) and geographic (it is related to Bozeman).

Another way to categorize postcards involves the method in which the postcard was produced. Almost all colored postcards, and some black and white ones, were manufactured using three- or four-color printing processes. These cards are known as "printed" cards, and when they are viewed under a magnifying glass, they will show a dot pattern. The other production process is called "real photo." This type of postcard is actually a photograph developed on photosensitive paper. In the case of a postcard, it has a postcard back (the word "postcard" is typically printed on the back) and a thick paper stock to allow it to better survive the rigors of the mail. When you look at a real-photo postcard (RPPC for short) under a magnifying glass, there are no dots. Almost all RPPCs will enlarge nicely and not lose clarity, contrary to the printed postcard, and most RPPCs are black and white. Those that are colored were individually hand tinted by a person.

Another way to characterize cards is by age. The earliest cards used to illustrate this book came from about 1905 to 1907. Most of the cards in this book were from the 1907 to 1915 era, often referred to as the "golden era of postcards," and are of the real-photo type. The first chapter is an exception, as most of the advertising cards are the printed type.

Cards made in the 1935–1955 era often have paper stock that has a linen cross-stitch pattern, if you look closely. These cards are appropriately called "linens." Most postcards made after 1955 fall under the category of photochromes and appear to be a colored photograph (but look out, if you try to enlarge one, it can lose clarity in a hurry). Only a few linen postcards are found in this book, and they appear in chapter one. And only a few photochromes are found, scattered across several chapters.

One final word about postcards—they are lots of fun to collect. And many are fun to look at. Most of you looking through this book will hopefully agree, and I hope you will have lots of fun with this book! May the postcard-collecting bug even bite a few of you!

Photographers in the Gallatin Valley

Almost every image found in this book was generated from a photograph that was originally taken by a photographer, mostly professional but a few by amateurs.

The top early-day photographers from the Gallatin Valley area that had postcards made showing their images were the Schlechten brothers, Alfred and Albert, of Bozeman; Charles Kinsey of Belgrade; and Niels Olson of Three Forks. Interestingly, F. J. Haynes and his son Jack, two of Montana's most famous postcard photographers, both of whom lived part-time in Bozeman, did not produce postcards of the Gallatin Valley area (as least none that I am aware of). Both of the Hayneses focused their attention on the vicinity in and around Yellowstone Park when they produced postcards. Another postcard photographer worthy of mention is F. Bertil Linfield of Bozeman. Albert Schlecthten sold his photography business to Linfield in 1923, and Linfield published many nice postcards over the next 30 years.

Many other photographers, professional and amateur alike, published at least a few postcards over the years. Names such as Alexander, Giles, Johnson, Rex, and Sensor will occasionally appear on postcards showing views of the Gallatin Valley. Among large-scale, out-of-state publishers whose names may appear on Gallatin Valley cards are Wesley Andrews of Baker, Oregon, and M. L. Zercher of Topeka, Kansas. These men probably hired local or traveling photographers to take pictures for them to use on postcards, as both studios published view cards from many different states, including Montana.

A Quirk Involving Bozeman Street Addresses

In researching locations for buildings and businesses in Bozeman, I discovered, after some initial confusion, a quirk in the naming of Bozeman streets prior to 1920. Main Street, which runs east to west in Bozeman, has always been the street that separates crossing avenues into north and south addresses. Do you know which avenue in Bozeman is the one that separates crossing streets into east and west addresses? The answer is Tracy Avenue. The quirk is that prior to 1920, Bozeman Avenue was the dividing avenue in Bozeman. The Bozeman Hotel, for example, was at 63 East Main Street prior to 1920. After 1920, its address became 325 East Main Street. For the purposes of this book, if an address is mentioned for a building or business shown on a pre-1920 postcard, I used the old address, the one that was in place at the time the card was made. This was done in part because some early businesses did not continue past the 1920s and their only address was the pre-1920 one. Hopefully, this explanation will help save future researchers of old Bozeman history from the confusion of how some locations seemed to radically change addresses after 1920.

Some Final Thoughts

Shortly before this book went to press, in early March 2009, a gas explosion ripped through the north side of the 200 block in Bozeman. Three buildings and at least five businesses were destroyed, and most sad, one human life was lost.

With the use of the Internet becoming quite popular by 2000, the use of postcards for advertising has seen a decline. There are still many nice scenic and street scene views being produced on postcards today. The Museum of the Rockies, located on the south edge of the MSU campus, has published many attractive and interesting postcards.

One

Advertising and Business

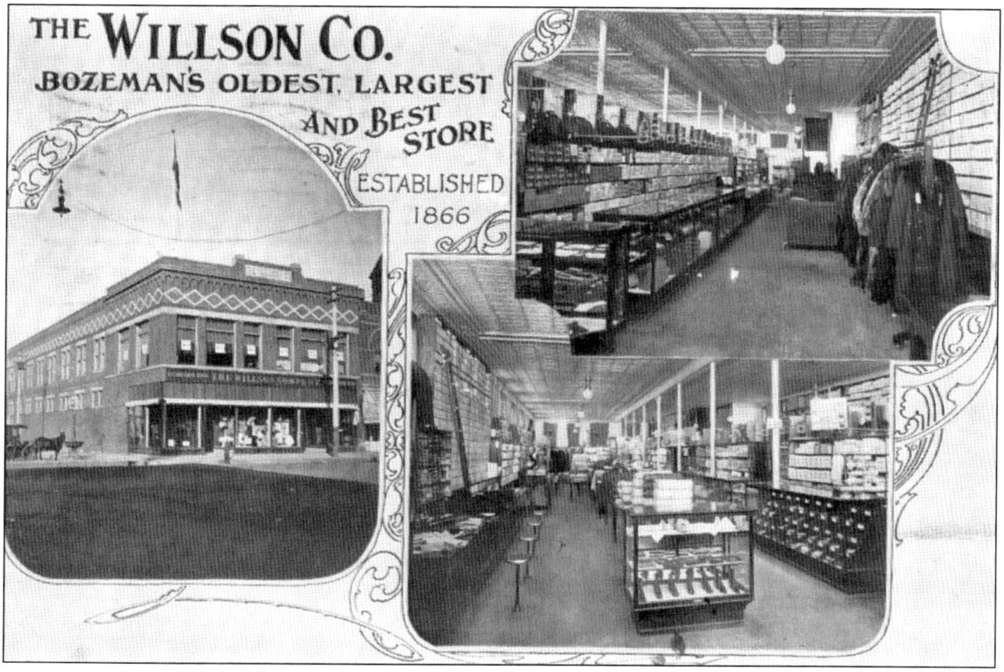

The Willson Company Store. Touting itself as "Bozeman's Oldest, Largest And Best Store—Established 1866," this prominent dry goods store was located at 35–37 West Main Street. This 1909 multi-view printed postcard shows two interior views and one exterior view. Mailed to an out-of-town patron, the message on the back includes, "You failed to give size wanted in pattern #3406."

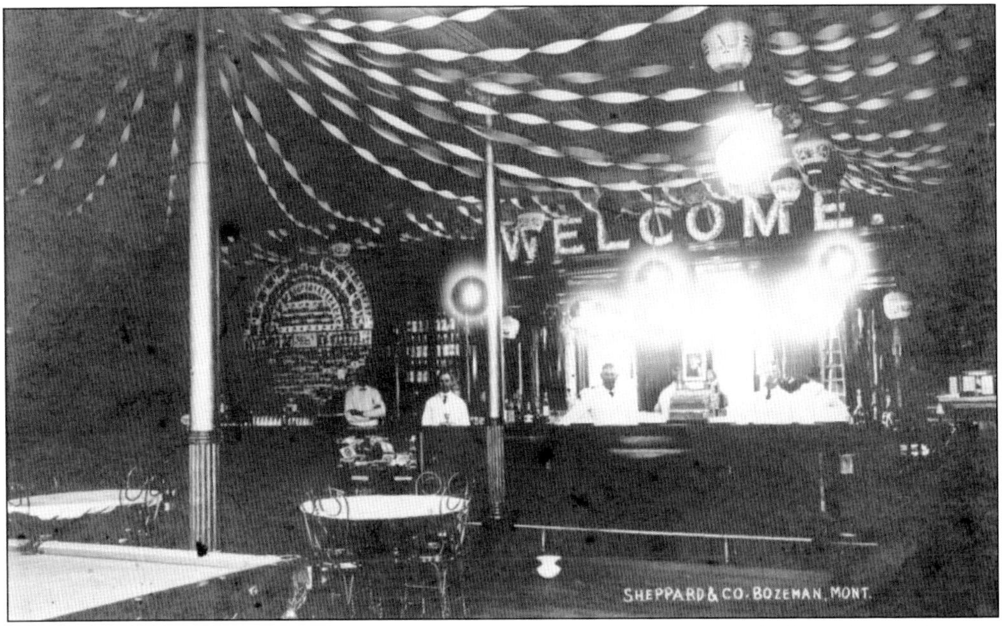

The Bozeman Bar. Located at 67 East Main Street, this *c.* 1910 real-photo image shows a well-decorated interior view with four men stationed behind the bar. Streamers twirl overhead, and a "welcome" sign is visible over the back bar mirror. The caption reads, "Sheppard & Co. Bozeman, Mont." Joseph F. Sheppard was the proprietor. (Photograph by Schlechten Studio, Bozeman, Montana; courtesy of Ken Hamlin.)

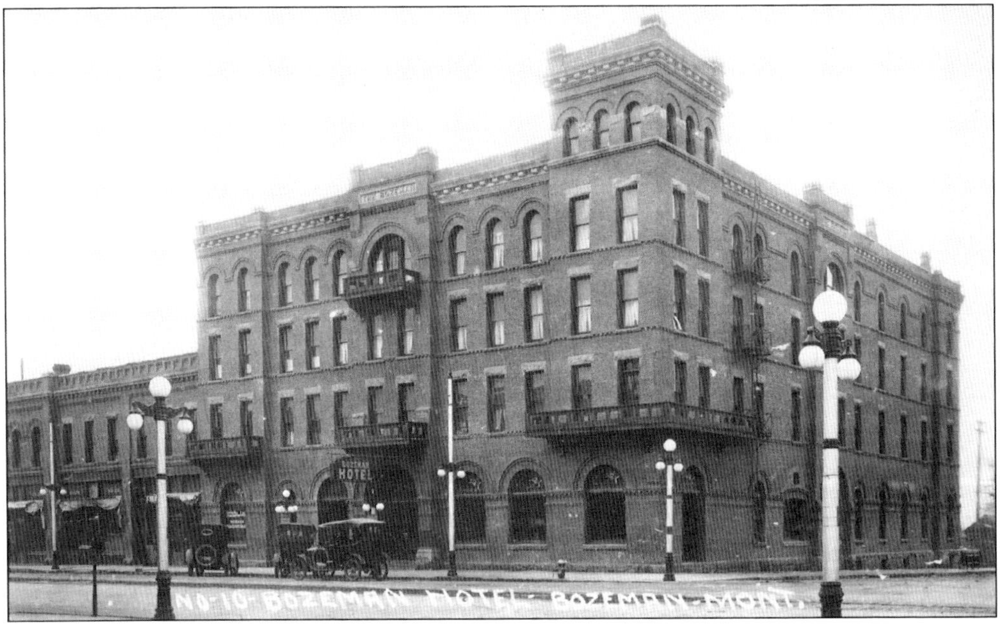

The Bozeman Hotel. Considered to be the town's best hotel from 1889 to 1929 (when the Baxter Hotel was built and took over the top spot), the Bozeman Hotel anchors the eastern end of Main Street in this *c.* 1915 real-photo postcard image. Its address at the time was 63 East Main Street. This hotel, which still stands today, was transformed into a shopping center with a variety of specialty shops and a restaurant in the mid-1970s.

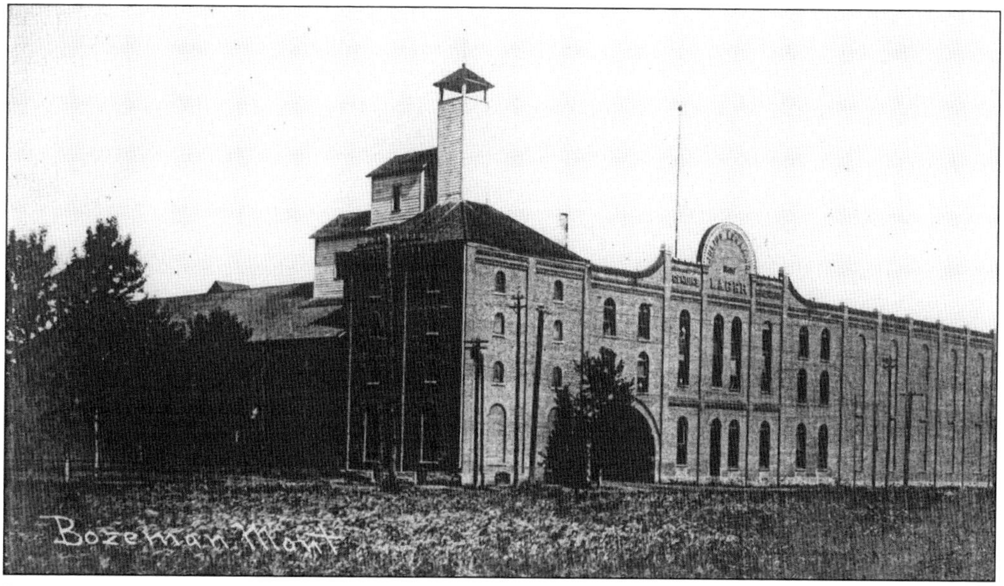

LEHRKIND BREWERY. Once the largest building in Bozeman, this impressive brick structure was constructed by Swiss brewer Julius Lehrkind. It stood at North Wallace Avenue and Plum Street. This *c.* 1915 real-photo view of the brewery was taken a few years before Prohibition forced Lehrkind to turn to other business ventures, including the marketing of coal and ice. After Prohibition, the brewery resumed and was famous for its Old Faithful Beer and lagers. (Courtesy of the Pioneer Museum Collection.)

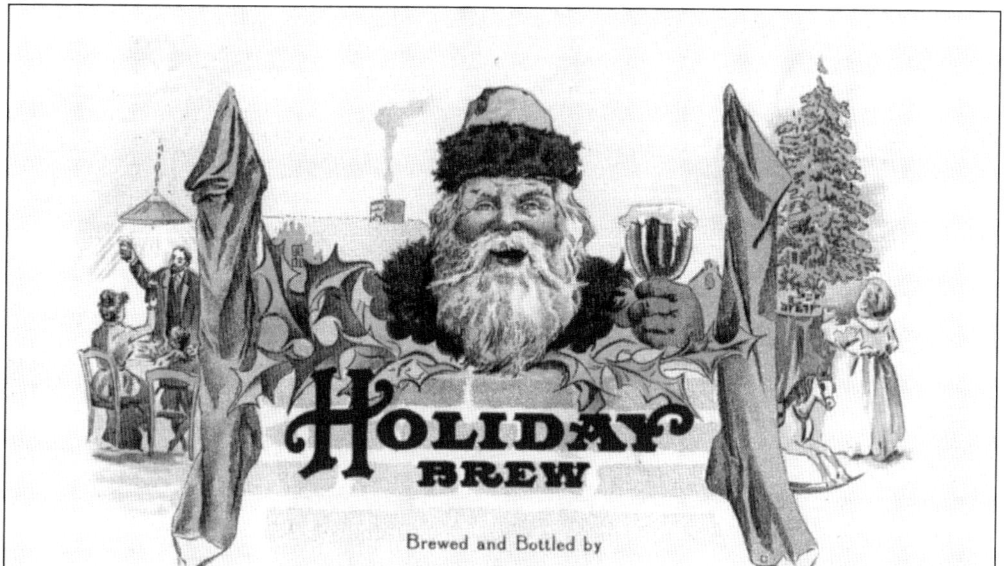

BOZEMAN BREWING COMPANY CHRISTMAS ADVERTISING. Even Santa Claus enjoyed a cold one during the Christmas season, as depicted on this 1910 postcard advertising Holiday Brew from the Bozeman Brewing Company. This postcard was mailed out by Julius Lehrkind's brewery to a local man and likely served as a Christmas greeting as well as an advertisement, based on its December 23 postmark.

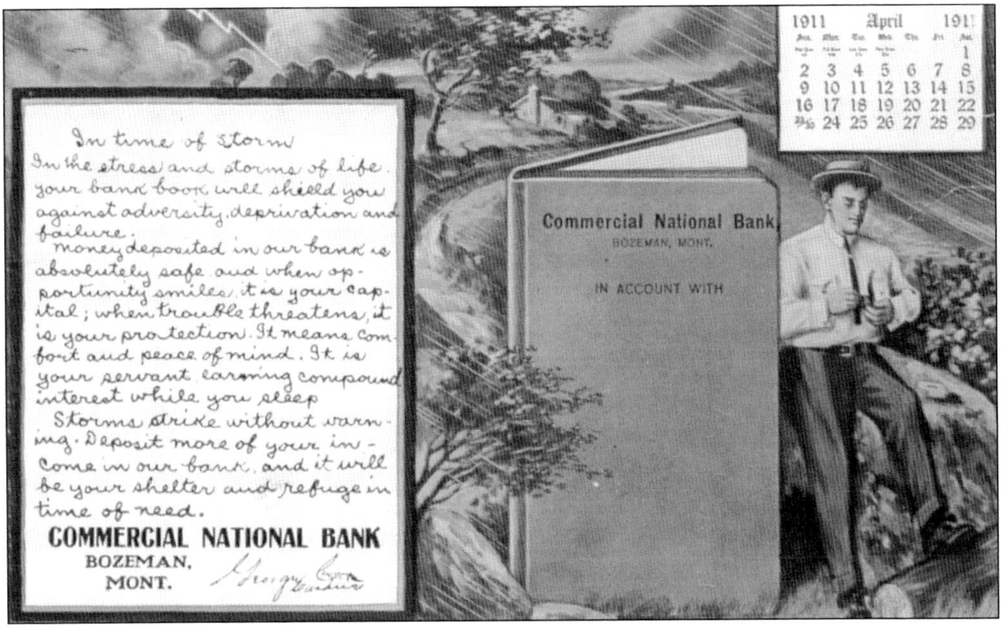

COMMERCIAL NATIONAL BANK. Part of this printed postcard reads, "Storms strike without warning. Deposit more of your income in our bank and it will be your shelter." Judging by the April 1911 calendar at the top right, this was the April card from a monthly series distributed by the bank to its customers. This bank was located at 40 West Main Street, and Joseph Kountz served as bank president. (Courtesy of Ken Hamlin.)

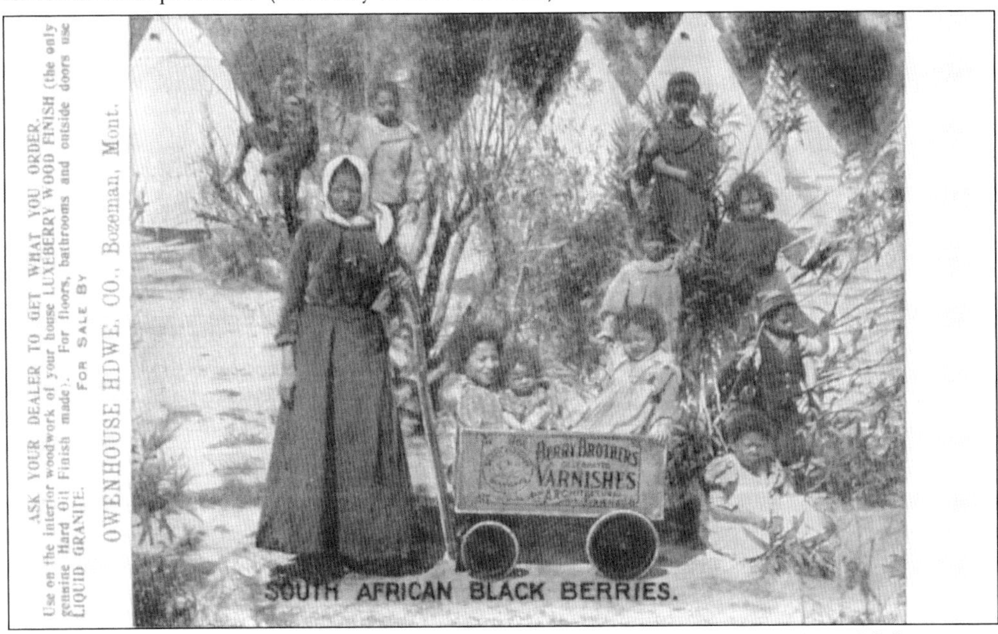

OWENHOUSE HARDWARE COMPANY STORE. Advertising "Luxeberry Wood Finish" for interior home woodwork, the illustration and caption on this *c.* 1905 printed postcard show the humor of a century ago, which occasionally included racial overtones. Captioned "South African Black Berries," the image shows three young Africans sitting in a small wooden wagon with "Berry Brothers Varnishes" printed on the side. This store was located at 108–112 West Main Street.

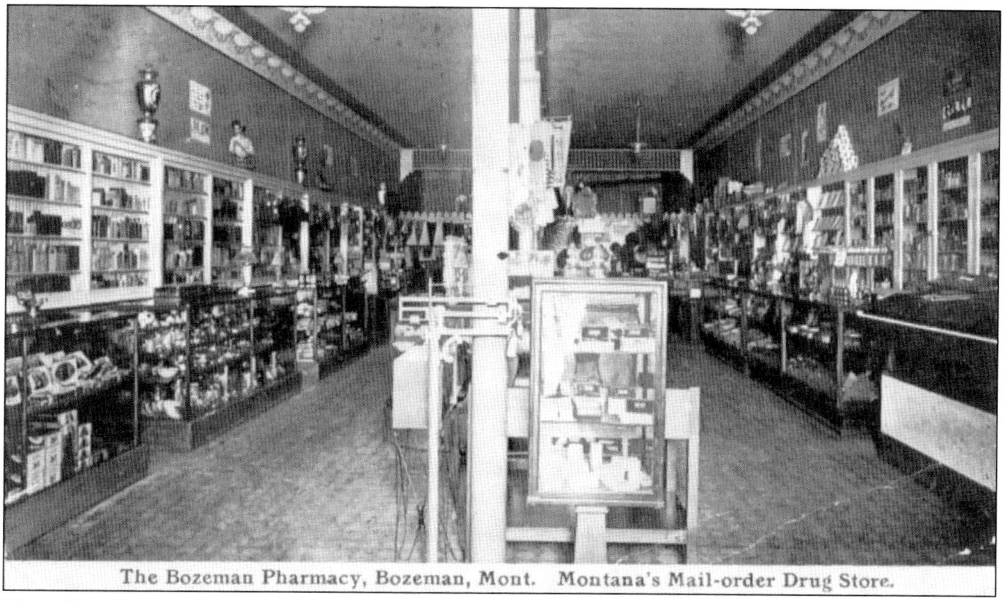

The Bozeman Pharmacy. Located at 114 West Main Street, this store was touted as "Montana's Mail-order Drug Store," according to the caption on this 1911 printed postcard. Advertising in the 1910 Bozeman Polk Directory indicated the store's efforts to market its photography wares with text that included, "Cameras, from $2.00 to $25.00 . . . All Days Are Good Days for Picture Taking." W. W. Trent was the proprietor.

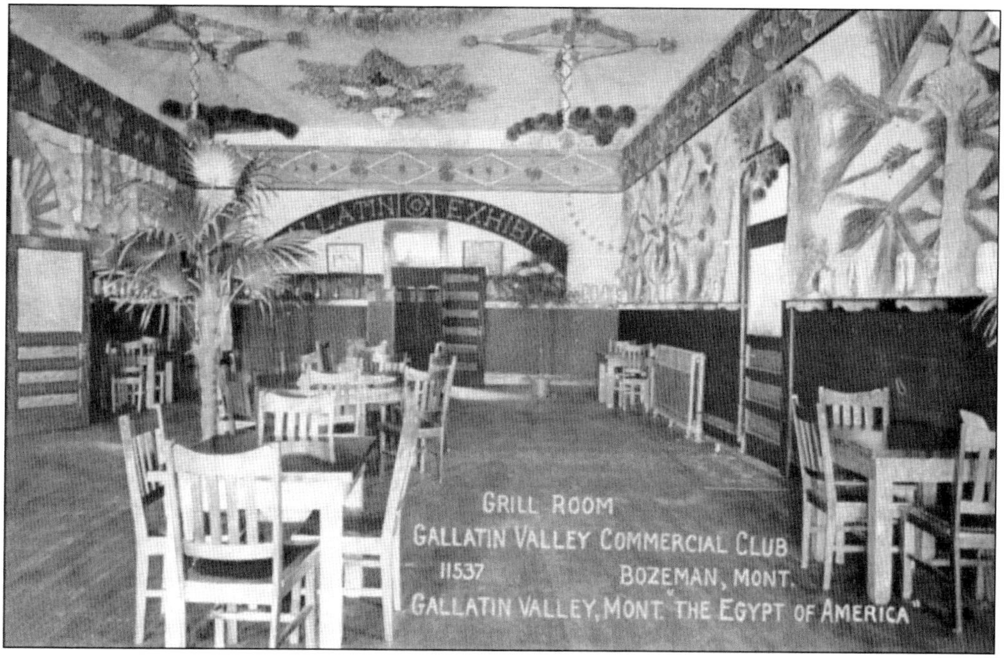

Gallatin Valley Commercial Club Interior. The caption of this *c.* 1910 printed postcard includes, "Gallatin Valley, Mont. 'The Egypt of America,'" a promotional reference to the fertile growing soil in the Gallatin Valley. This building was situated at 101 West Main Street. Albert Brandley served as president of the club, which was a precursor to the present-day chamber of commerce.

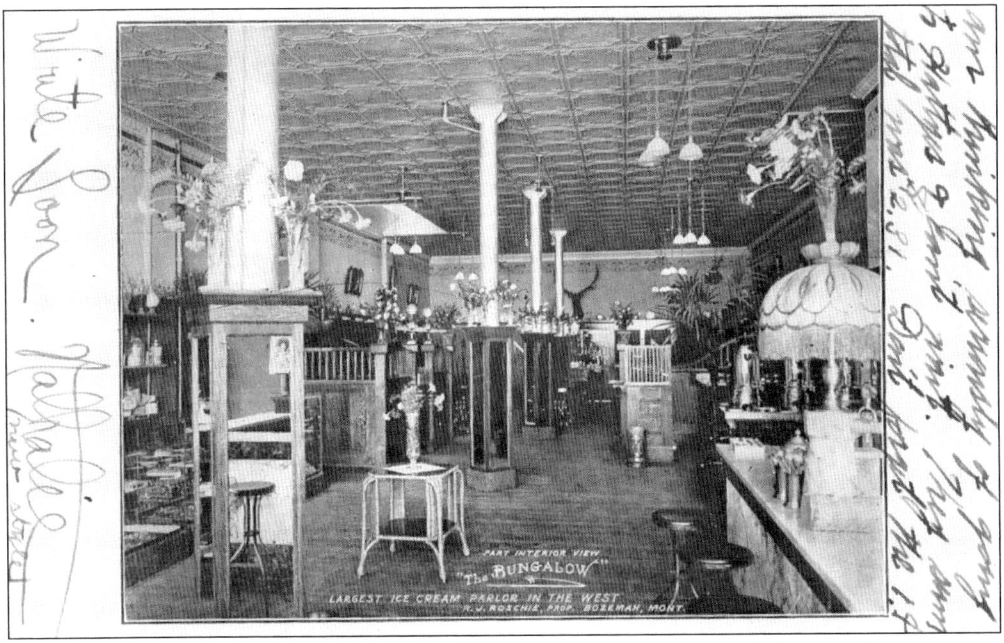

The Bungalow Ice Cream Parlor. This *c.* 1910 printed postcard shows a "Part Interior View" of the "Largest Ice Cream Parlor in the West." The soda fountain bar is visible at the far right. This upscale parlor was located at the "1st Door w. of the Postoffice," at 210 West Main Street, and R. J. Roschie was the proprietor. Advertising in the 1910 Bozeman Polk Directory included, "Mfrs. of High Grade Candies, Ice Cream and Ices, Dainty Lunches." The bungalow closed in 1994.

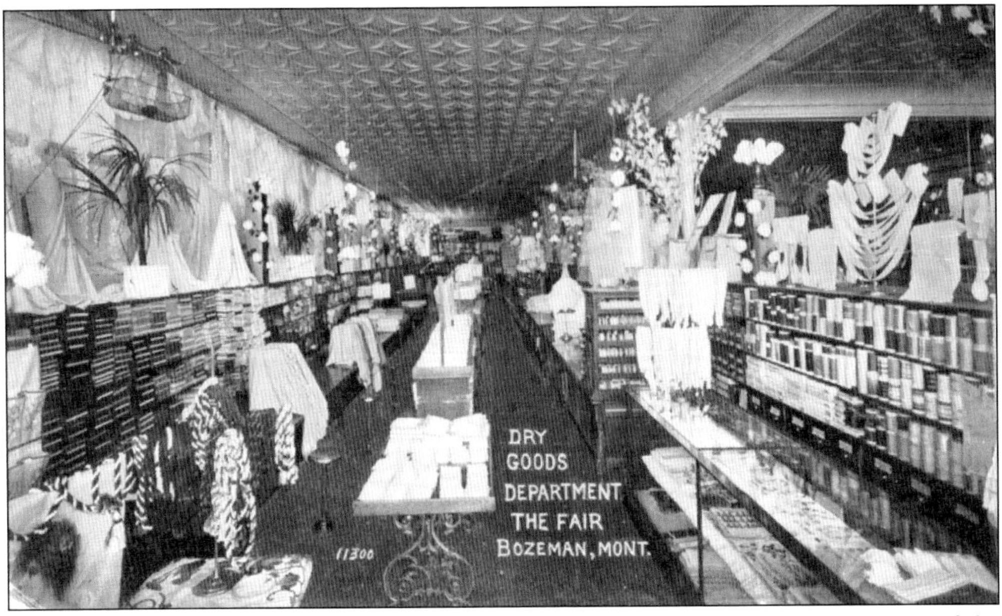

The Fair Department Store. This 1910 printed postcard shows an interior view of the dry goods department at the Fair. Located on the southwest corner of Main Street and Black Avenue, this store specialized in fabrics and textiles and carried a large selection of clothing. The Fair also carried Buster Brown shoes.

HOTEL BAXTER. This impressive art deco hotel became Bozeman's tallest building when it was constructed in 1929, and it remains so today from its location at 105 West Main Street. Text printed on the back of this *c.* 1940 linen advertising postcard states, "'Montana's Pacemaker'—100 Outside Rooms—10 Apartments. Coffee Shop, Private Dining Rooms, Ballroom, The Robin Lounge, Studios of Radio Station KRBM. Mac Nab Hotel Company, Operators. Robin MacNab, Resident Mgr."

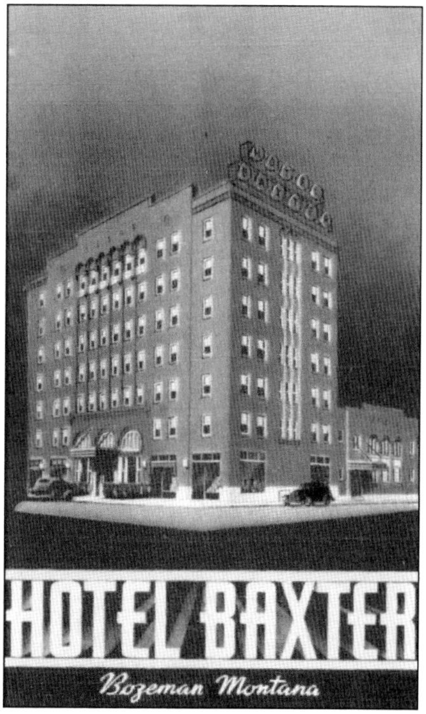

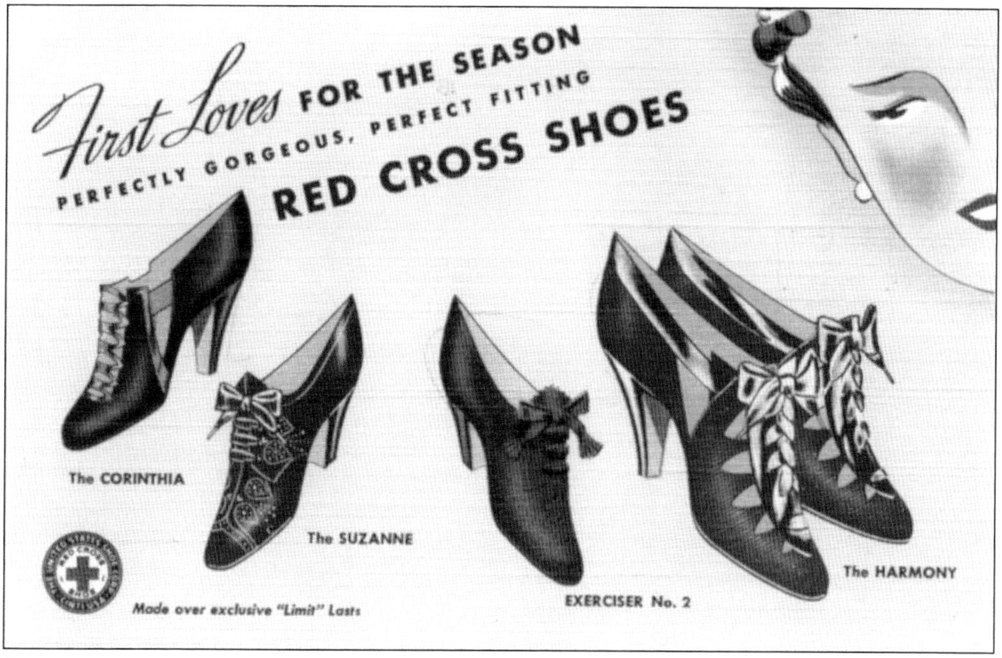

CHAMBERS-FISHER COMPANY SHOE ADVERTISING. Red Cross Shoes were a popular brand of women's shoes in the 1930s. Text printed on the back of this 1938 linen advertising postcard states, "We predict a case of love-at-first-sight when you see these brilliant new Red Cross Shoes . . . Now only $6.85—Chambers-Fisher Co.—Bozeman, Montana." Located at 7–11 West Main Street, this store was touted as "Bozeman's Leading Department Store." (Courtesy of Ken Hamlin.)

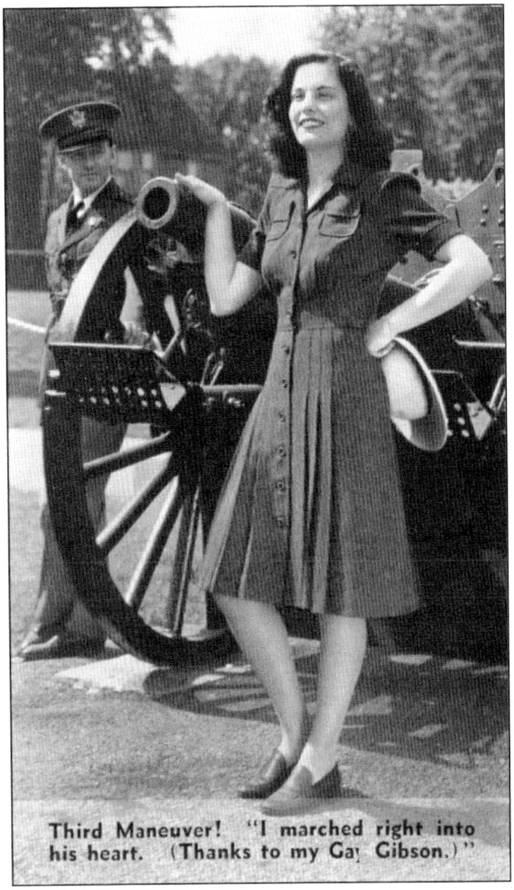

RIDDLE'S WOMEN'S CLOTHING STORE ADVERTISING. Located at 5 East Main Street, this store employed clever advertising themes on its postcards relating to America's military focus at the onset of World War II. A model in a Gay Gibson–brand dress wins a look of approval from her man in uniform in each of these images. Both cards were postmarked from Bozeman in August 1941, just months before the Pearl Harbor attack. (Both courtesy of Ken Hamlin.)

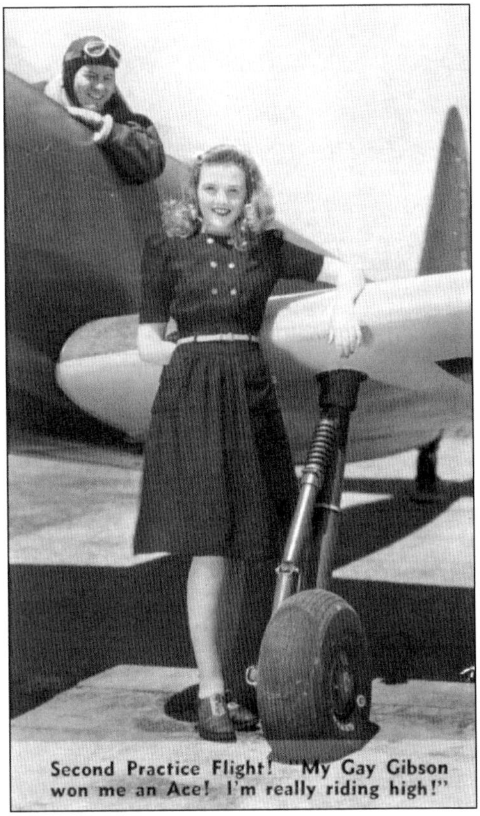

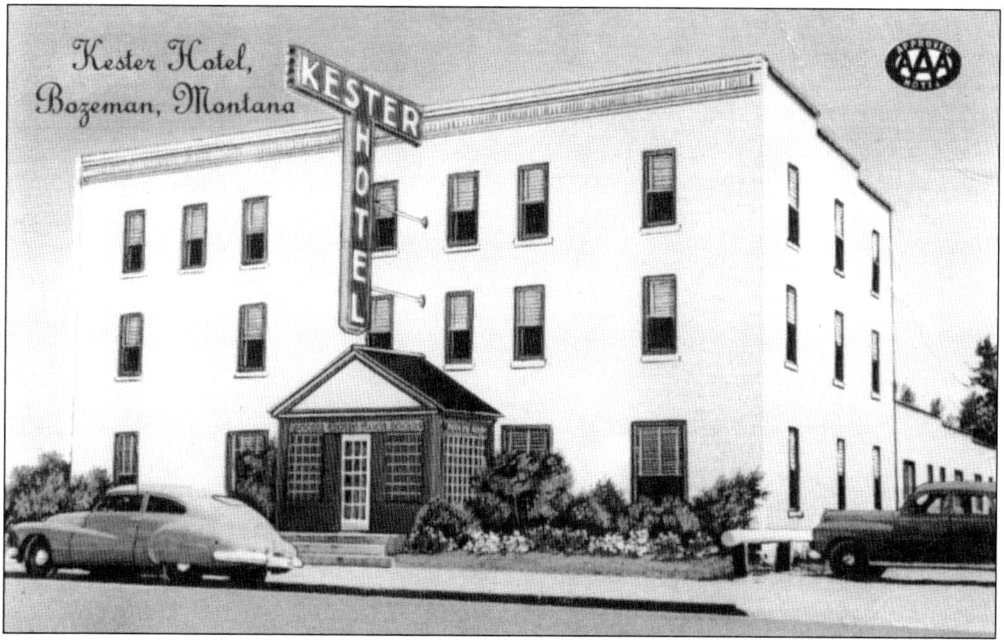

KESTER HOTEL. Located at 440 East Main Street, the Kester Hotel is featured in this *c.* 1950 linen advertising postcard. Text printed on the back includes, "Nicely Furnished, Spacious Ground Floor—Rooms all with Phone and Soft Water." Alma Kester Gebo and Homer Gebo were the proprietors. The card included a Triple A logo designation.

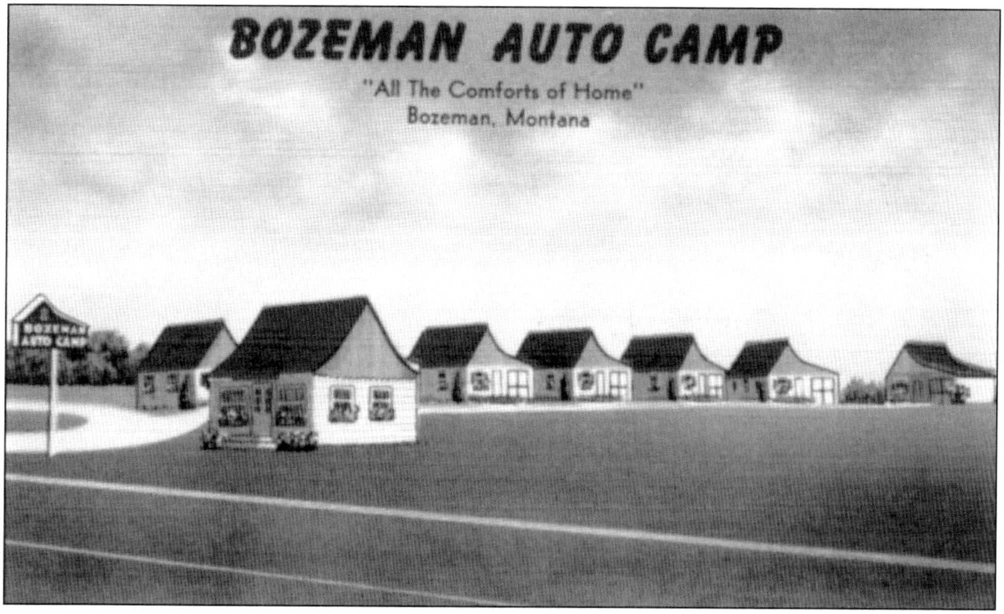

BOZEMAN AUTO CAMP. This *c.* 1940 linen advertising postcard shows small cabins providing "All the Comforts of Home." Bozeman and the Gallatin Valley were emerging as a tourist destination, and most of the courts and auto camps (the word "motel" was just coming into use) were run by local people. Text on the back of this card includes, "At the Entrance of Scenic Bozeman Canyon—Leading to Lewis and Clark Divide. U.S. Highway No. 10, East of Bozeman . . . Forest Noel, Proprietor."

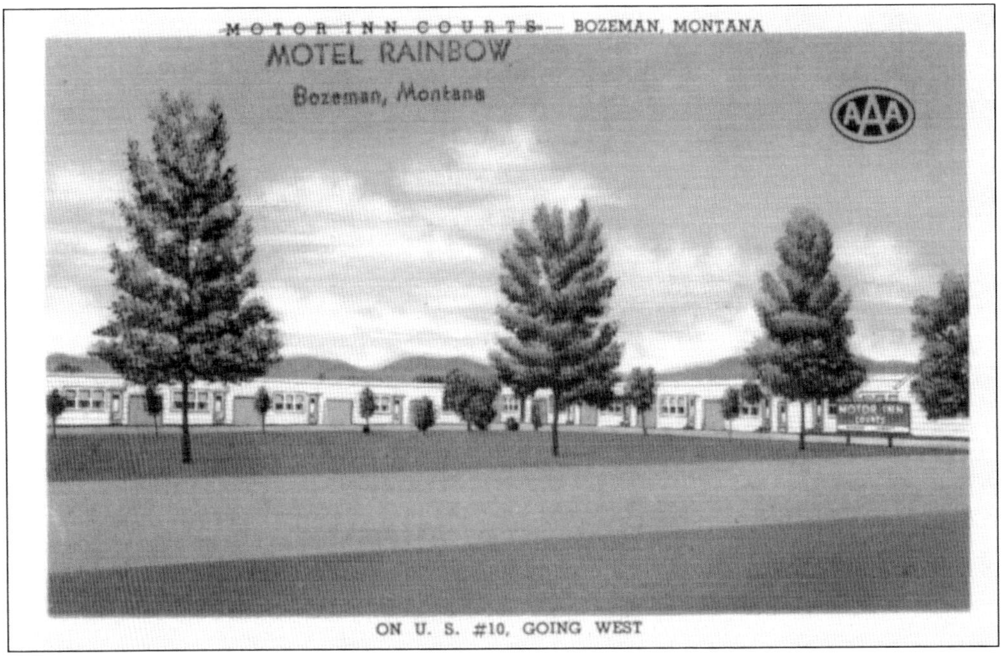

MOTEL RAINBOW (MOTOR INN COURTS). Located at 510 North Seventh Avenue, the Rainbow Motel is still in operation today. This linen advertising postcard, printed in 1951, indicates the motel's previous name was Motor Inn Courts and that Paul Doran was the owner-manager. The name change to Motel Rainbow took place after 1954, resulting in the use of an overstamp on this postcard to note the change.

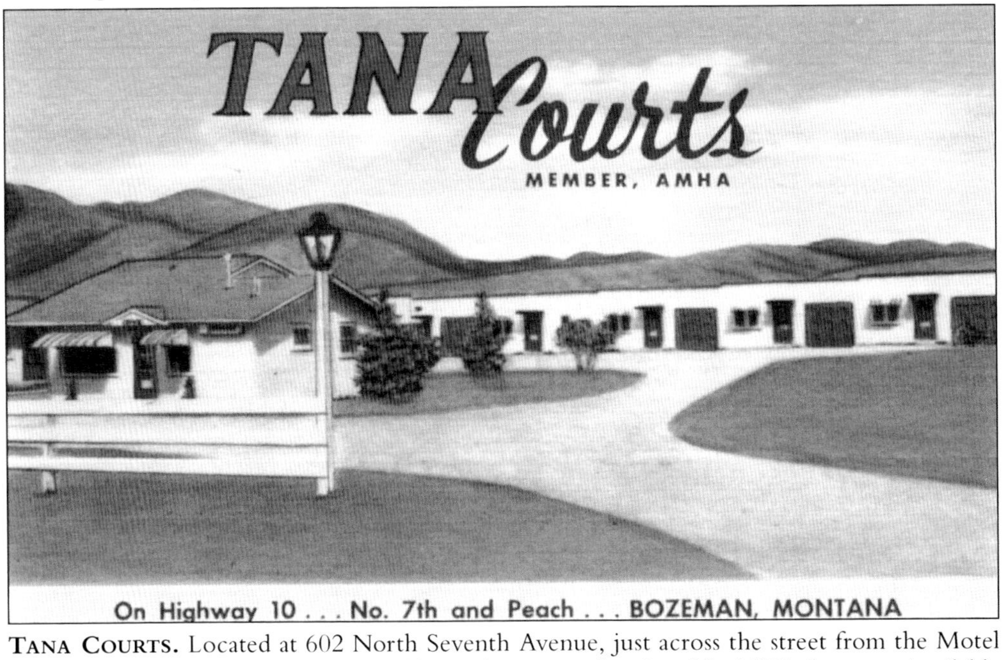

TANA COURTS. Located at 602 North Seventh Avenue, just across the street from the Motel Rainbow, Tana Courts advertised itself as "Clean—Modern" and had "Kitchenettes Available with Refrigerators." John Bareither was the proprietor at the time this *c.* 1950 linen advertising postcard was published.

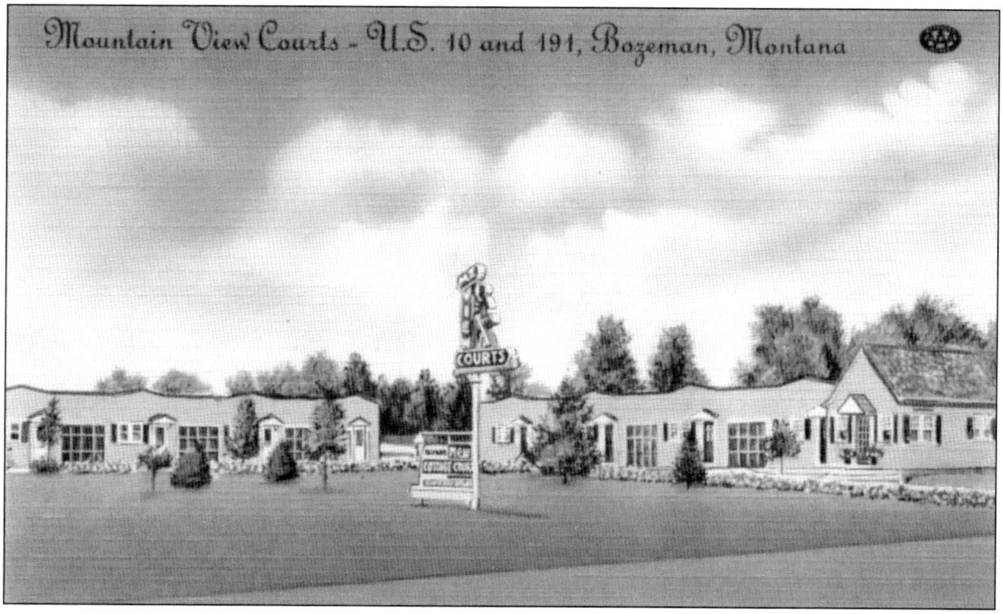

Mountain View Courts. This linen advertising postcard, postmarked from Bozeman in 1953, has text on the back billing the Mountain View Courts as "Bozeman's Finest Motel" and "Gallatin way to Yellowstone Park." Located at 1010 East Main Street, this was originally an auto camp, and it later became the Mountain View Motel. Noel Simmons was the proprietor at the time this card was used.

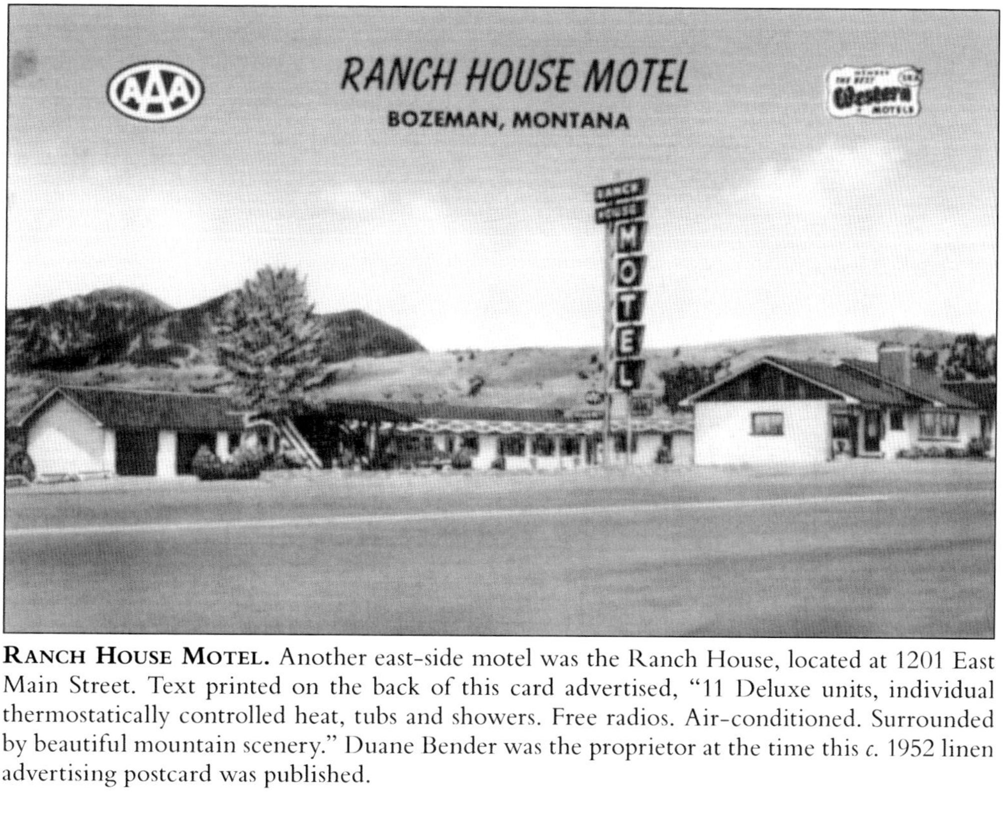

Ranch House Motel. Another east-side motel was the Ranch House, located at 1201 East Main Street. Text printed on the back of this card advertised, "11 Deluxe units, individual thermostatically controlled heat, tubs and showers. Free radios. Air-conditioned. Surrounded by beautiful mountain scenery." Duane Bender was the proprietor at the time this *c.* 1952 linen advertising postcard was published.

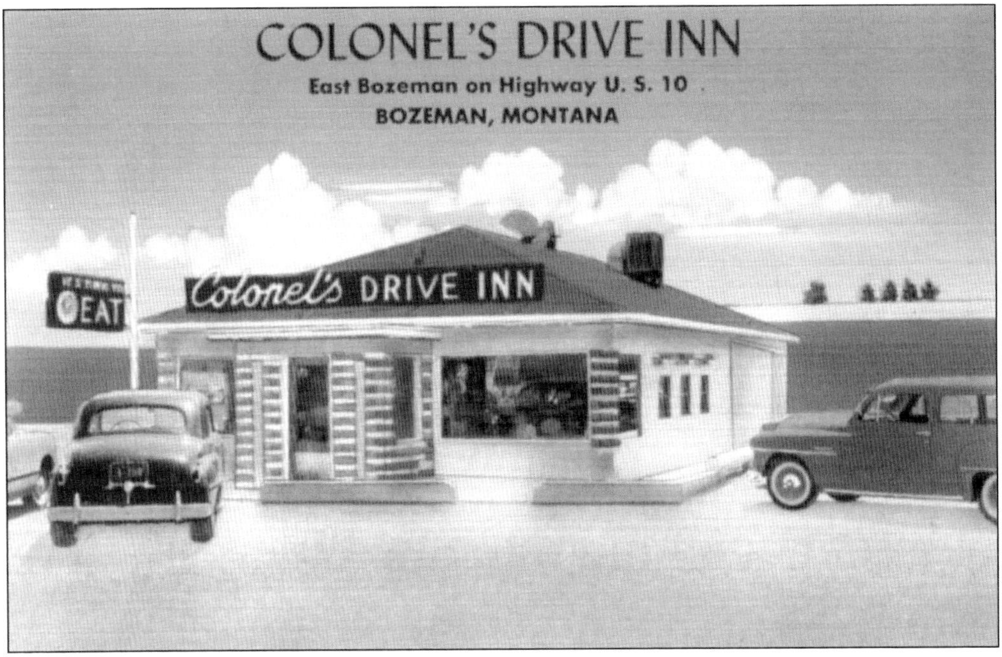

COLONEL'S DRIVE INN. Located at 1104 East Main Street near the east-side motels, this early Bozeman drive-in was a popular spot. At the time this *c.* 1950 linen advertising postcard was made, Interstate 90 was still 20 years in the future. Traffic on Highway U.S. 10, as noted on this card, ran through Bozeman's main street and then on to North Seventh Avenue.

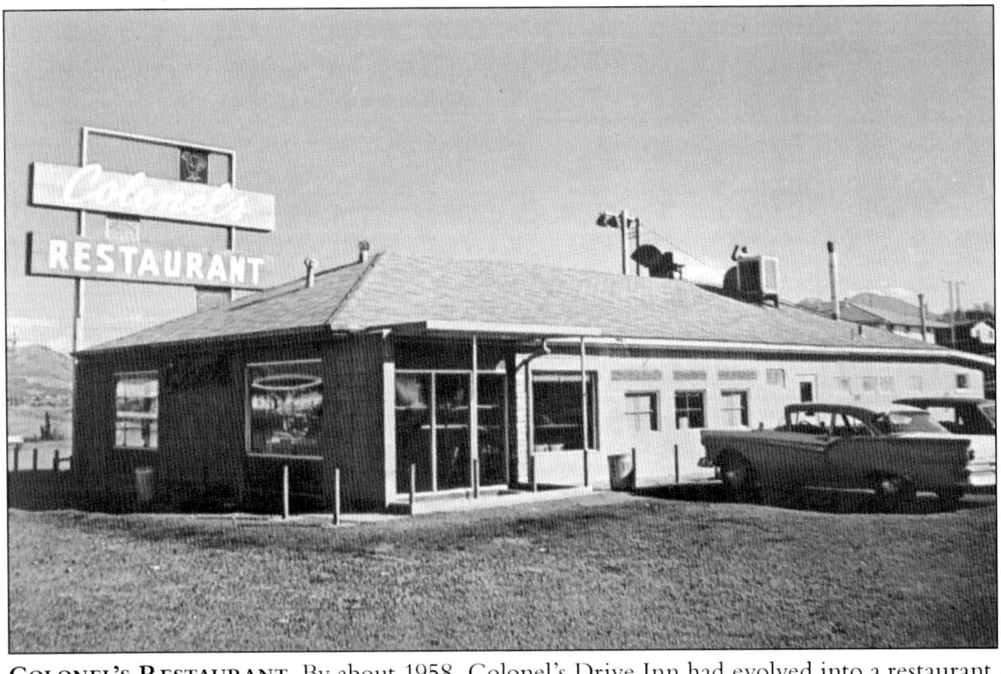

COLONEL'S RESTAURANT. By about 1958, Colonel's Drive Inn had evolved into a restaurant. This *c.* 1958 chrome advertising postcard has text on the back stating, "Enjoy Good Food . . . Convenient to Good Motels—East Edge of Town." This café advertised, "Complete meals, lunches and fountain services . . . steak, chicken and seafood dinners."

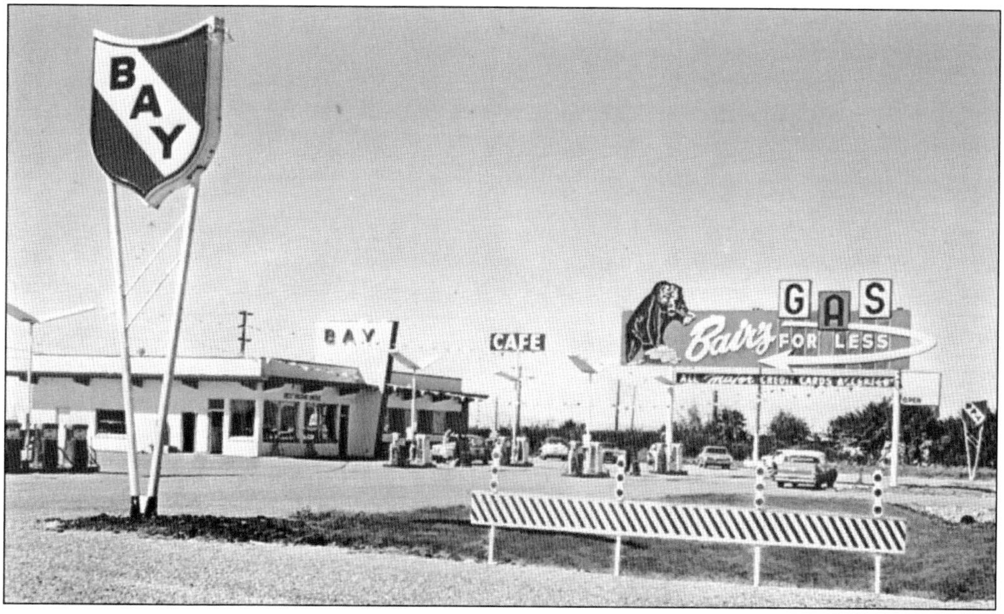

BAIR'S TRUCK STOP AND COFFEE SHOP. Located at 815 North Seventh Avenue, on Highway 10, Bair's featured a large gasoline bay for the time and was open 24 hours. Text printed on the back of this *c.* 1962 chrome advertising postcard includes, "Located in the heart of Bozeman's motel district. Featuring a complete family Coffee Shop, plus quality petroleum products for the trucking and motoring public."

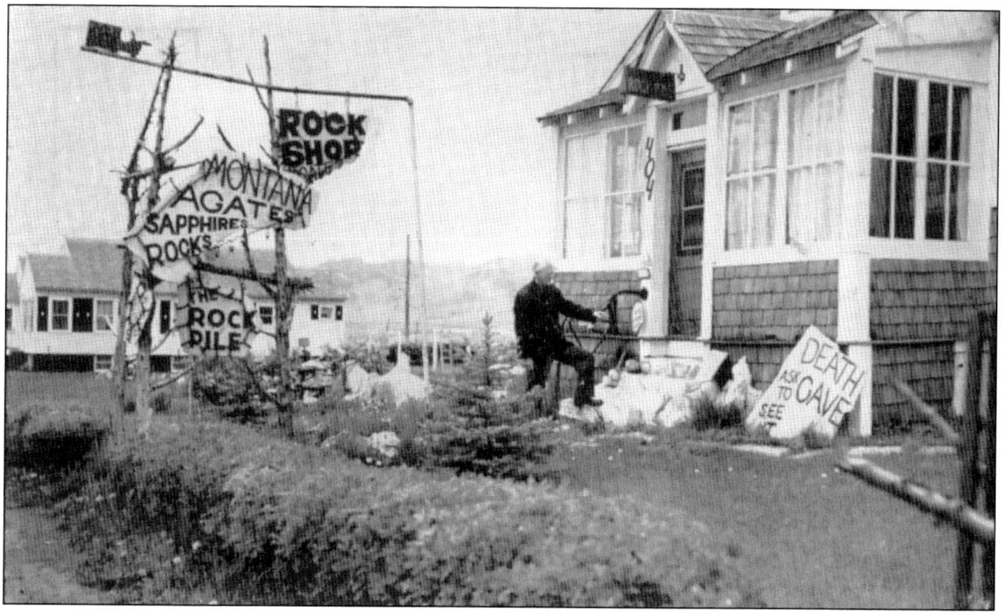

THE ROCK PILE ROCK SHOP. This rock shop advertised Montana agates and sapphires on the homemade signs in front of the shop. Another sign, visible at right, states, "Death Cave—Ask to See It." If a person was a rock hound around 1950, when this printed postcard was made, how could he or she resist checking this place out when in Bozeman? This shop was probably located on Bozeman's north side, but no information about it could be found in either city phone books or business directories.

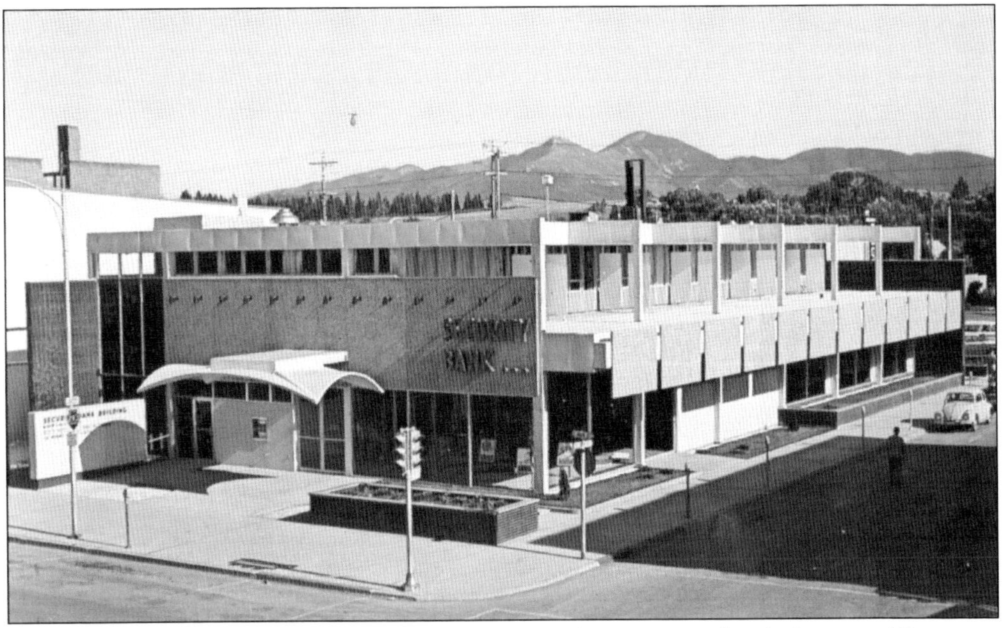

THE SECURITY BANK BUILDING. Located on the southeast corner of Main Street and Bozeman Avenue, the new home of Bozeman's First Security Bank is featured on this *c.* 1961 chrome postcard. The staff moved to this new location in September 1960 after outgrowing the bank's previous location at 110 East Main Street. This bank underwent major renovations in 2009.

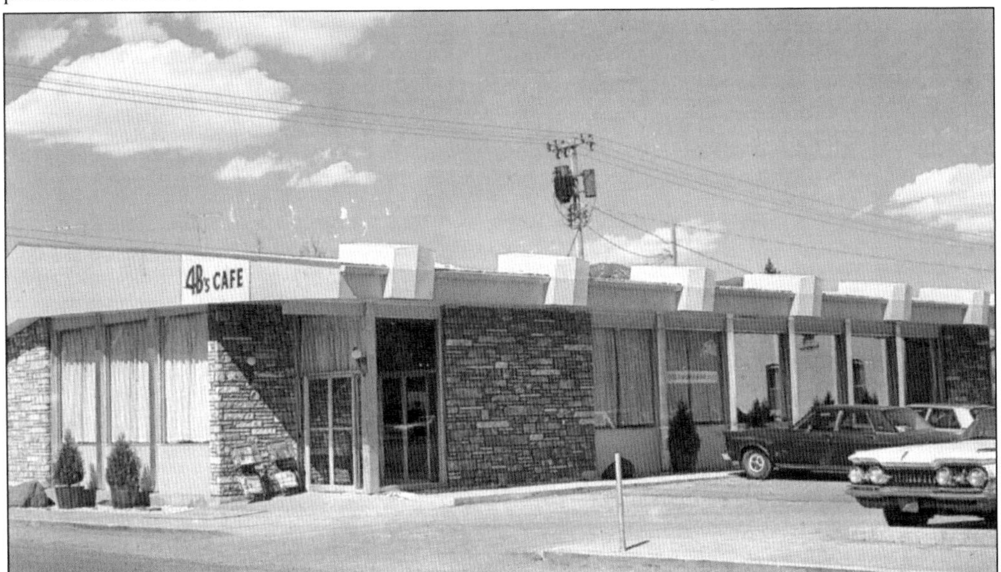

4B'S CAFÉ. This *c.* 1962 chrome postcard shows the Bozeman version of the popular restaurant chain, which once had a dozen locations in Montana. This café was located at 421 East Main Street and open 24 hours. Bill Hainline, who named the family-style eatery after his own family—himself, his wife Barbara, his son Bill Jr., and daughter Barbara—established 4B's in 1947. Menu staples included their original guaranteed steaks, meatloaf, oyster stew, and navy bean and cream of tomato soups. Most of the 4B's locations are now closed, including this one.

Two

CELEBRATIONS AND EVENTS

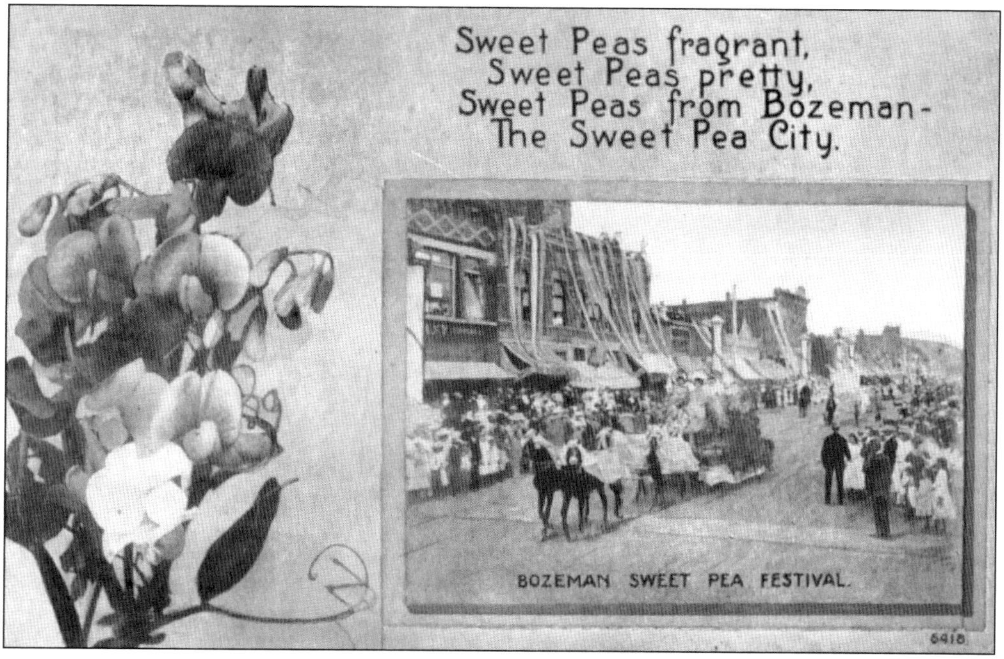

SWEET PEA FESTIVAL POSTER ART. With the success of the initial Sweet Pea Festival in 1906, the Bozeman community worked to promote it as an annual event. Bozeman was even labeled "The Sweet Pea City," as depicted in the verse on this *c.* 1910 printed postcard. The early Sweet Pea Festivals carried on for nearly a decade before being discontinued. This festival was resurrected in 1977 and continues today as an annual event held in early August.

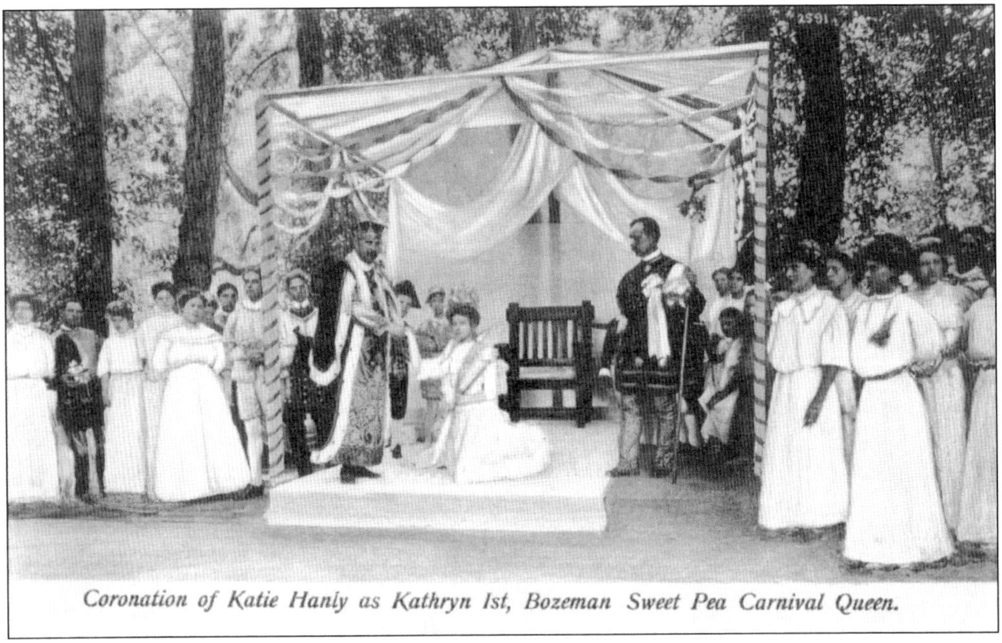

KATIE HANLY, FIRST CARNIVAL QUEEN. This vintage printed postcard shows the crowning of the queen at the first Sweet Pea Festival in 1906. The caption reads, "Coronation of Katie Hanly as Kathryn 1st, Bozeman Sweet Pea Carnival Queen." This first parade consisted of some 200 floats, most decorated with sweet peas.

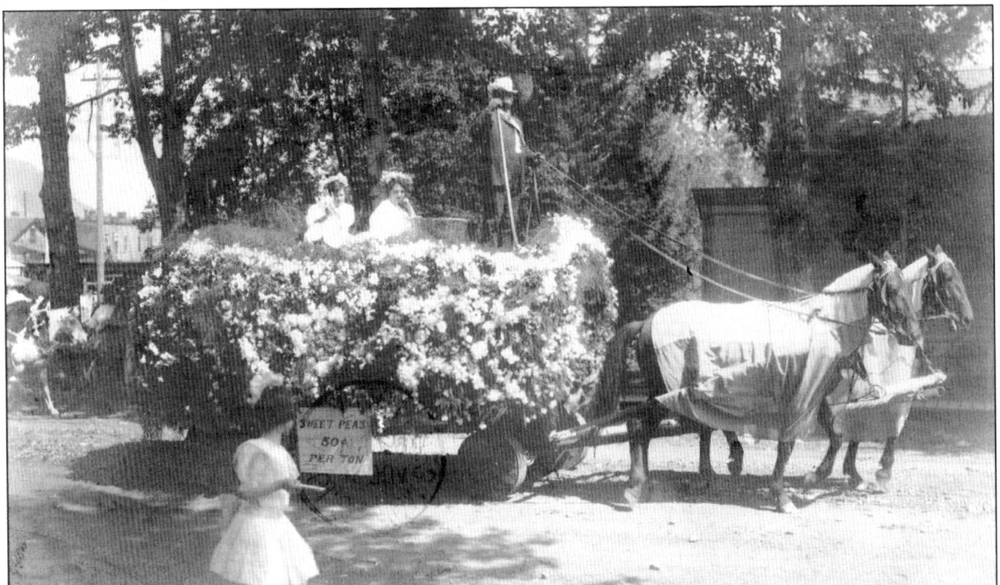

SWEET PEAS—50¢ PER TON. The sweet pea, one of the traditional bumper crops in the Gallatin Valley, was chosen as the symbol of the festival because of its fragrance, beauty, and ample supply. This real-photo postcard view, from the 1907 festival parade, shows a girl waving from the top of a horse-drawn float laden with sweet peas. The float bears a sign at its center bottom stating, "Sweet Peas 50¢ Per Ton," a testimony to the ready availability of this flower. (Courtesy of R. Dale Beland.)

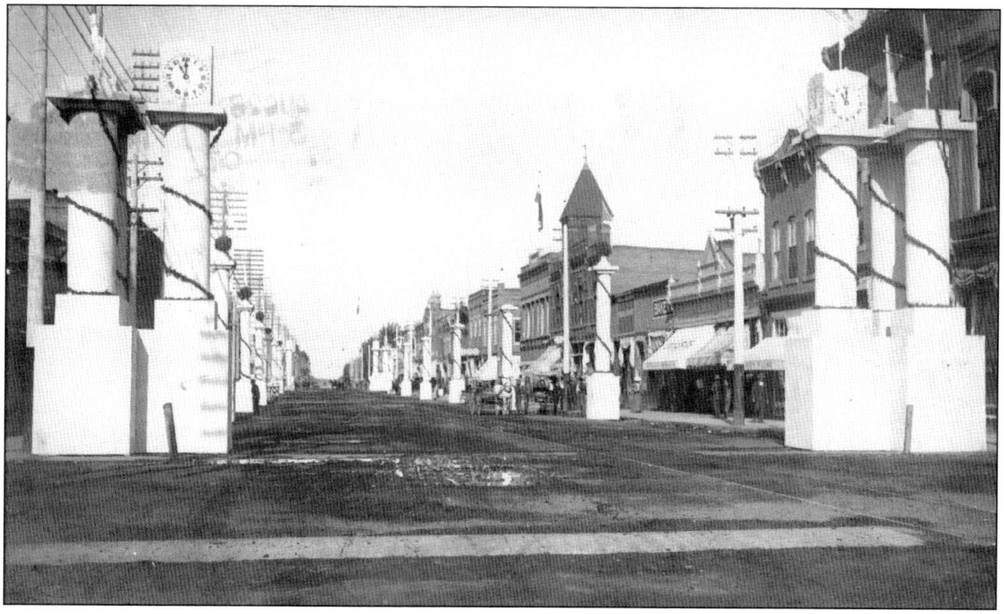

MAIN STREET READY FOR THE CARNIVAL. Postmarked August 23, 1907, just after the second Sweet Pea Festival, this real-photo postcard image shows how Bozeman's Main Street was set up with giant decorative columns for the big parade. The message on the back includes, "The way the street looked for carnival. The streets were beautiful."

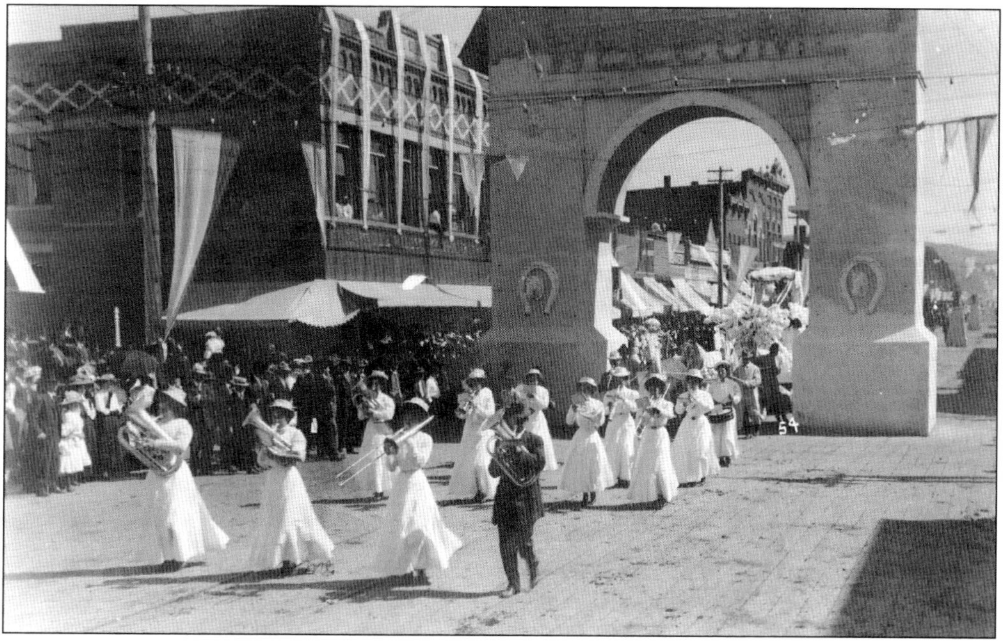

BAND MARCHING UNDER THE ARCH. The Ladies Imperial Band, with help from a single gentleman, march through the giant arch during the 1909 Sweet Pea Festival parade. The message on the back of this real-photo postcard, postmarked from Bozeman in September 1909, reads, "This is us in the Sweet Pea Carnival don't we look fine. Nina." The Willson Company store at 35–37 West Main Street can be seen in the background. (Photograph by Schlechten Studio, Bozeman, Montana.)

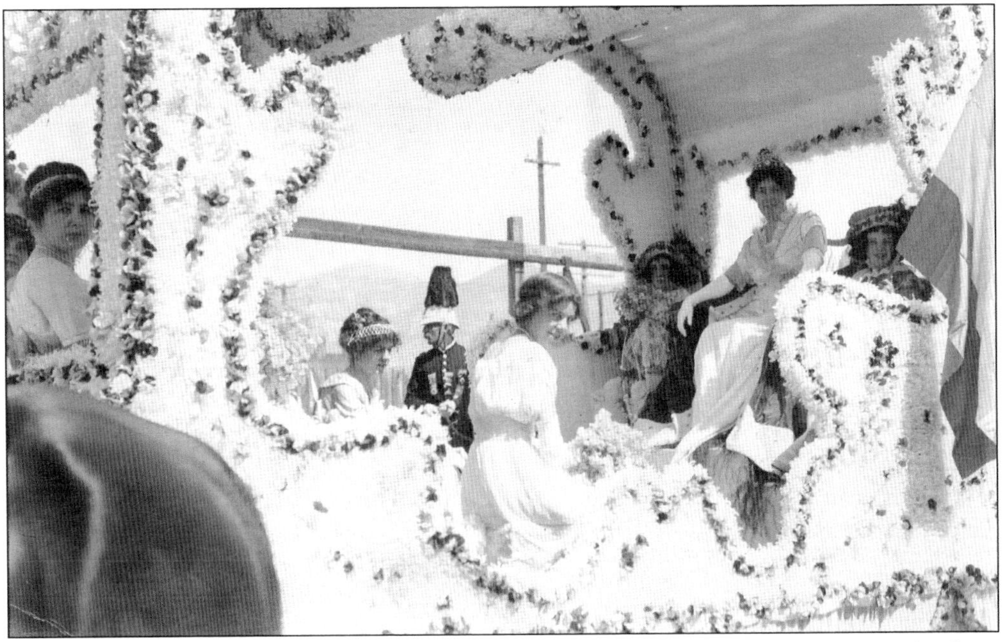

Queen's Float, 1913 Sweet Pea Parade. The 1913 queen, Mignon Quaw, smiles from her flowery throne as her attendants look on. The queen was the daughter of Thomas Quaw, who was the founder of the city of Belgrade, 9 miles west of Bozeman. The message on the back of this real-photo postcard reads, "This is the queen's float. I wish you could have seen the lovely flower-trimmed carriages and autos."

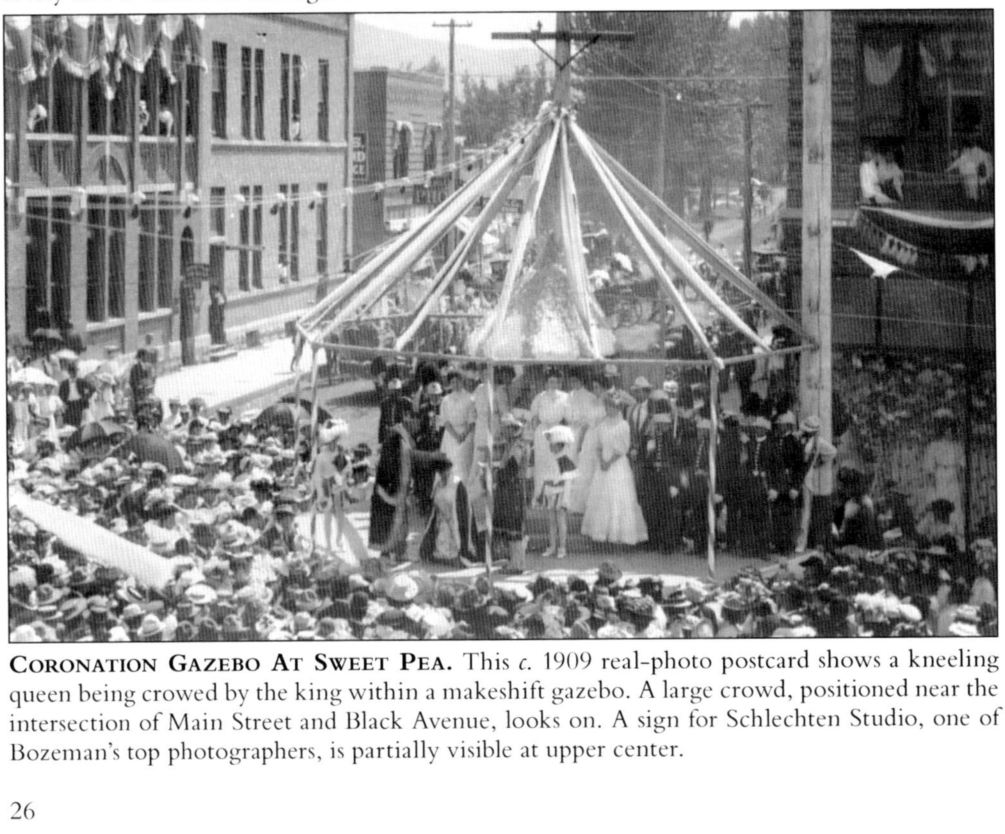

Coronation Gazebo At Sweet Pea. This *c.* 1909 real-photo postcard shows a kneeling queen being crowed by the king within a makeshift gazebo. A large crowd, positioned near the intersection of Main Street and Black Avenue, looks on. A sign for Schlechten Studio, one of Bozeman's top photographers, is partially visible at upper center.

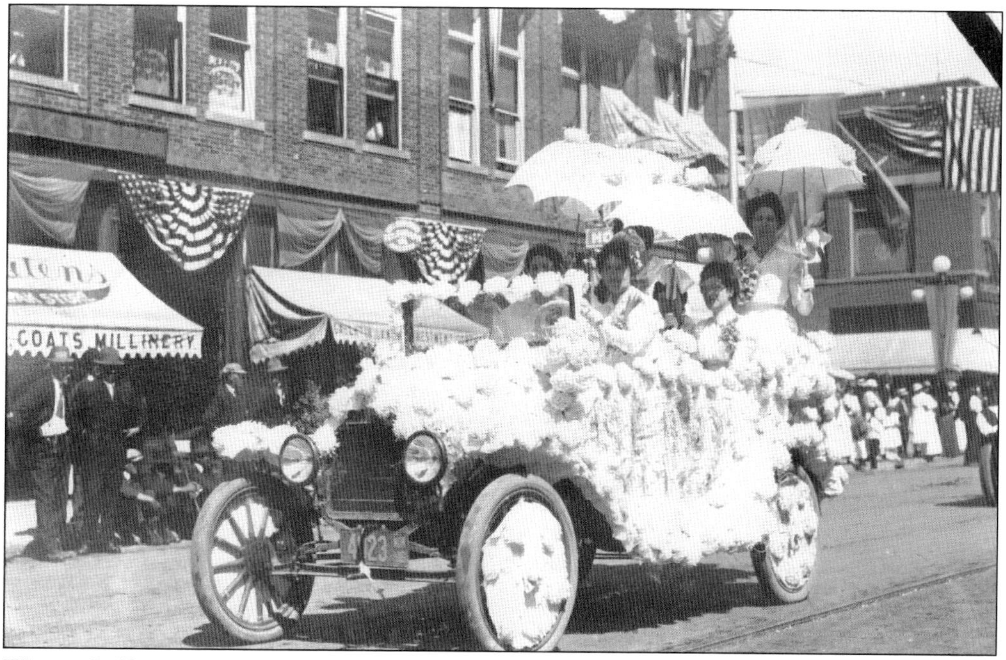

Women's Decorated Car At Sweet Pea. This *c.* 1912 real-photo postcard shows a well-decorated car in the parade procession. Note that all of the car's occupants are women, including the driver. The car is passing by the Gallatin Land Investment Company on Main Street.

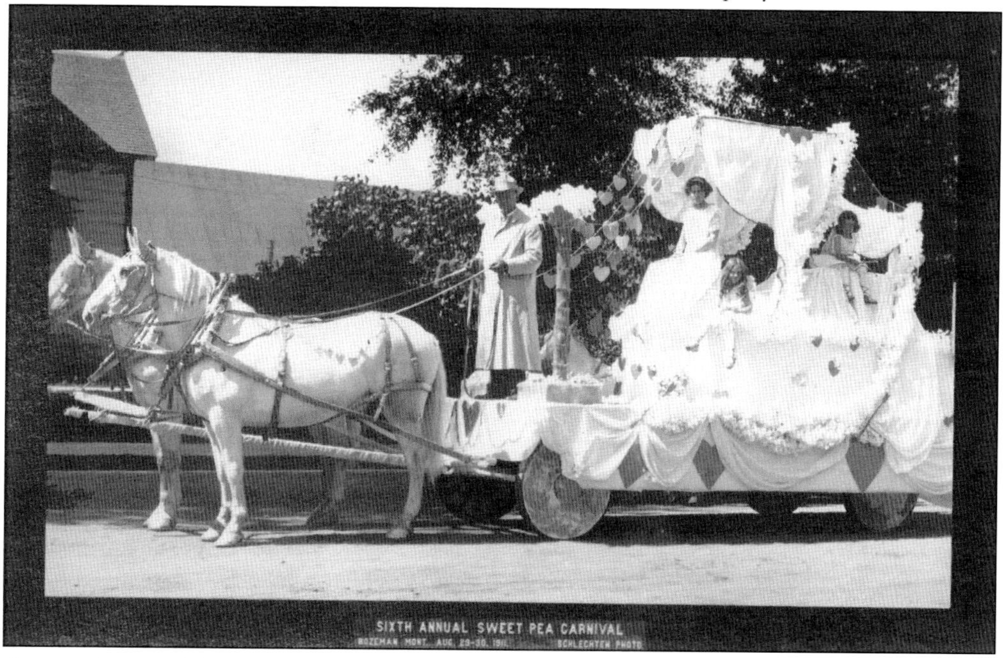

Horse-Drawn Float, 1911 Sweet Pea Festival. Two big, strong, white horses await the driver's command to begin their parade route. This real-photo postcard, unlike most postcards showing images of the Sweet Pea Festival, is captioned at the bottom with "Sixth Annual Sweet Pea Carnival—Bozeman, Mont. Aug. 29-30, 1911." (Photograph by Schlechten Studio, Bozeman, Montana.)

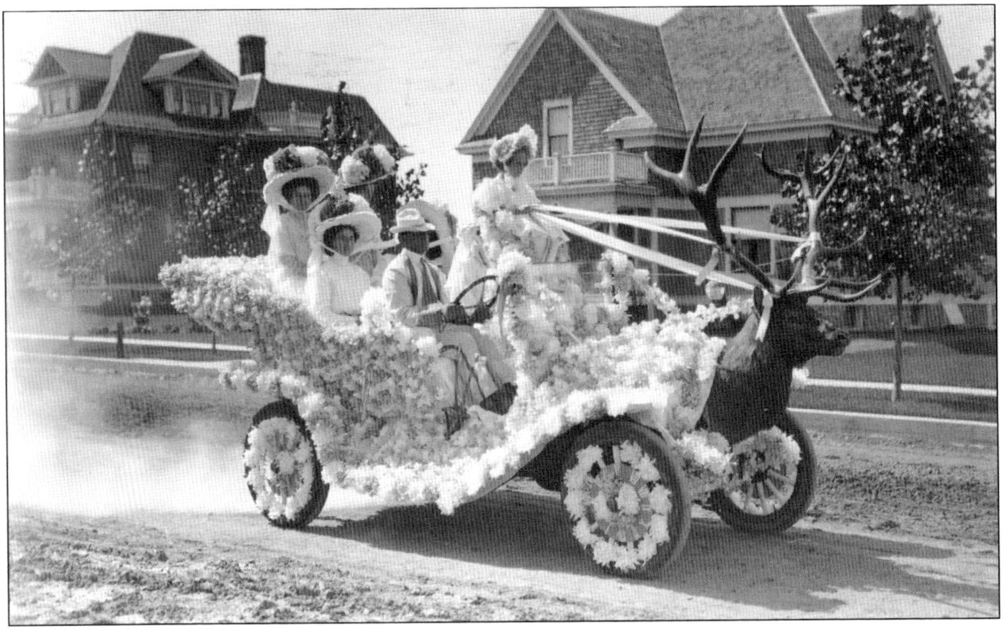

Decorated Car Float At Sweet Pea. This real-photo postcard, postmarked from Bozeman in 1909, shows Frank Esgar driving his sweet-pea decorated auto north on Central Avenue (now Willson Avenue) to prepare for the gathering on Main Street. A large, antlered elk head is attached to the front hood of his auto. (Photograph by Schlechten Studio, Bozeman, Montana.)

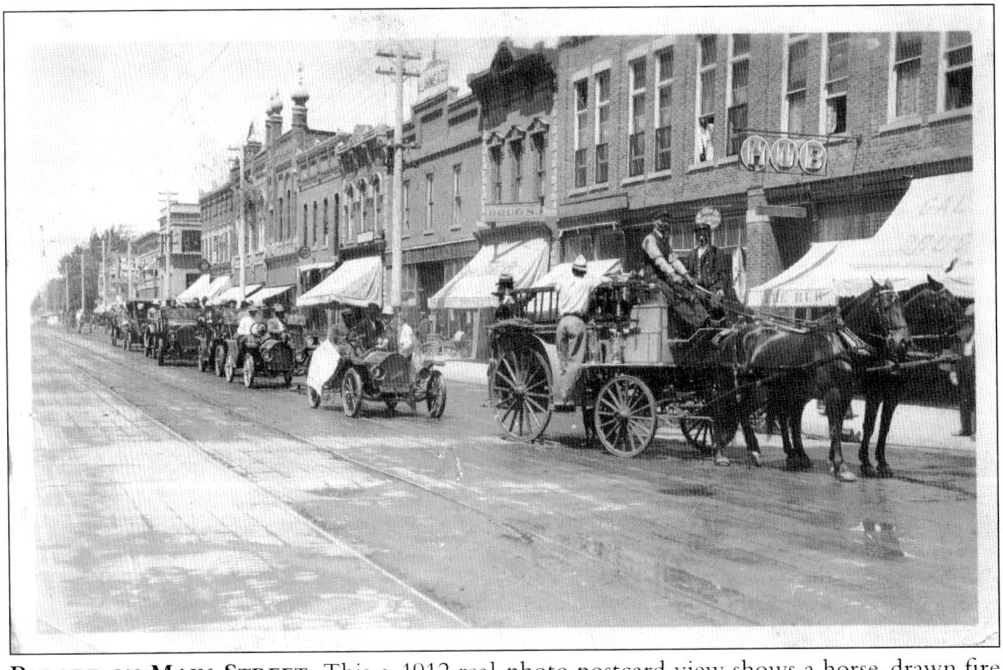

Parade on Main Street. This *c.* 1912 real-photo postcard view shows a horse-drawn fire wagon in front of a long string of cars during a parade on Bozeman's Main Street. The Hub, a men's furnishing and clothing store, is visible at far right. (Photograph by Schlechten Studio, Bozeman, Montana.)

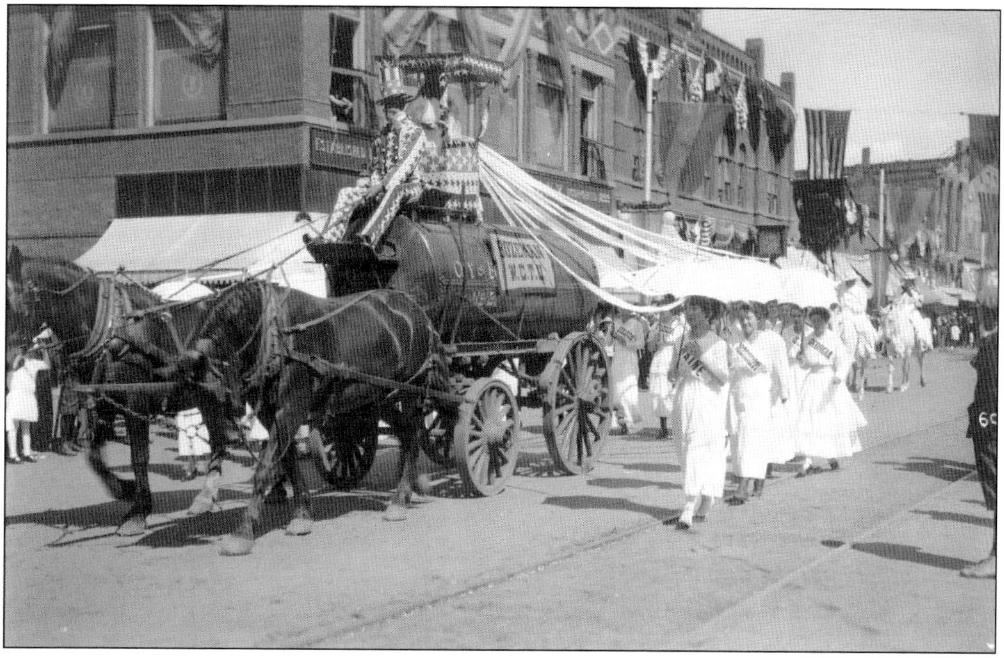

WCTU AND UNCLE SAM AT SWEET PEA. This *c.* 1910 real-photo postcard shows the Bozeman Women's Christian Temperance Union horse-drawn "float" with Uncle Sam at the reins. Walking beside are ladies dressed in white with banners for various states. This group spearheaded the crusade for Prohibition, which went into effect in 1920 and lasted until 1933.

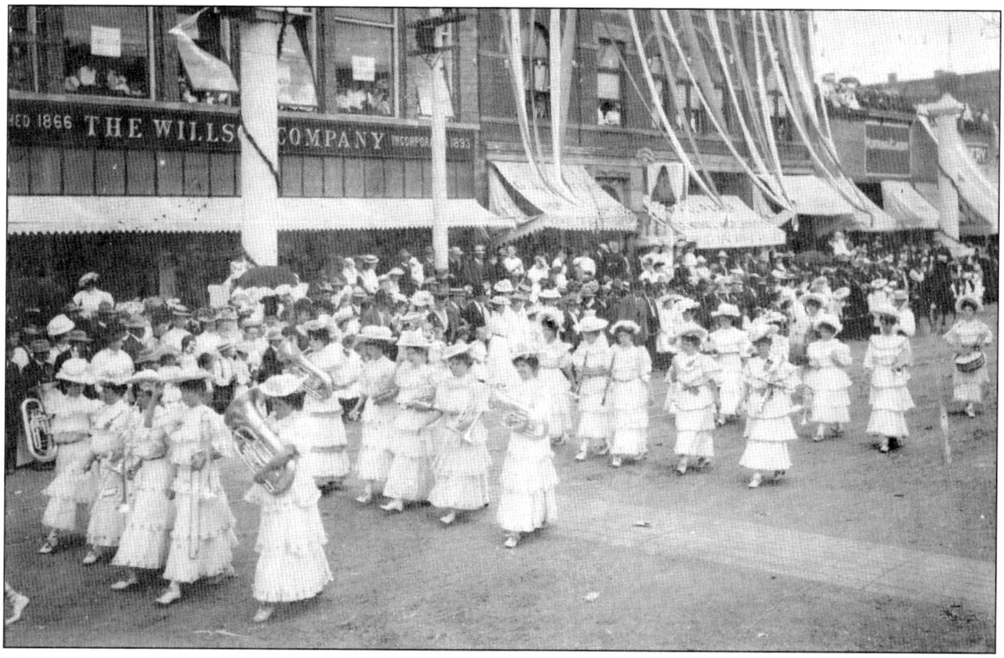

WOMEN'S MARCHING BAND AT SWEET PEA. This real-photo postcard, postmarked from Bozeman in 1909, shows the Ladies Imperial Band of Bozeman and the Gallatin County area. The band performed at many events and were regulars at the early Sweet Pea Festival parades. (Photograph by Schlechten Studio, Bozeman, Montana.)

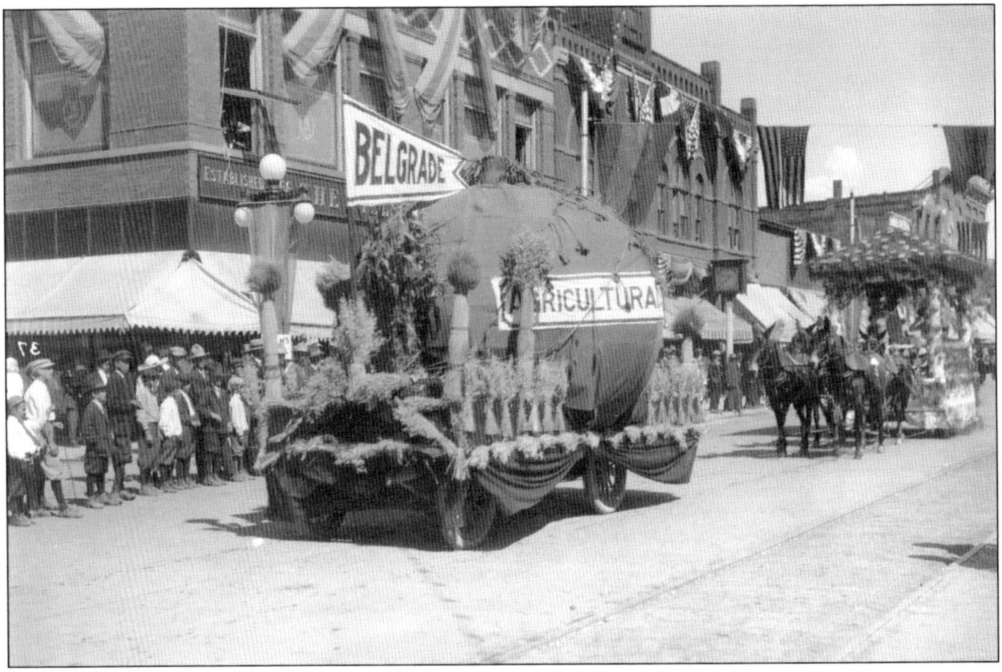

BELGRADE AGRICULTURAL FLOAT AT SWEET PEA. This *c.* 1910 real-photo postcard image shows the parade in progress near the Willson Company store on Main Street. The town of Belgrade, 9 miles to the west, was an active participant in the Sweet Pea Festival.

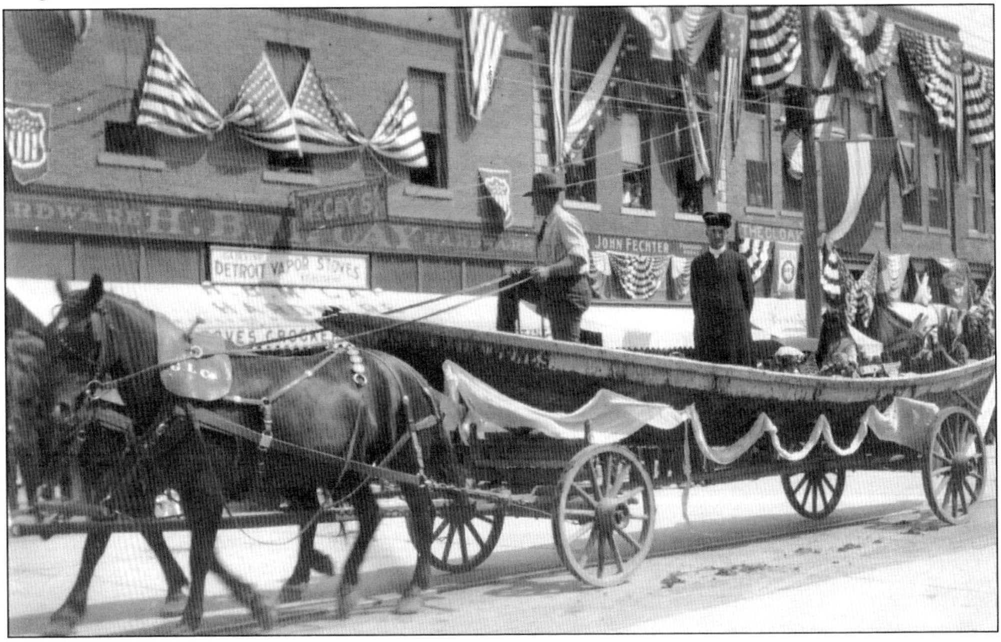

FATHER DESMET FLOAT AT SWEET PEA. This 1914 real-photo postcard view shows a parade in progress as it passes in front of the H. B. McCay hardware store on Main Street. A message penned on back reads, "This is another float in our parade. It represents Father [Peter John] DeSmet and the Indians. 50 yrs. ago Bozeman was started and 25 yrs. ago Montana was admitted as a state."

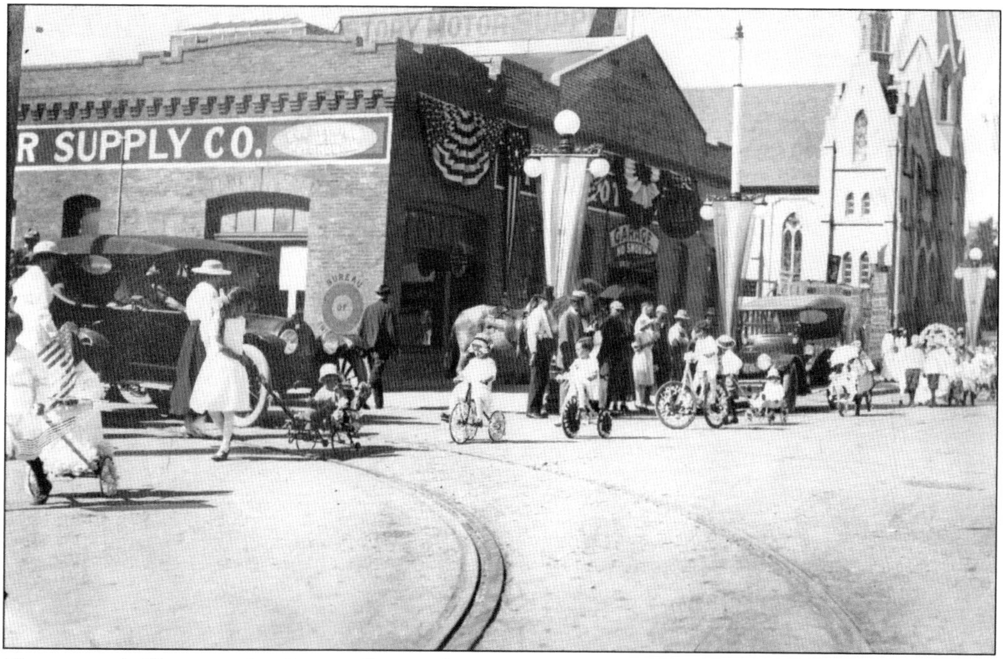

CHILDREN'S PARADE AT SWEET PEA. This 1914 real-photo postcard shows a children's parade in progress as it passes in front of Story Motor Supply Company on West Main Street. Many of the tricycles and wagons are decorated with flowers and some with flags as well.

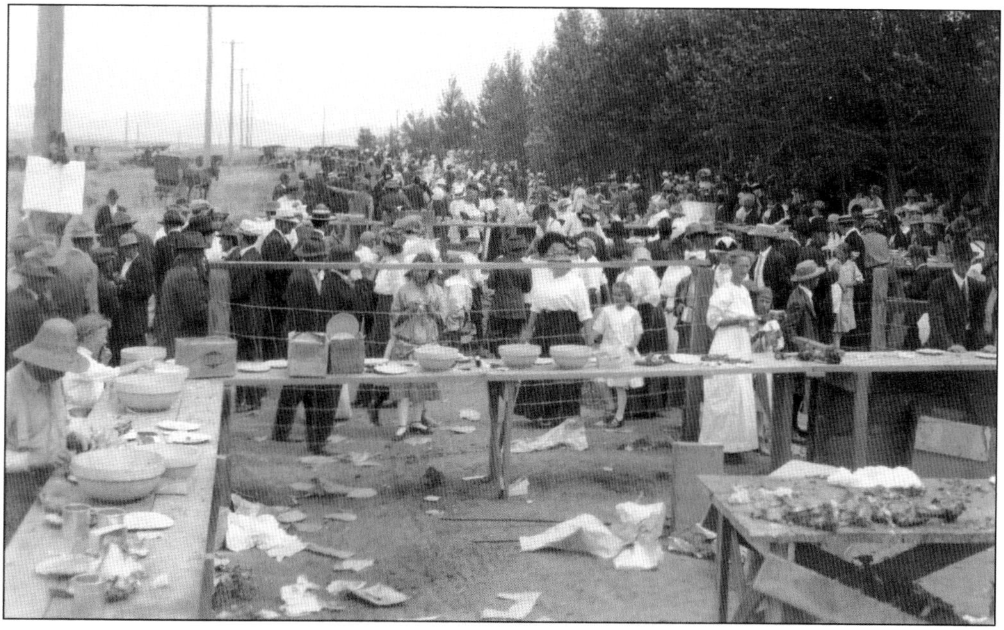

FUN AND TRASH AT SWEET PEA. This candid *c.* 1908 real-photo postcard shows the aftermath of a large crowd's picnic. The garbage detail will have its work cut out for it when the parade and celebration are over for the day.

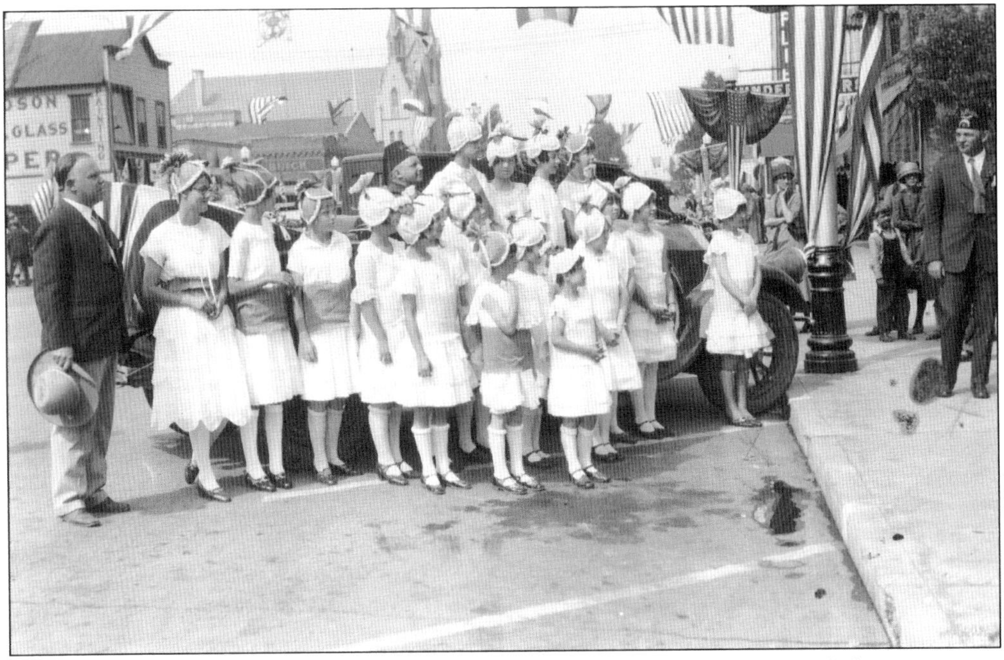

Flower Girls at Shriner's Parade. This *c.* 1920 real-photo postcard shows a group of flower girls standing amidst flags and Shriners on Main Street. The flower girls presented bouquets to the Imperial party. One of the girls may be Maxine McBride, as noted on the back of this card. The Holy Rosary Catholic Church is visible in the background.

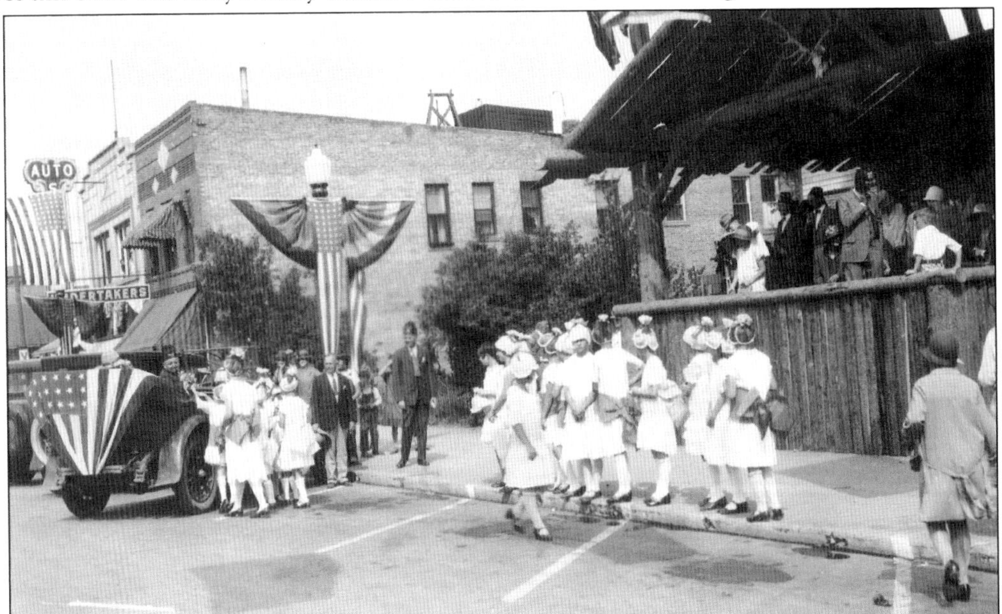

Viewing Cabin for Shriner's Parade. Message penned on the back of this *c.* 1920 real-photo postcard reads, "A log cabin built especially for the Imperial party to view the parade. Man standing in cabin is Imperial Pote." Flower girls dressed in white and wearing "flower bonnets" are visible in the foreground.

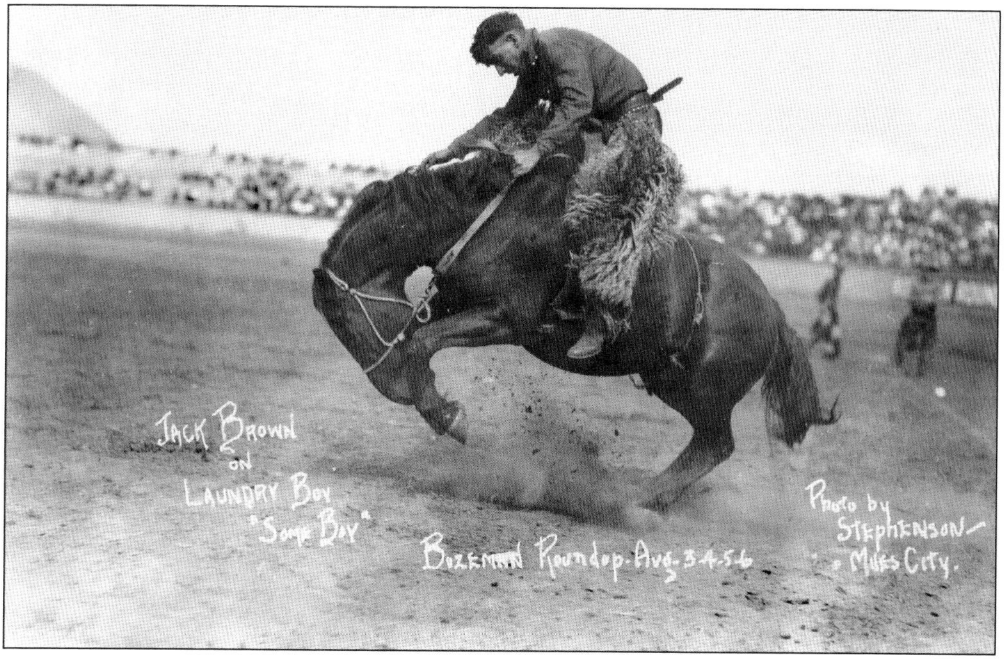

BRONC RIDING AT THE BOZEMAN ROUNDUP. Jack Brown works to stay on a bucking broncho named Laundry Boy, as shown on this *c.* 1918 real-photo postcard view. The Bozeman Roundup was an annual event from 1919 to 1926. (Photograph by Stephenson, Miles City, Montana.)

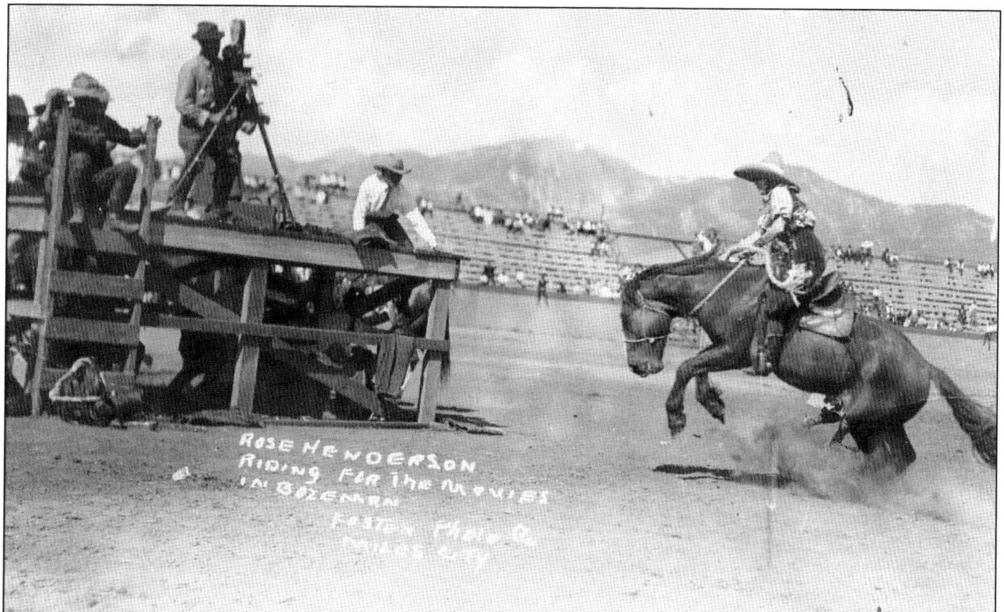

ROSE HENDERSON AT THE BOZEMAN ROUNDUP. A movie camera, at left, captures a ride by cowgirl Rose Henderson, seen here in this *c.* 1918 real-photo postcard image. Henderson, named posthumously to the National Cowgirl Hall of Fame, made a name for herself during the golden age of rodeo as a champion bronc rider and relay racer. (Photograph by Foster Photo Company, Miles City, Montana.)

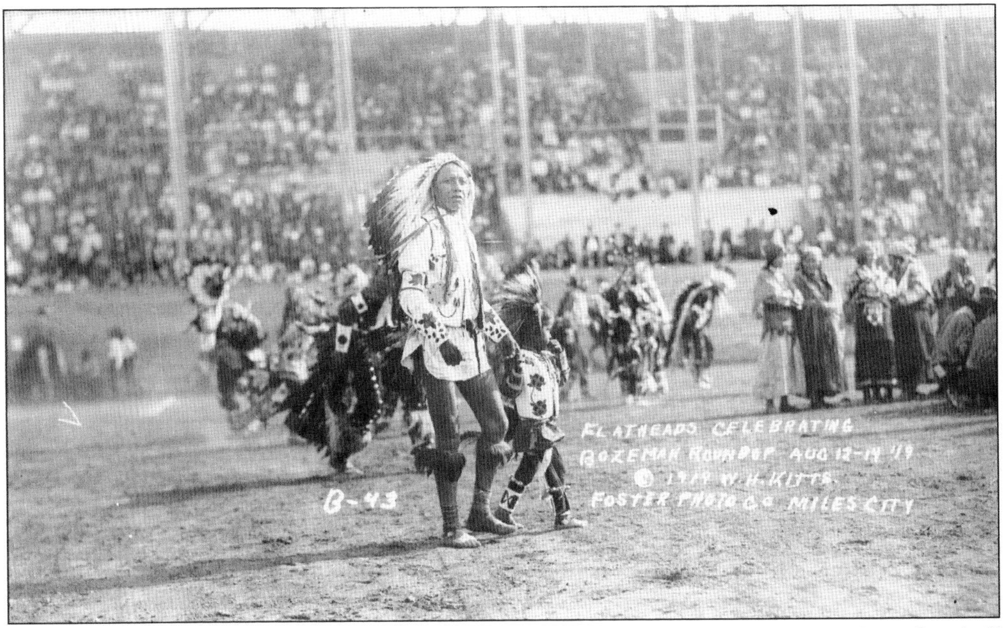

FLATHEAD INDIAN CELEBRATING. The Bozeman Roundup featured a parade, a baseball game, and a carnival prior to the featured rodeo competition. Participants in the parade, which included Native Americans, the rodeo queen and her court, and other dignitaries, often made an appearance at the rodeo arena. Attired in full regalia, a Flathead Indian is shown in this *c.* 1918 real-photo postcard. (Photograph by Foster Photo Company, Miles City, Montana; courtesy of Ken Hamlin.)

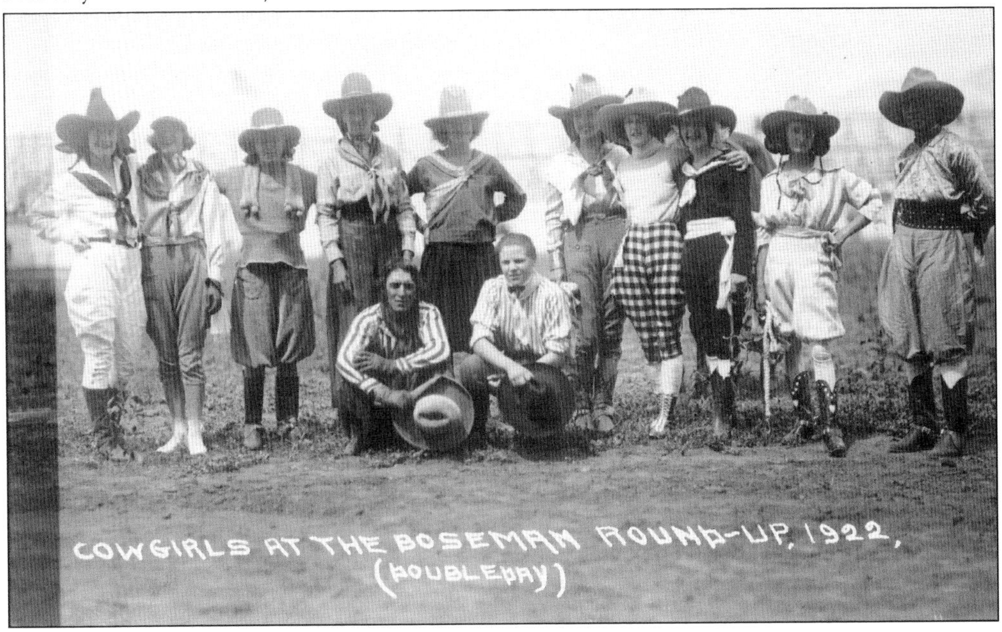

COWGIRLS AT THE ROUNDUP, 1922. This vintage real-photo postcard provides an interesting group picture of the cowgirls participating in the 1922 rodeo. Note that each cowgirl has her own distinct outfit. The only identified cowgirl in this image is Mabel Strickland, at far left. (Photograph by Ralph R. Doubleday, traveling rodeo photographer.)

Three

Churches and Schools

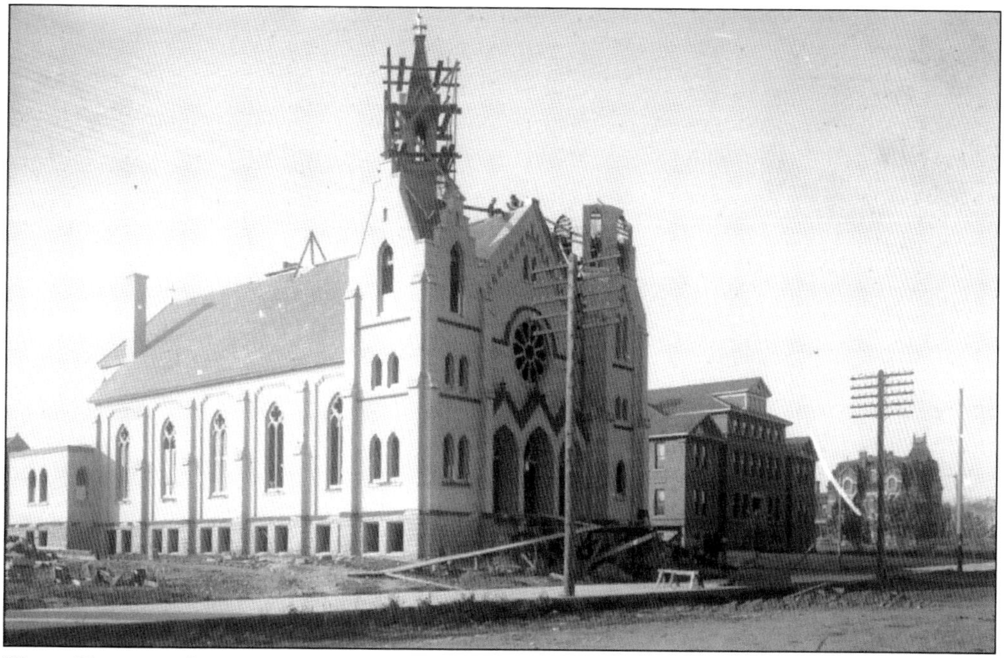

Holy Rosary Church Under Construction. This vintage real-photo postcard shows the new Catholic church nearing completion. The cornerstone had been laid on June 9, 1907, and construction was completed in 1908. This church, located at the corner of Main Street and South Third Avenue, recently celebrated its centennial.

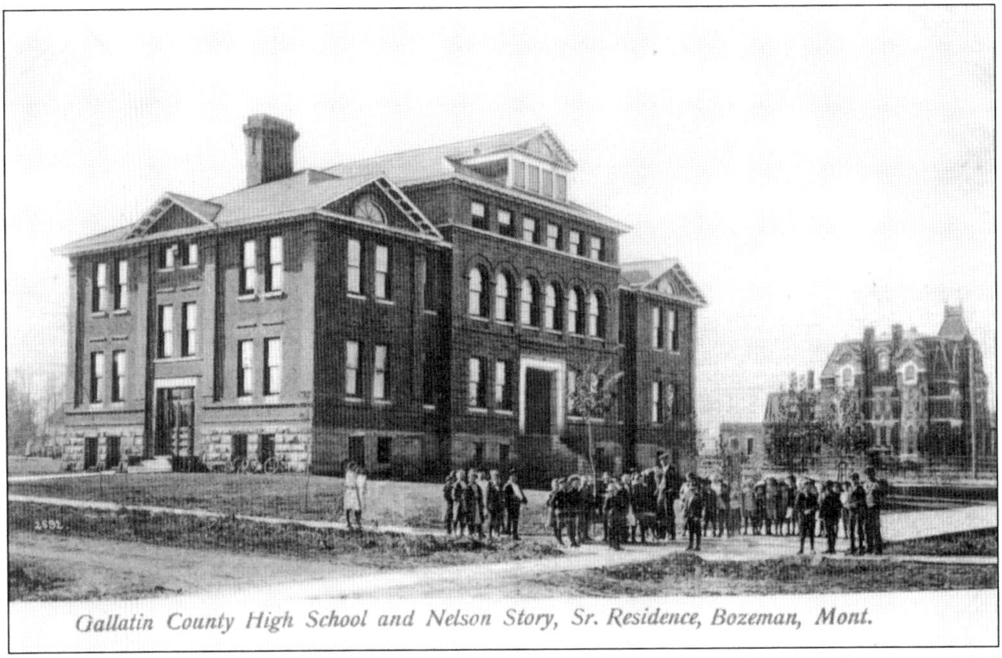

High School and Story Mansion. This *c.* 1910 printed postcard shows students assembled in front of the Gallatin County High School on West Main Street. The mansion at right belonged to one of Bozeman's prominent early businessmen, Nelson Story. The old high school shown here was built in 1902. It was adjoined by a new high school in 1937. The Story mansion was demolished in 1936 to provide needed area for the new school's construction.

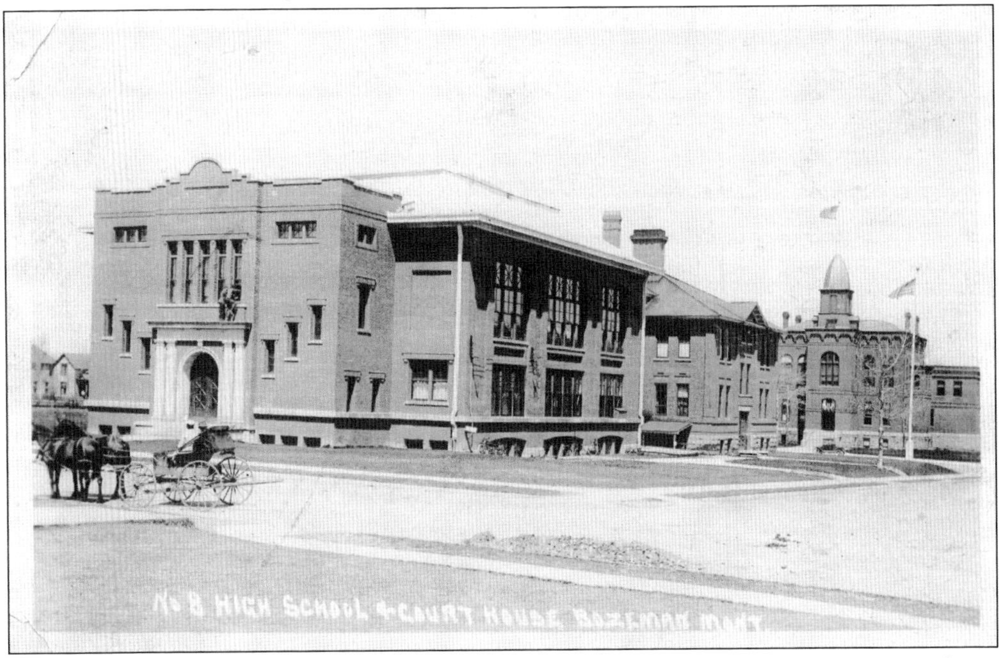

High School With South-Side Addition. This *c.* 1920 real-photo postcard image shows the new addition to the south end of the old high school. This view looks north from Babcock Street toward Main Street and the old courthouse, which is visible in the background.

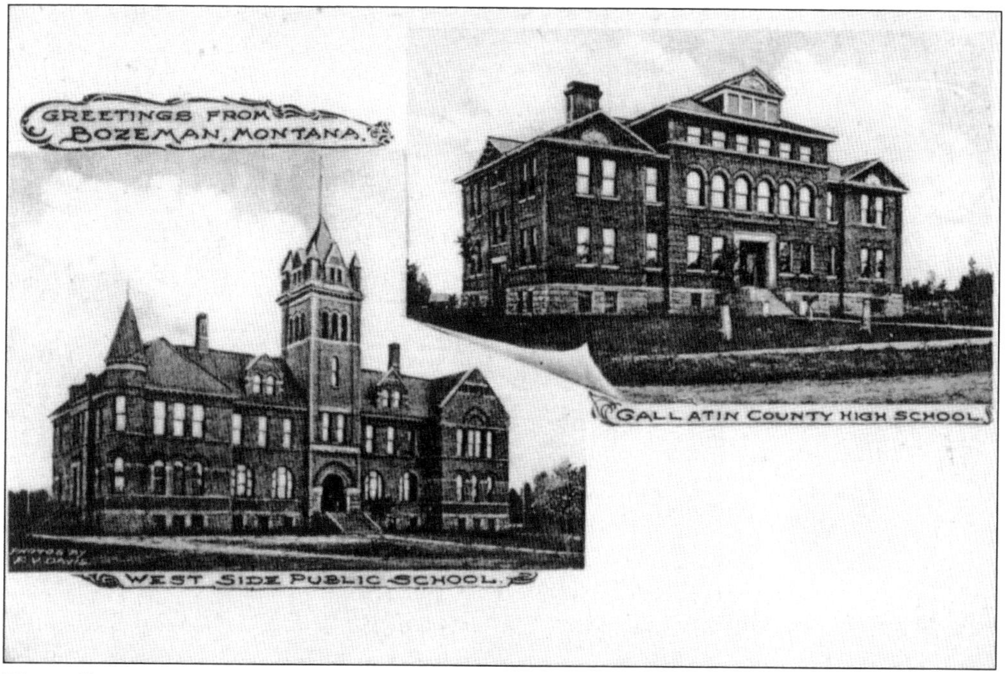

High School and West Side School. This *c.* 1910 printed postcard shows the two prominent schools on Bozeman's west side. The West Side School was located on Babcock Street, between Third and Fourth Avenues, and a block south of the high school, which was on Main Street. The West Side School would soon be renamed Irving School.

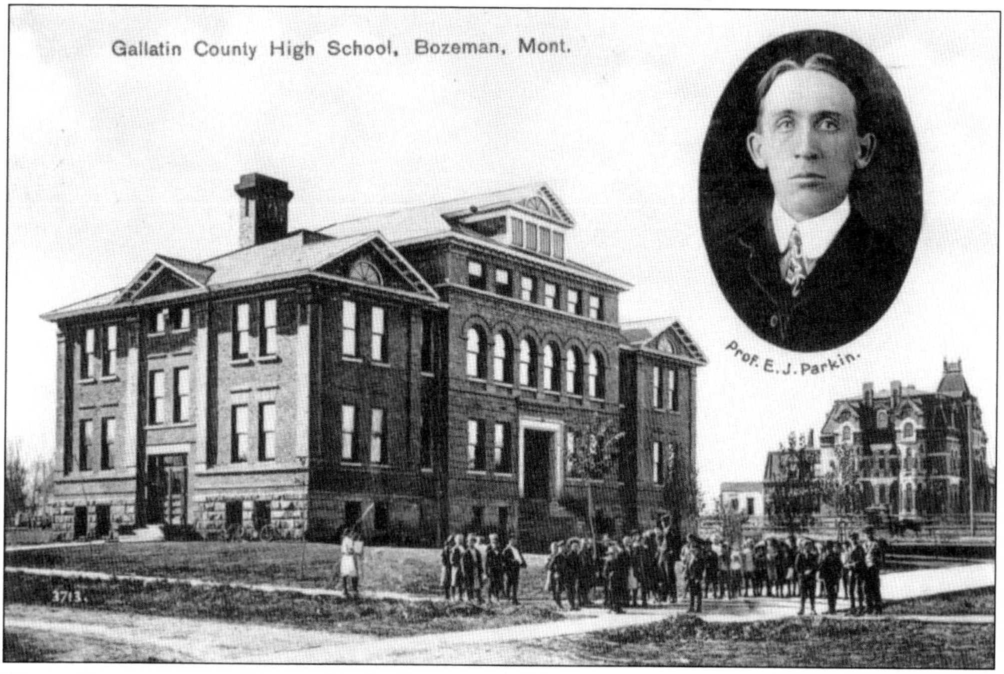

High School and Prof. E. J. Parkin. This *c.* 1910 printed postcard shows students assembled in front of Gallatin County High School on West Main Street. This building still stands today and is used mainly as a storage facility.

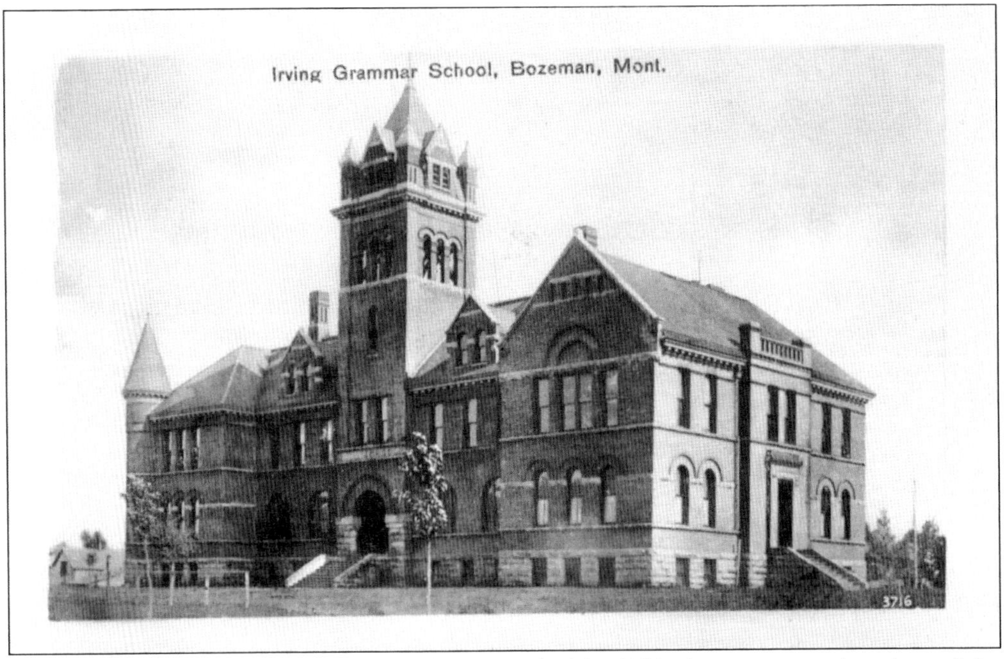

Irving School. This printed postcard, postmarked in 1911, shows an exterior view of the elementary school. It was located on the south side of Babcock Street, between Third and Fourth Avenues. B. W. Spaulding served as the principal at the time.

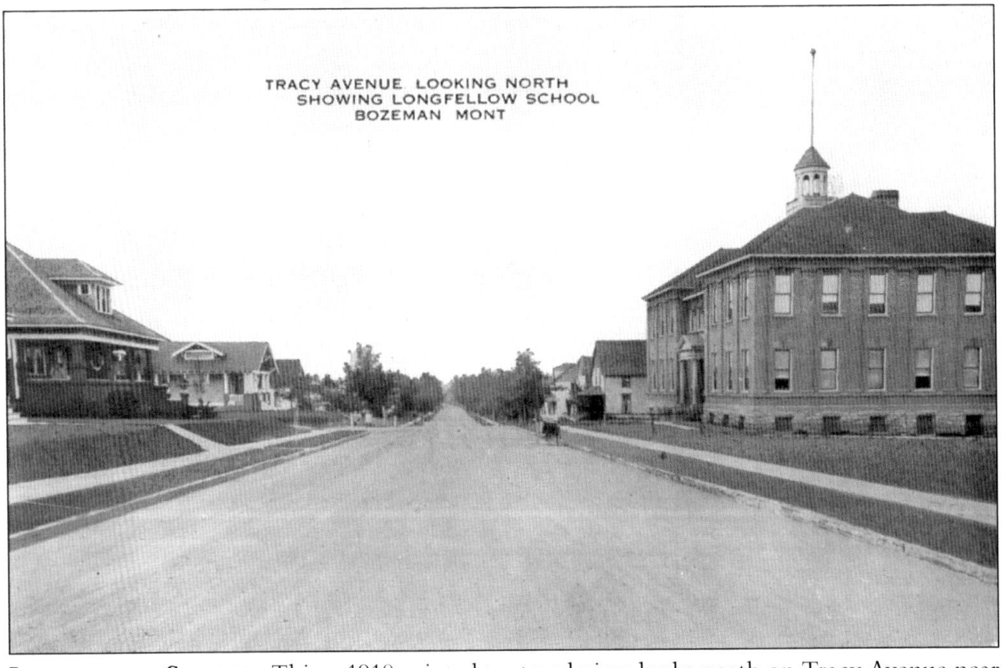

Longfellow School. This *c.* 1910 printed postcard view looks north on Tracy Avenue near the intersection with Dickerson Street and shows the old brick elementary school at right. This school was later rebuilt in the flat-roofed art deco/moderne style, in the same fashion as the Irving and Hawthorne schools. Leora Hapner was the school's principal at the time this postcard was made.

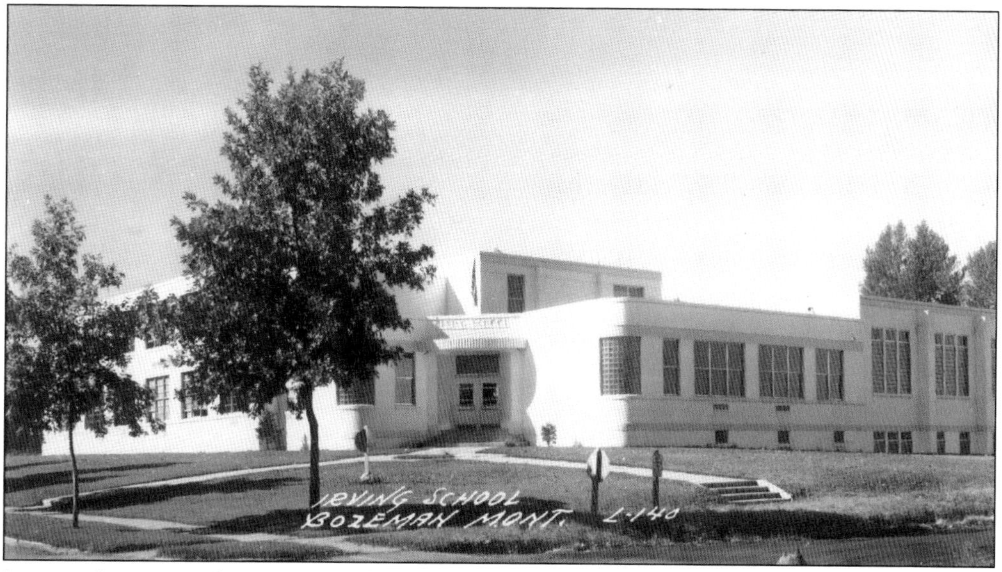

IRVING SCHOOL. This *c.* 1940 real-photo postcard shows the new Irving School shortly after it was built. The exterior view shows the popular art deco style used in this time period. The architect was Fred Willson, who also designed the county courthouse, the high school (see caption below), and several other Bozeman buildings. This school is located a few blocks north of the Montana State University (MSU) campus in the southern section of Bozeman.

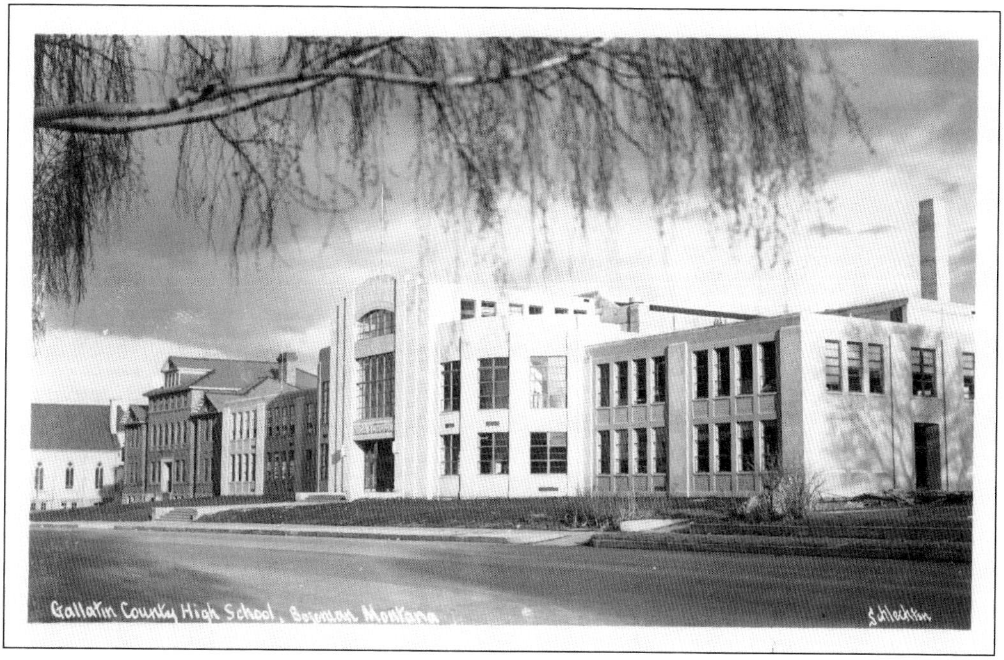

NEW HIGH SCHOOL, 1937. This vintage real-photo postcard shows the new high school shortly after it was built. This school was later named Willson School in honor of architect Fred Willson. It served the community well until growth required that a new high school be built in the late 1950s. The current Bozeman High School is about 1 mile to the west on Main Street. Willson School later served as a junior high and elementary school and, more recently, as an alternative high school.

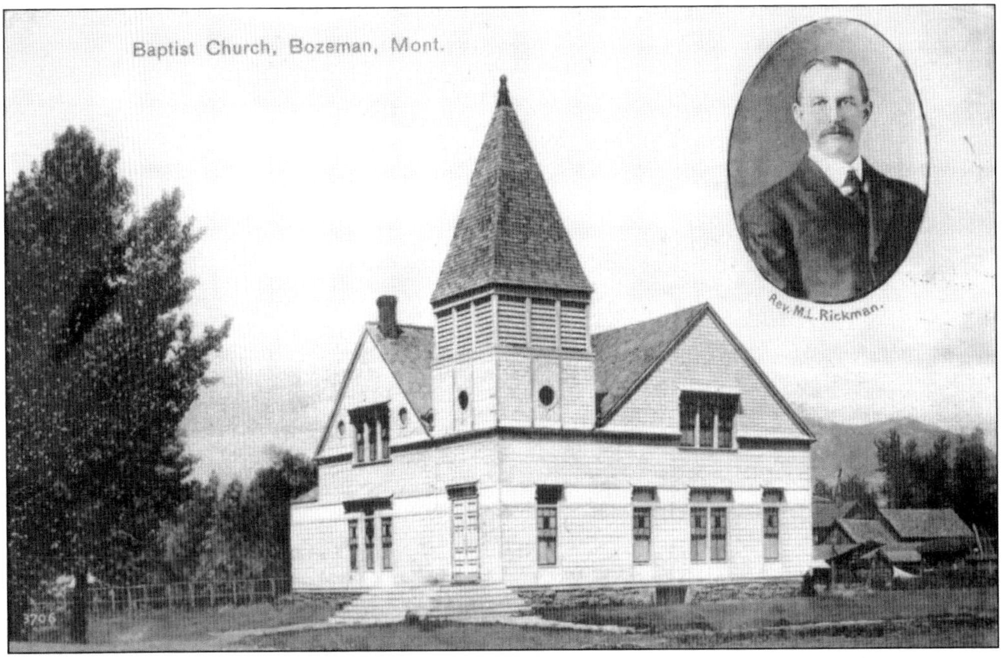

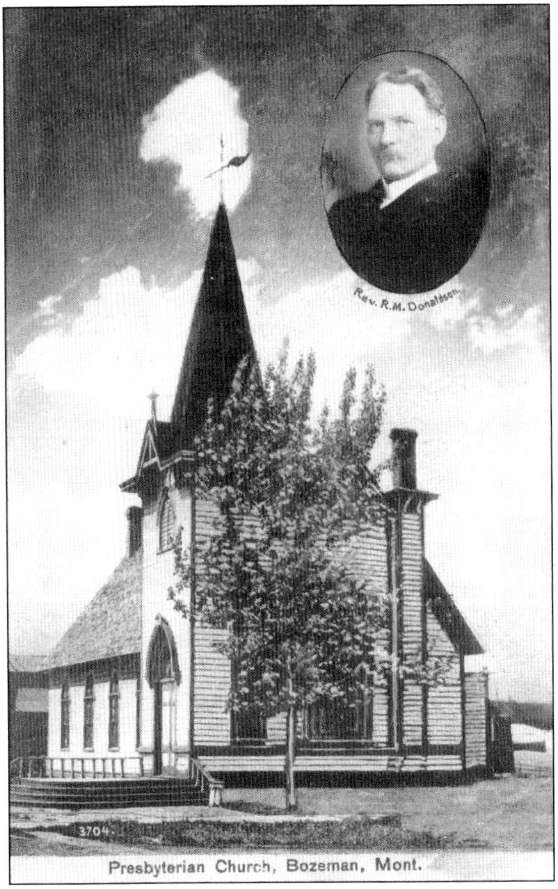

BAPTIST CHURCH AND REVEREND RICKMAN. This *c.* 1908 printed postcard shows the early First Baptist Church located on the corner of Black Avenue and Olive Street. The congregation numbered about 130 members at the time this view was made. The pastor was Rev. M. L. Rickman.

PRESBYTERIAN CHURCH AND REVEREND DONALDSON. This is a view of the old First Presbyterian Church, which had stood at the corner of Willson Avenue and Babcock Street since 1879. A new church replaced this one shortly after this *c.* 1908 postcard view was taken. The congregation had reached almost 350 members at this time. R. M. Donaldson was the church pastor. The new Presbyterian church was constructed near this one.

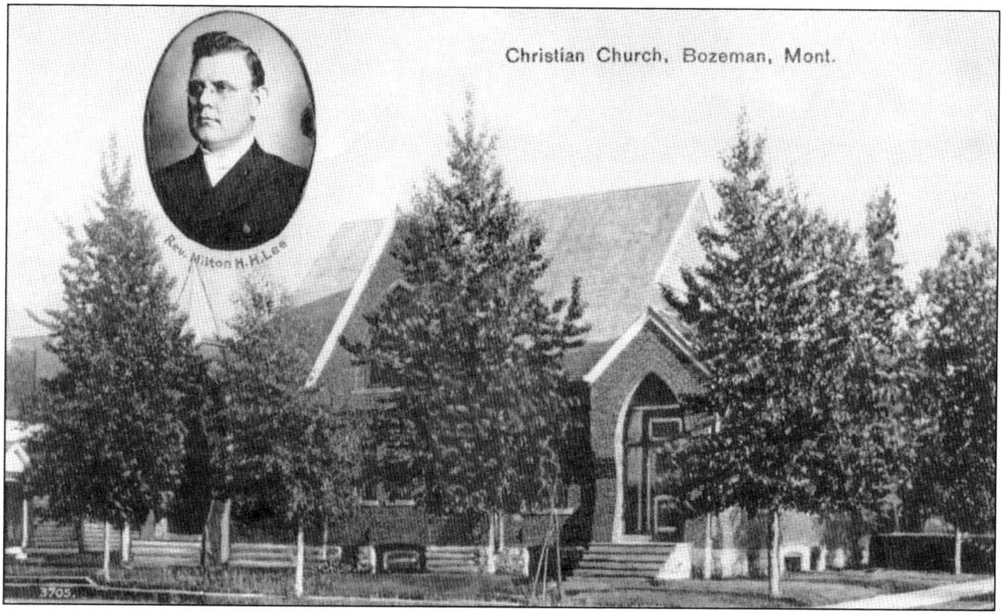

CHRISTIAN CHURCH AND REVEREND LEE. Located at the corner of Babcock Street and Grand Avenue, the Grand Avenue Christian Church had a congregation of approximately 400 members a century ago. The inset at upper left on this *c.* 1908 printed postcard view shows the pastor, Rev. Milton H. H. Lee.

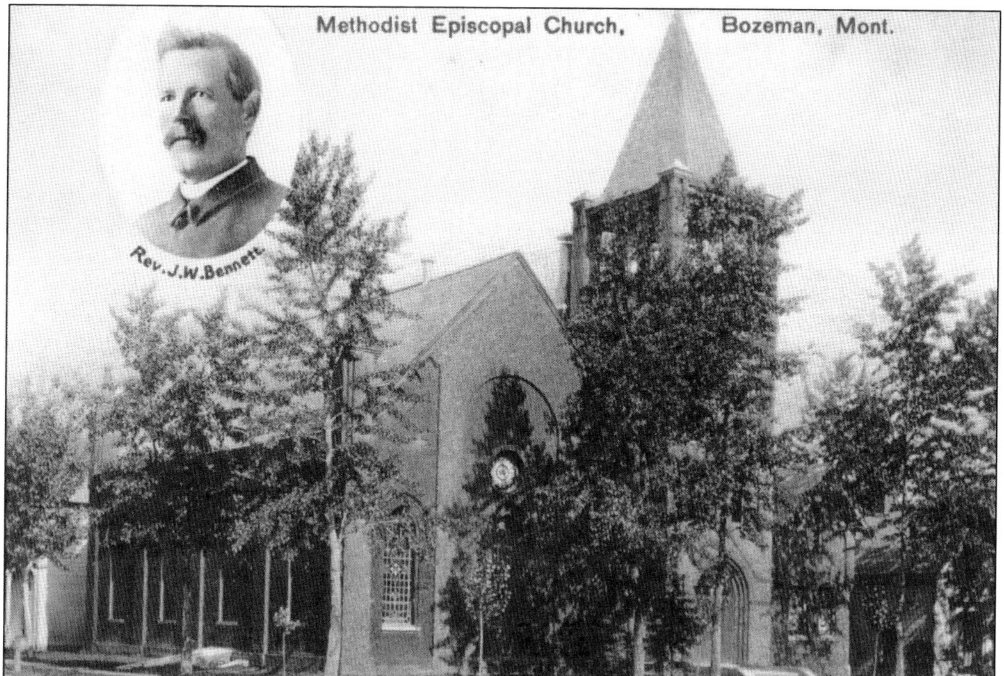

METHODIST EPISCOPAL CHURCH AND REVEREND BENNETT. This church stood at the corner of Olive Street and Central (now Willson) Avenue, as shown on this printed postcard that dates to about 1908. Rev. J. W. Bennett served as pastor to a congregation of about 300. This church still stands today and is known as the United Methodist Church.

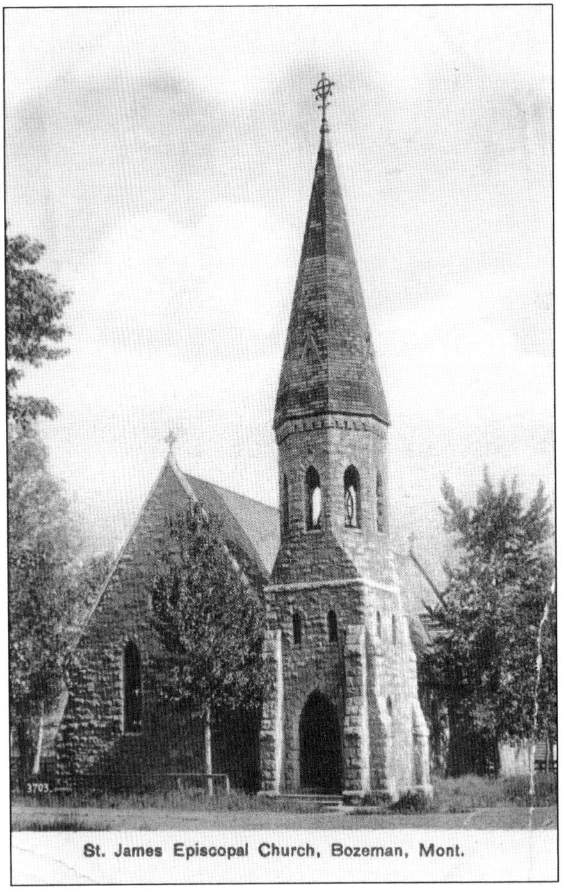

St. James Episcopal Church. The membership of this church was more than 200 when this *c.* 1908 printed postcard was made. This church stood at the corner of Tracy Avenue and Olive Street, and the pastor at the time was Rev. Frank B. Lewis.

Four Bozeman Churches. This *c.* 1908 printed multi-view postcard shows four Bozeman churches from a century ago. Pictured, from the top left, are the Christian church, the Methodist church, a second Methodist church, and the Presbyterian church.

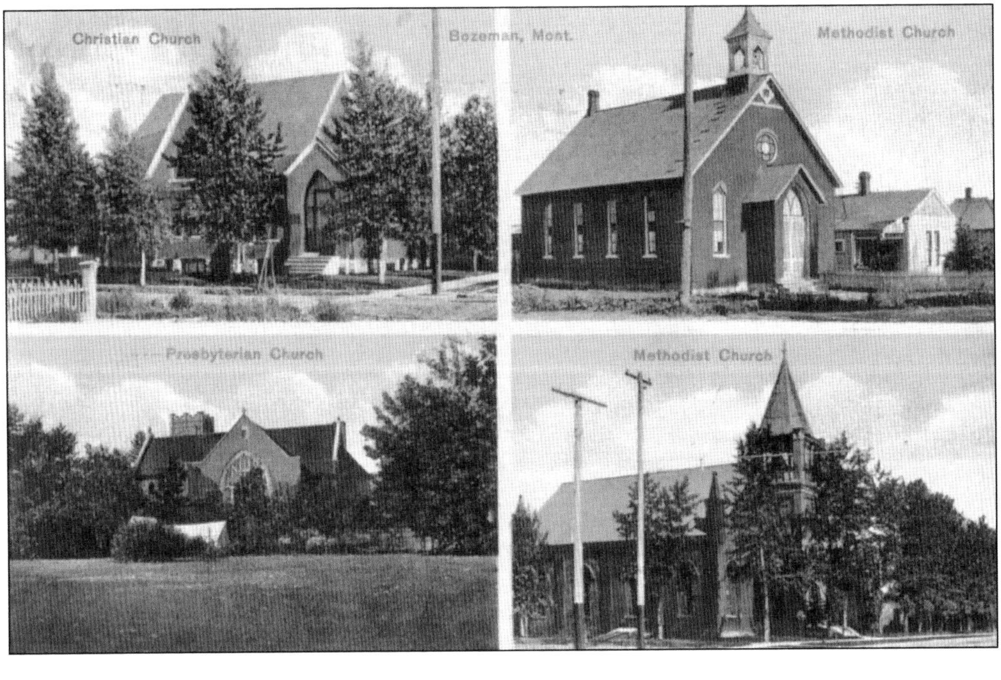

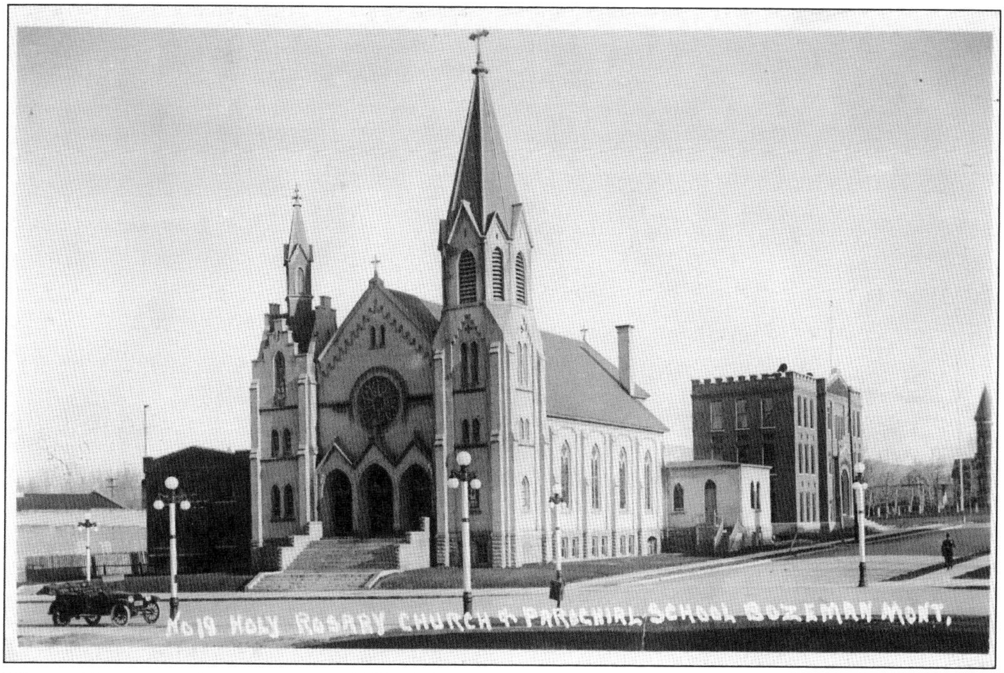

Holy Rosary Church, c. 1918. This *c.* 1918 real-photo postcard was taken from the courthouse lawn and looks south across Main Street and down South Third Street. The parsonage is behind the church, and the brick building in the background is the Holy Rosary parochial school, which no longer stands.

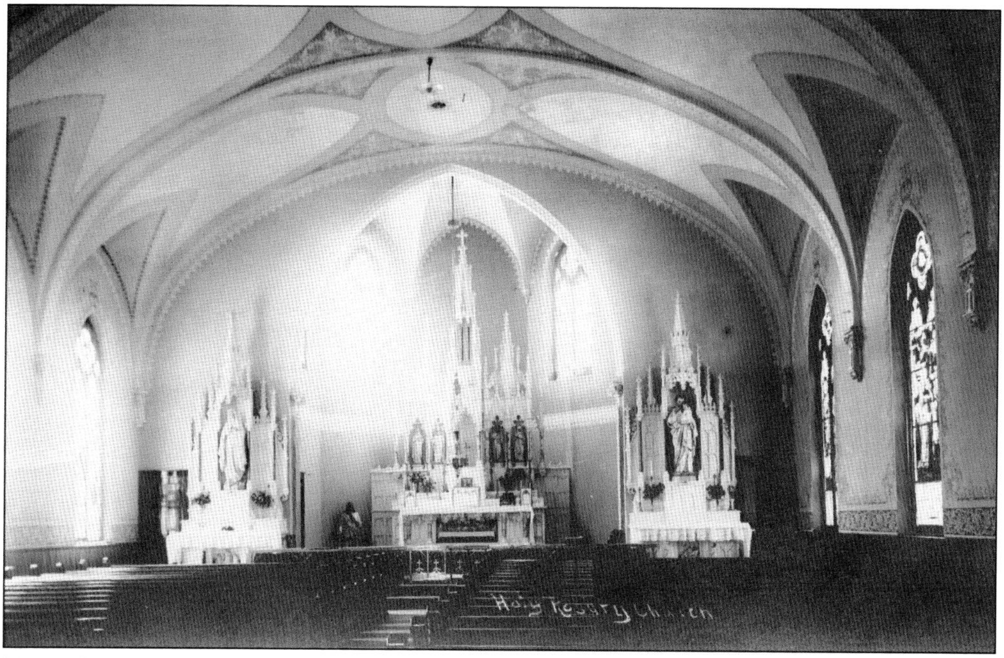

Holy Rosary Church, Interior View. This real-photo postcard was postmarked 1908, the year that this church was constructed. Pictured is the original sanctuary, with a center altar and two side altars. The Catholic church was organized in Bozeman about 1887.

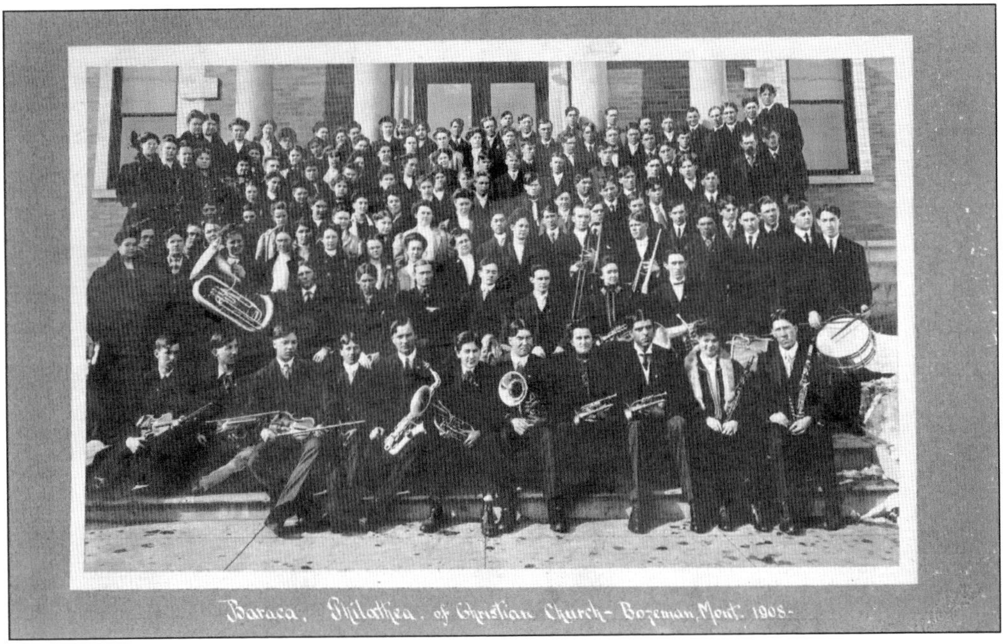

CHRISTIAN CHURCH BAND. Captioned "Baraca, Philathea, of Christian Church—Bozeman, Mont. 1908," this real-photo postcard image shows the young people's Sunday school class at the Christian church. As many as 150 members attended the class, which included an orchestra. The organizer and director was Mrs. Lee, wife of the church pastor. Both she and her husband, Rev. Milton H. H. Lee, were ordained ministers. Mrs. Lee is in the second row, second from right.

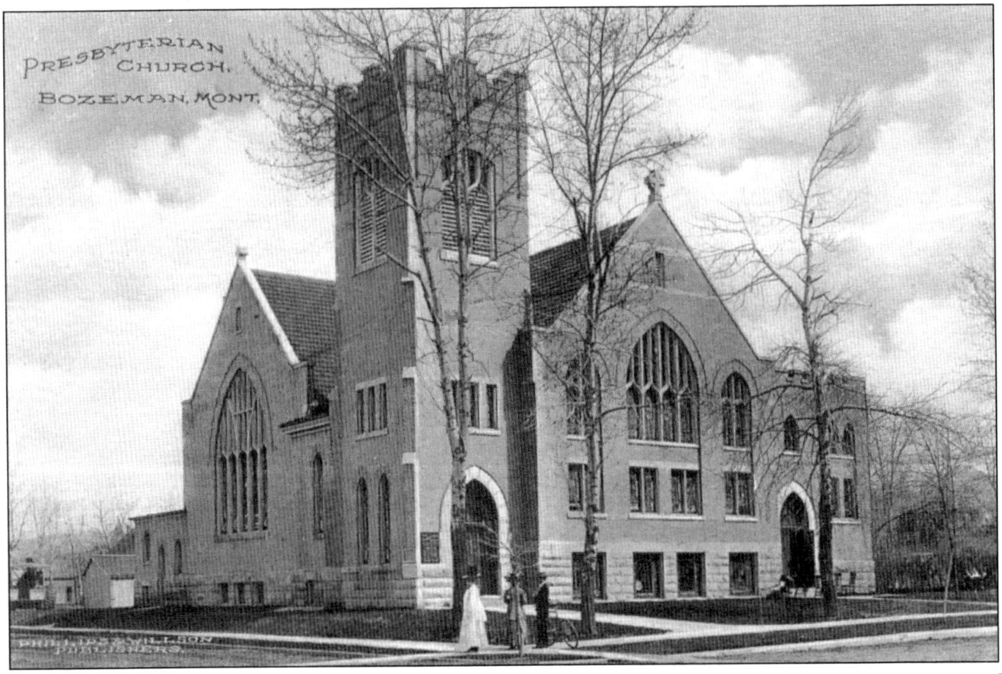

PRESBYTERIAN CHURCH. Three people stand in the foreground at the southeast corner of Babcock Street and Central Avenue. Behind them is the impressive new Presbyterian church, which had recently been completed at the time this *c.* 1910 printed postcard view was made.

Four

MAIN STREET

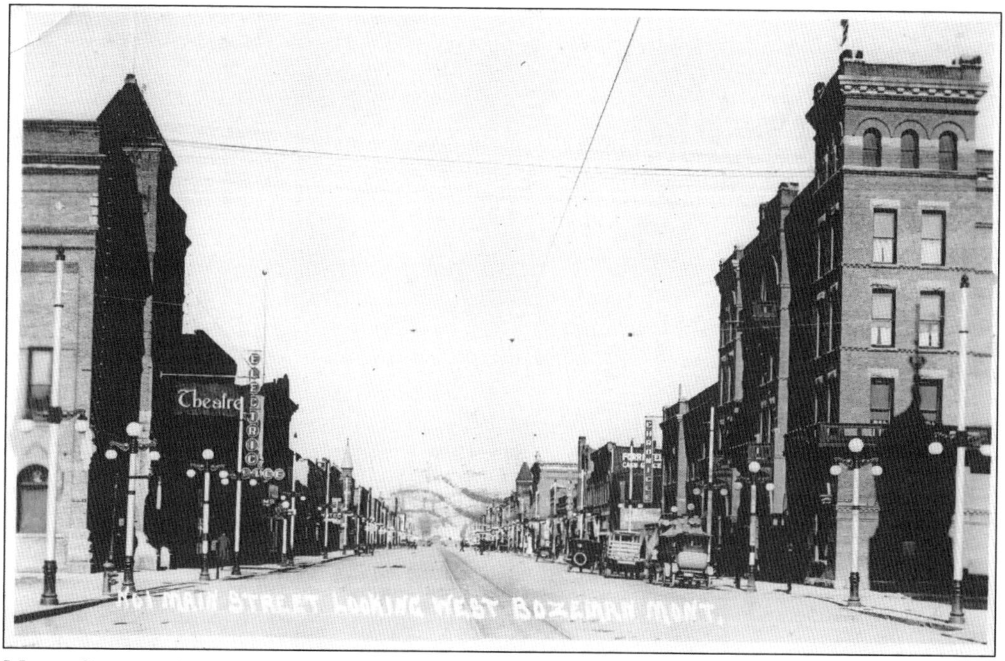

MAIN STREET LOOKING WEST. The Bozeman Hotel, at right, anchors the eastern end of Bozeman's Main Street as shown on this real-photo postcard, postmarked 1917. This hotel still stands today. The building across the street was the Bozeman Opera House.

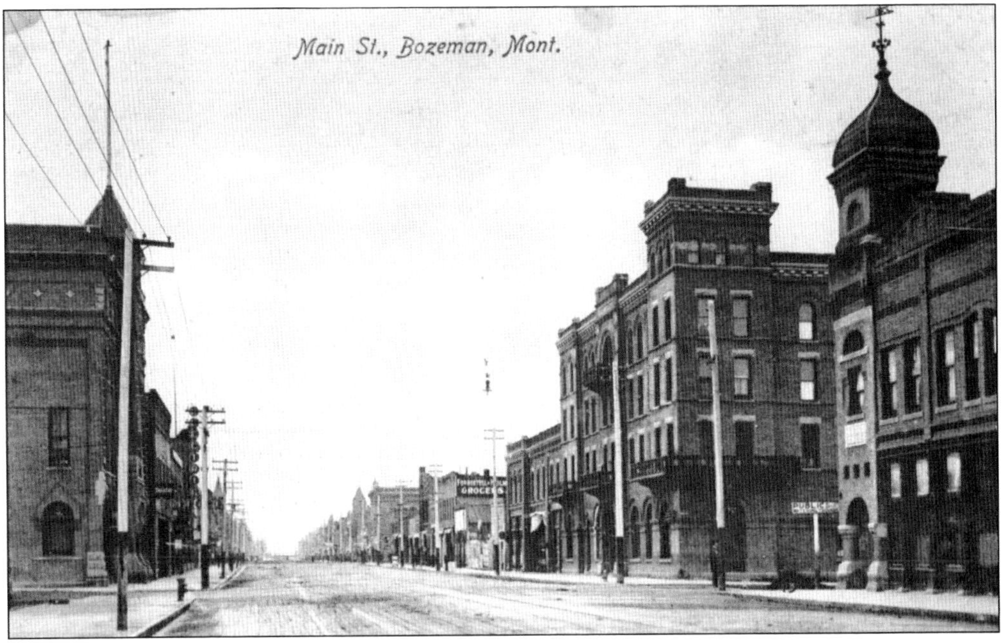

MAIN STREET LOOKING NORTHWEST. This printed postcard view of Main Street dates to about 1908 and is one of the earliest street views of Bozeman found on a postcard. The building at the far right is the Tilton Building, a mercantile. It was razed about 1963, and the city hall was built there. The Bozeman Hotel, with its corner tower, then the valley's premier hotel, is just to the west across Rouse Avenue.

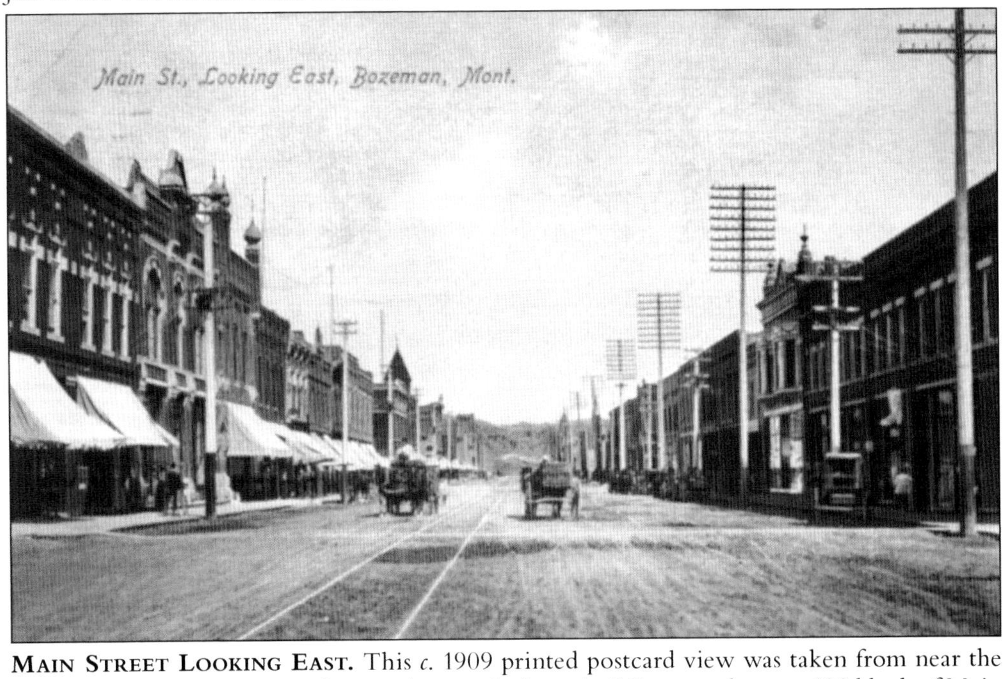

MAIN STREET LOOKING EAST. This *c.* 1909 printed postcard view was taken from near the intersection of Main Street and Tracy Avenue. It shows buildings on the west 100 block of Main Street. Horse-drawn wagons and buggies were still the most common transportation mode, but automobiles would be predominant on Main Street within a few years.

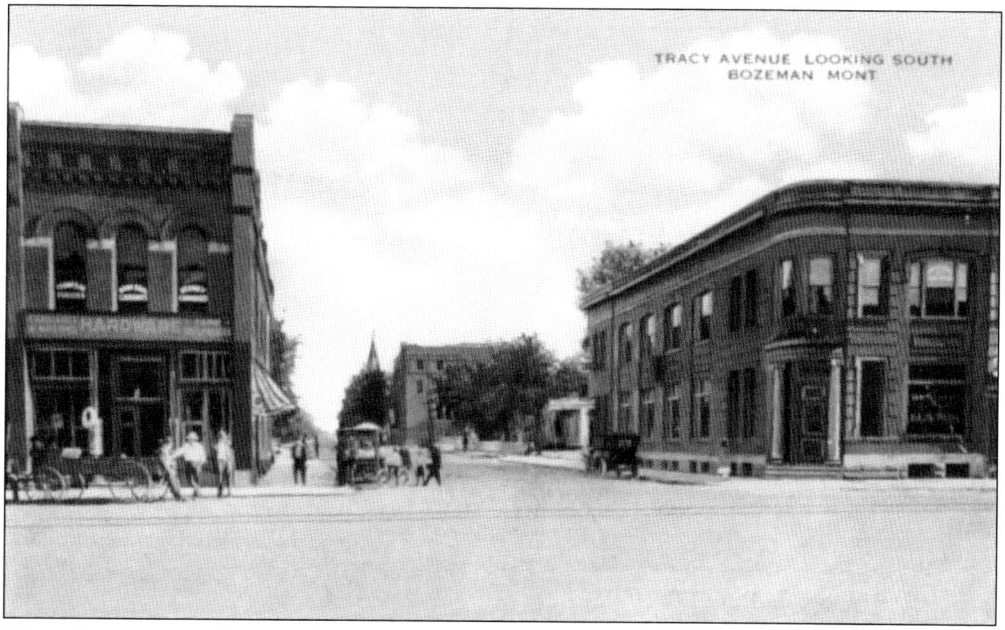

MAIN STREET AND TRACY AVENUE INTERSECTION. This *c.* 1912 printed postcard view, taken from the intersection of Main Street and Tracy Avenue, shows two prominent businesses on Bozeman's Main Street. At left is Ellis-Brandley and Company Hardware with signs advertising "Carriages & Wagon—Hardware—Farm Implements." The Gallatin Trust and Savings Bank is on the right. The church steeple in the background belongs to St. James Episcopal Cathedral.

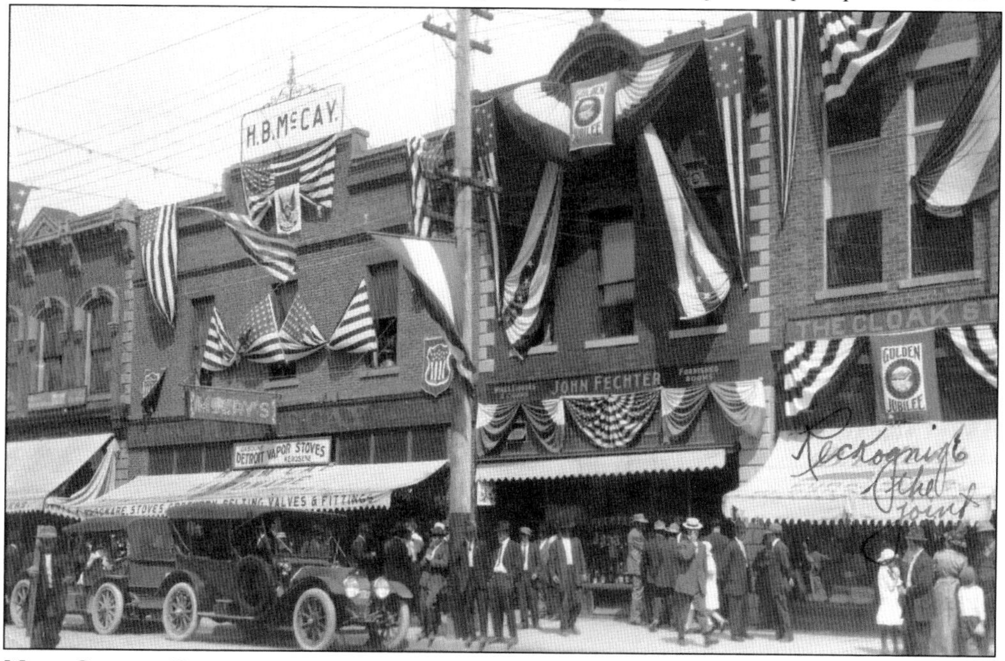

MAIN STREET DECORATED FOR GOLDEN JUBILEE. Patriotic flags and streamers along with Golden Jubilee banners mark this celebration along a north side section of Main Street on the west 100 block. The H. B. McCay hardware store is on the left. John Fechter's cigar store is center, and Braten's Fur Store is on the right, as shown on this *c.* 1916 real-photo postcard.

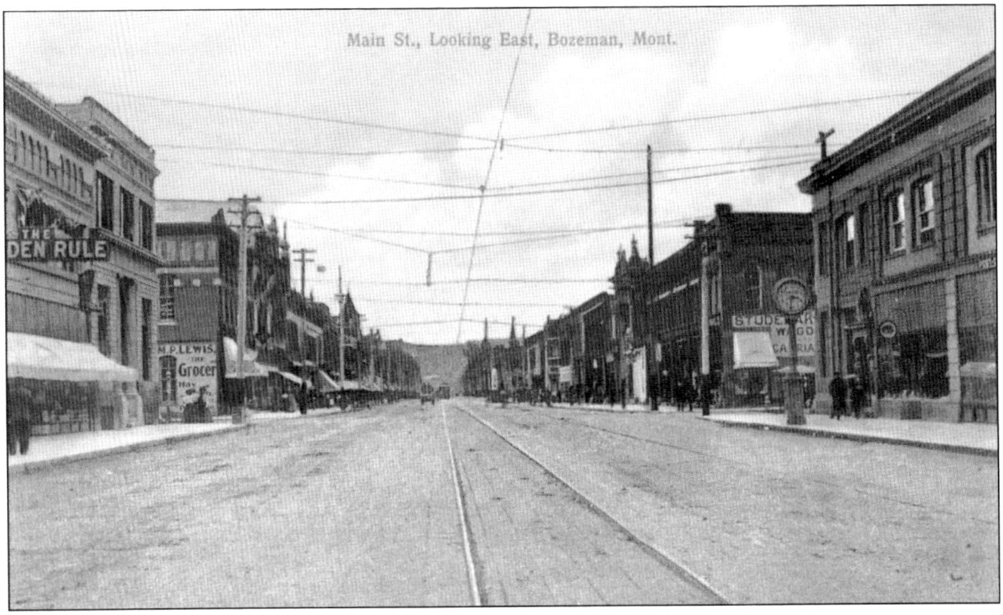

Main Street Looking East, About 1910. This view looks toward the intersection of Tracy Avenue and beyond. Visible at far left is the Golden Rule department store. The Gallatin Valley National Bank, one of Bozeman's earliest banks, and the M. P. Lewis grocery store are also at left. At the far right is the post office, which was located at 208 W. Main Street. A streetcar can be seen in the distance on this *c.* 1910 printed postcard view.

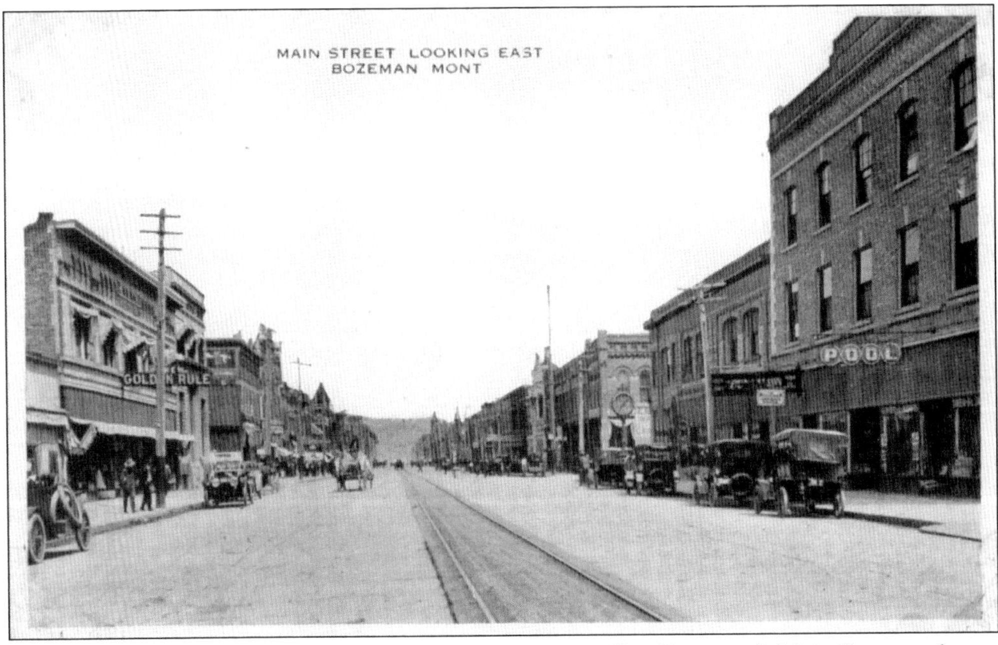

Main Street Looking East, About 1920. Cars now line Bozeman's Main Street as shown in this *c.* 1920 printed postcard view, taken from nearly the same vantage point as the image above. Note that angle parking for cars had not yet been implemented. Streetcar tracks are still in place, but this service was likely out of operation by this time. The Golden Rule building, visible at left, still stands and underwent a major renovation in 2007.

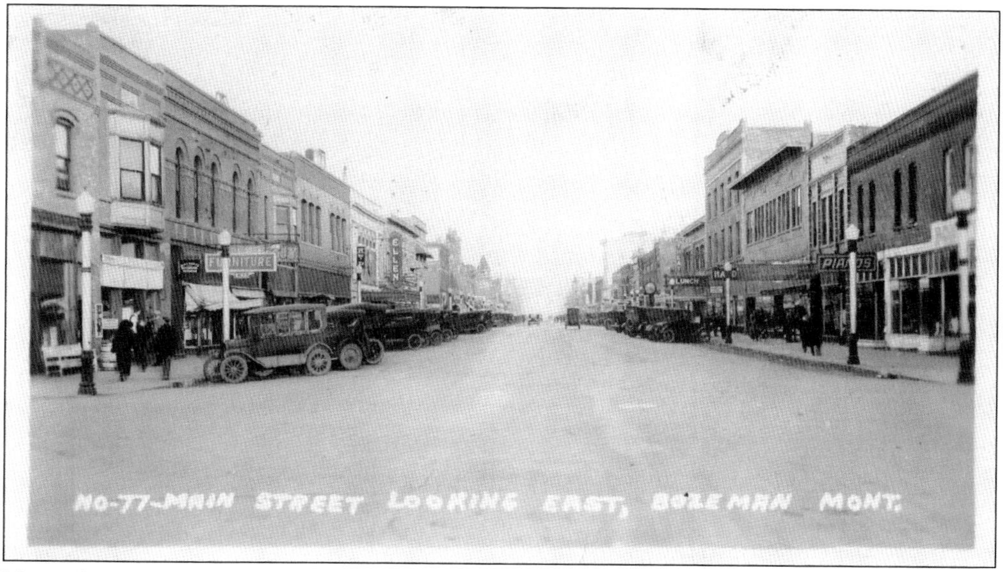

MAIN STREET LOOKING EAST, ABOUT 1925. This real-photo postcard view was taken near the intersection of Main Street and Willson Avenue. The image includes an early view of the Ellen Theater, which is visible at center left. The Ellen Theater opened its doors in 1919 and specialized in the showing of motion pictures. Across the street from the Ellen was the newly opened Rialto Theater. The Gem Theater was Bozeman's other movie theater at the time.

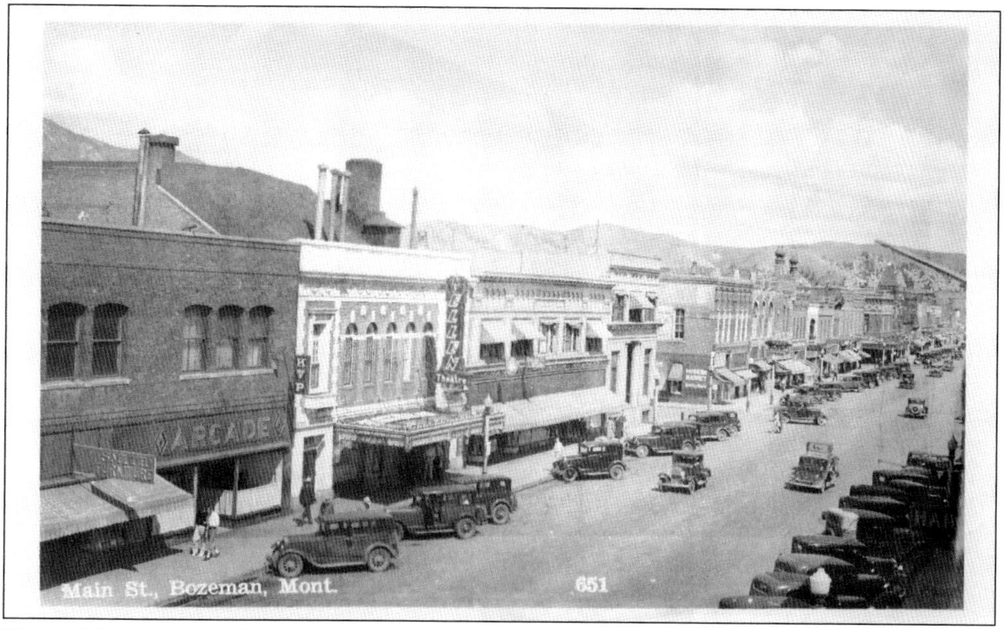

ELLEN THEATER ON MAIN STREET. A new but short-lived sign advertising the Ellen Theater is visible near the center of this *c.* 1930 real-photo postcard view. Designed by renowned architect Fred Willson, the theater was named for Ellen Trent Story, wife of the prominent Gallatin Valley entrepreneur and cattle rancher Nelson Story. This view looks east down the north side of Main Street to the Tracy Avenue intersection and beyond. Smith Furniture and the Arcade can be seen at left. (Photograph by Schlechten Studio, Bozeman, Montana; courtesy of R. Dale Beland.)

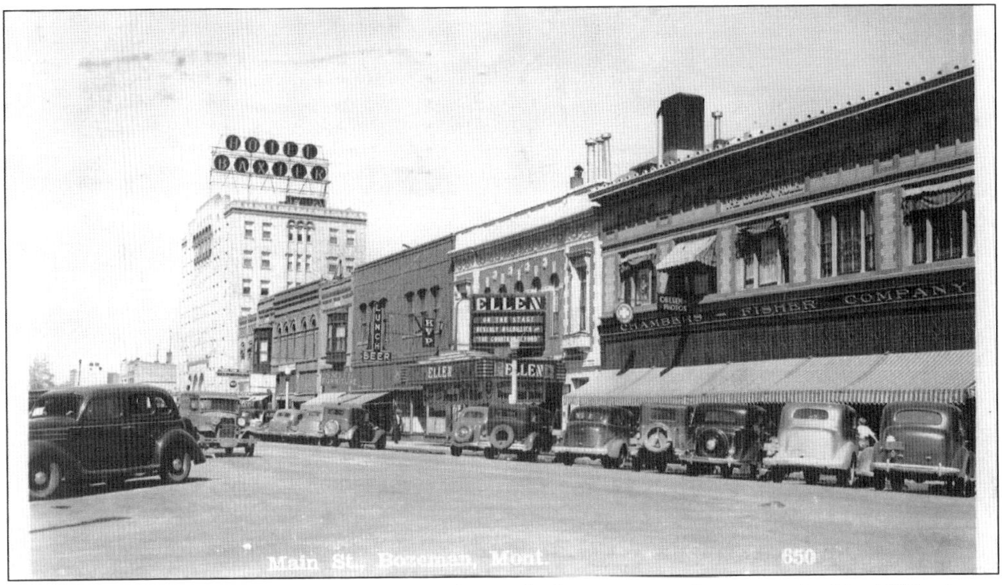

NORTH SIDE OF WEST MAIN STREET. This real-photo postcard, postmarked in 1936, shows the north side of much of the business district on West Main Street. Prominent at right are the Chambers-Fisher Company department store and the Ellen Theatre. The theater's marquee reads, "On the Stage—Beverly Hillbillies and 'The Country Beyond.'" The Baxter Hotel rises tall in the background. (Photograph by Schlechten Studio, Bozeman, Montana.)

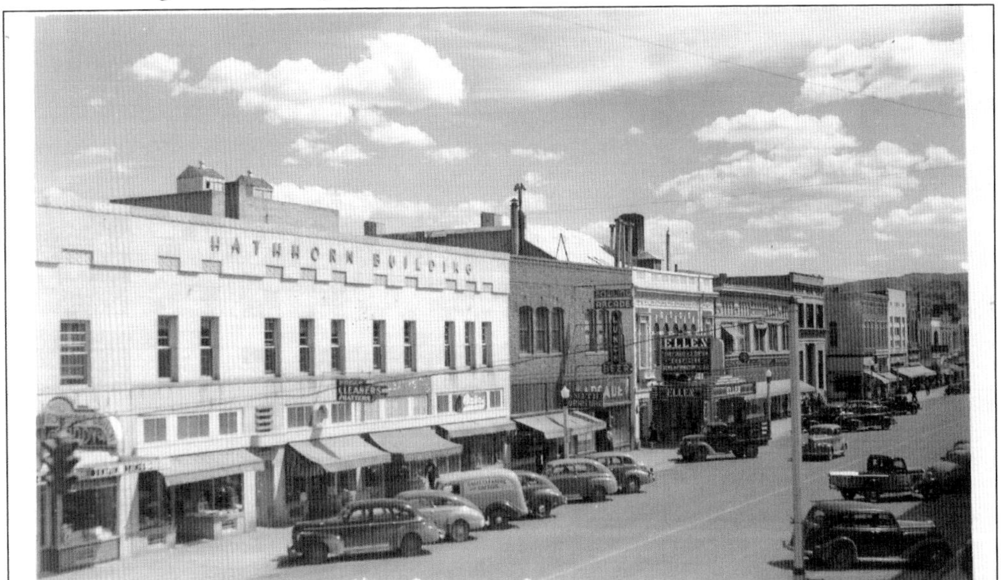

HATHHORN BUILDING AND ELLEN THEATRE. Angle parking was still used on Main Street when this *c.* 1948 real-photo postcard view was made. This view looks east from near the Willson Avenue intersection. The Hathhorn Building and the Ellen Theater are clearly visible. In recent years, the Ellen fell into disrepair, but a major renovation project is now underway to rejuvenate this beloved theater. The first live theatrical performance presented on the Ellen stage in over 30 years was held in December 2008. (Photograph by Schlechten Studio, Bozeman, Montana.)

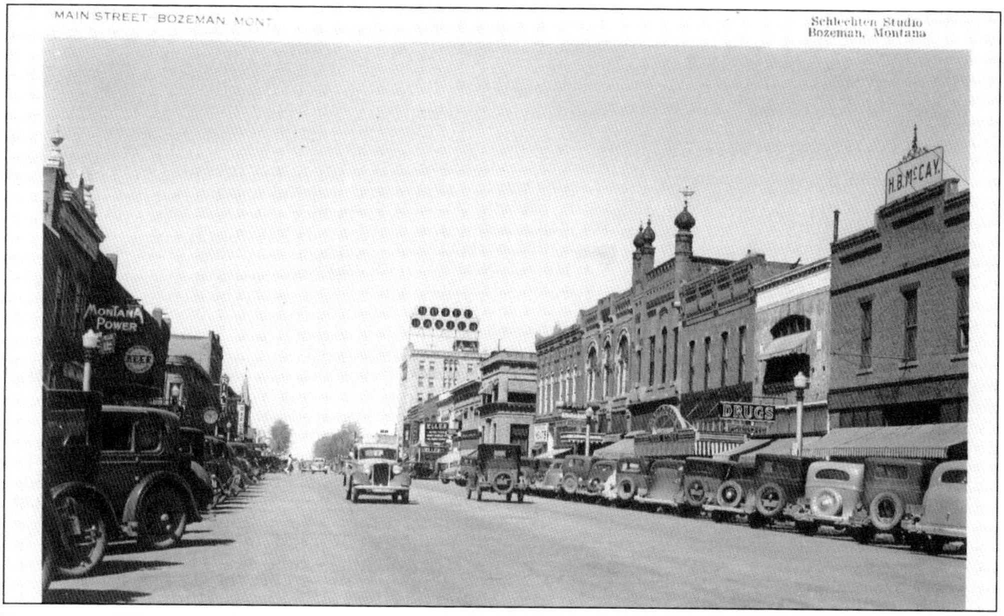

Looking West on Busy Main Street. The western end of Main Street's business district is featured in this *c.* 1940 real-photo postcard. H. B. McCay hardware is at right, and the Montana Power Company office is on the far left. Farther down, on the right side of the street, the Ellen Theater marquee can be seen. The Baxter Hotel stands tall in the background. (Photograph by Schlechten Studio, Bozeman, Montana.)

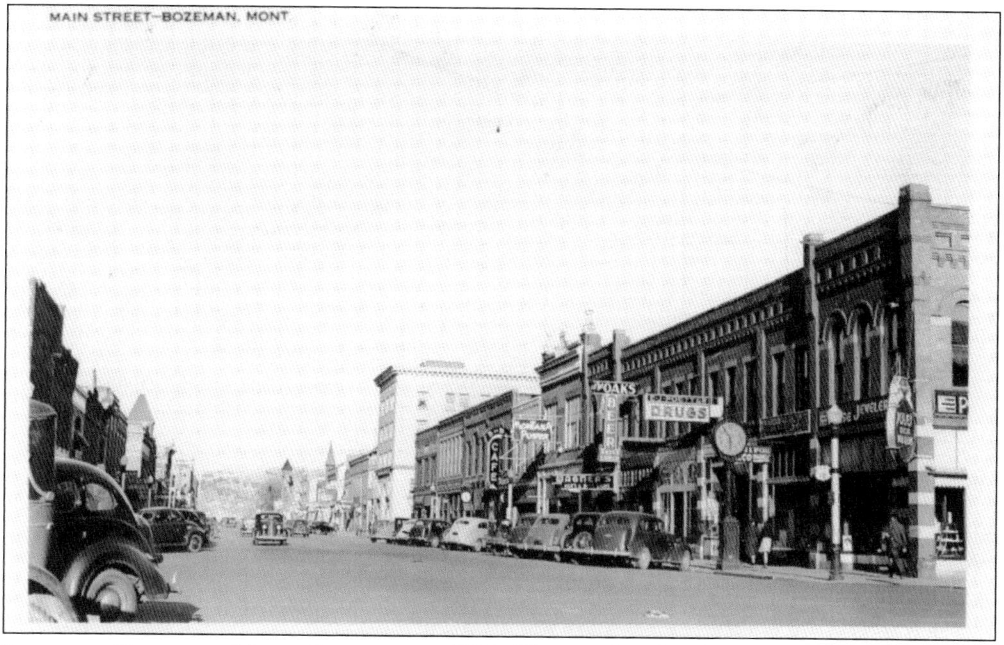

Looking East on Main Street, c. 1938. The south side of Main Street's 200 block is pictured in this *c.* 1940 real-photo postcard. Pease Jewelry (now Miller Jewelry) is at right, and signs for E. J. Poetter Drugs, Wagner's Men's and Boy's Store, Montana Power, and B-B Café are clearly visible. Although the photographer is not identified, the image is similar to a picture Schlechten Studio in Bozeman, Montana, would produce.

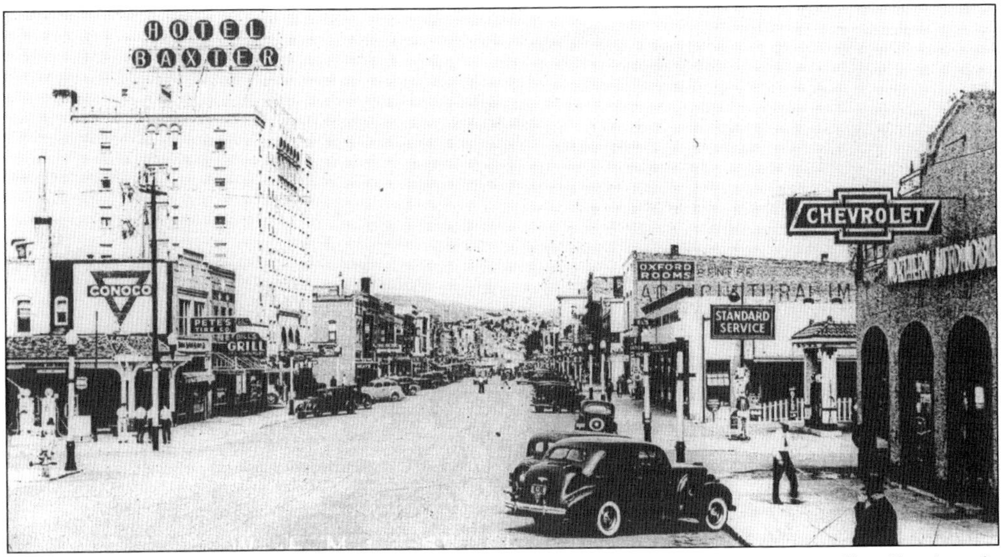

LOOKING EAST ON MAIN STREET, C. 1948. With the west-side shopping mall still a decade away, most businesses were nestled on a six-block stretch on Main Street. This real-photo postcard shows part of the West Main Street business district. Pete's Tire Company, Bill's Grill (later Doug's Grill), and the Baxter Hotel are prominent at left, while the Oxford Hotel is visible at right. A Conoco gas station (later a Texaco station) and a Standard service station can be seen in the foreground. Most of these businesses, including the two gas stations, are gone now. (Photograph by Johnson.)

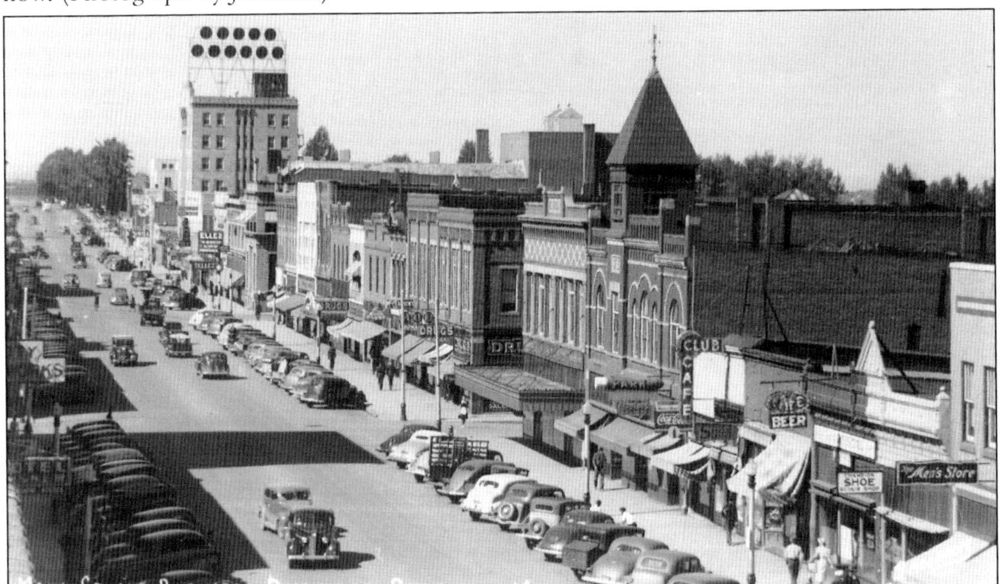

CENTRAL BUSINESS DISTRICT, C. 1945. No empty parking spaces, as shown in this real-photo postcard image depicting the north side near the center of the business district on Bozeman's Main Street, indicated that business was good. Many signs are visible, including the Men's Store, Champion Shoe Repair Shop, and Club Café at right. The Baxter Hotel anchors the west end of Main Street in the background. (Photograph by Sanborn Souvenir Company, Denver, Colorado.)

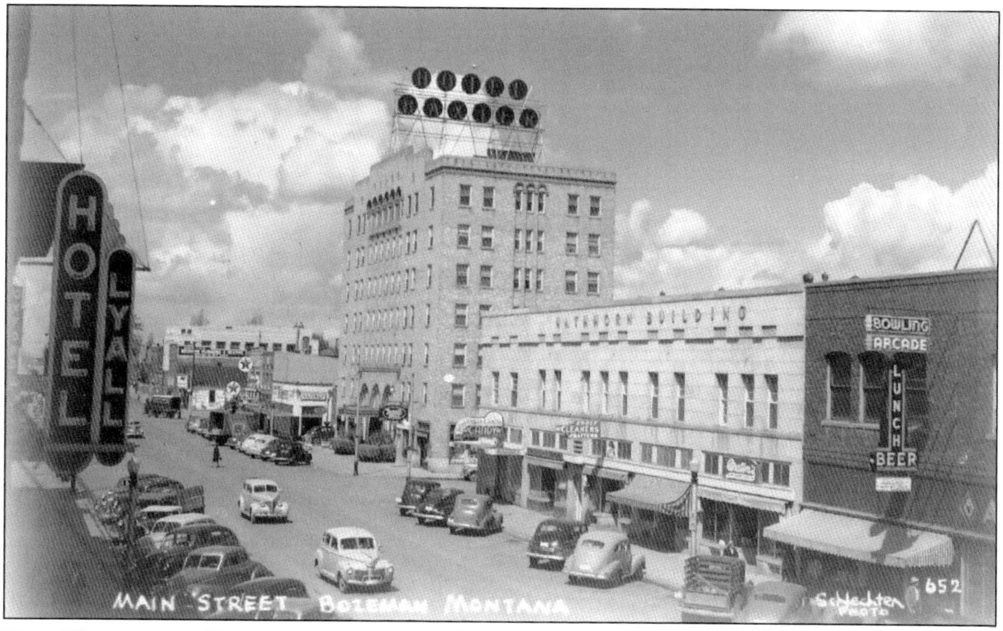

THE HATHHORN BUILDING, *c.* 1945. The Hathhorn Building hosted several businesses in Bozeman's business district, including a candy store and a cleaning business. This image appears to have been taken from a window perch at the Lyall Hotel (the sign visible at far left). Bozeman's tallest hotel, the Baxter, dominates the north side of the 100 block of West Main Street. The seven-story Baxter hosted a Rexall Drug Store on the corner. A Safeway grocery store, left, is also seen in this real-photo postcard. (Photograph by Schlechten Studio, Bozeman, Montana.)

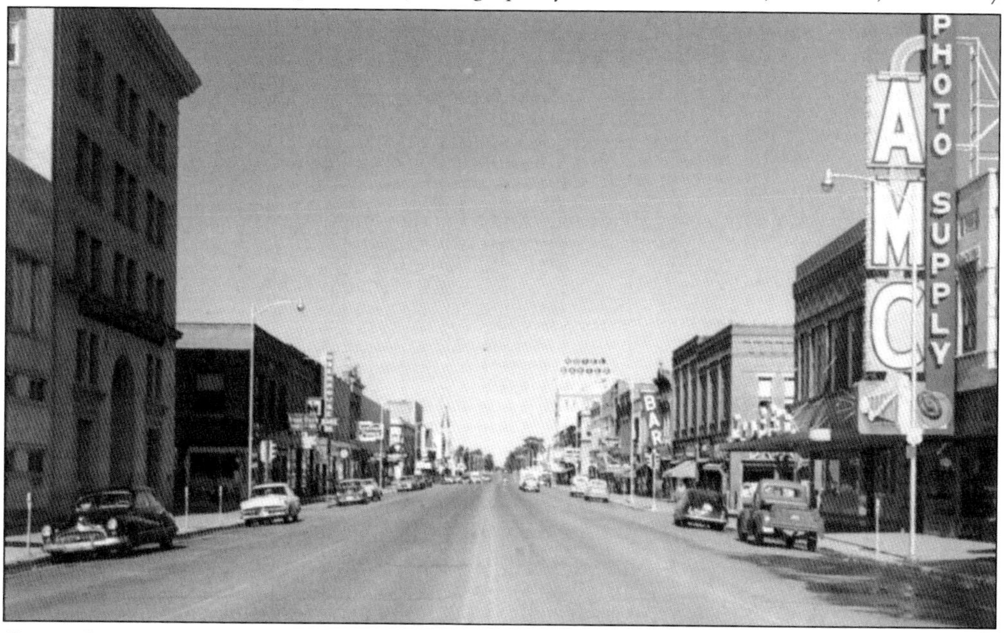

GIANT NEON SIGN ON MAIN STREET. The Automatic Machine Company Photo Supply sign at right was the largest neon sign in Montana at the time this *c.* 1955 chrome postcard image was taken. It advertised Bill Sullivan's business. This view looks west toward the central business district on Main Street near the intersection with Black Avenue.

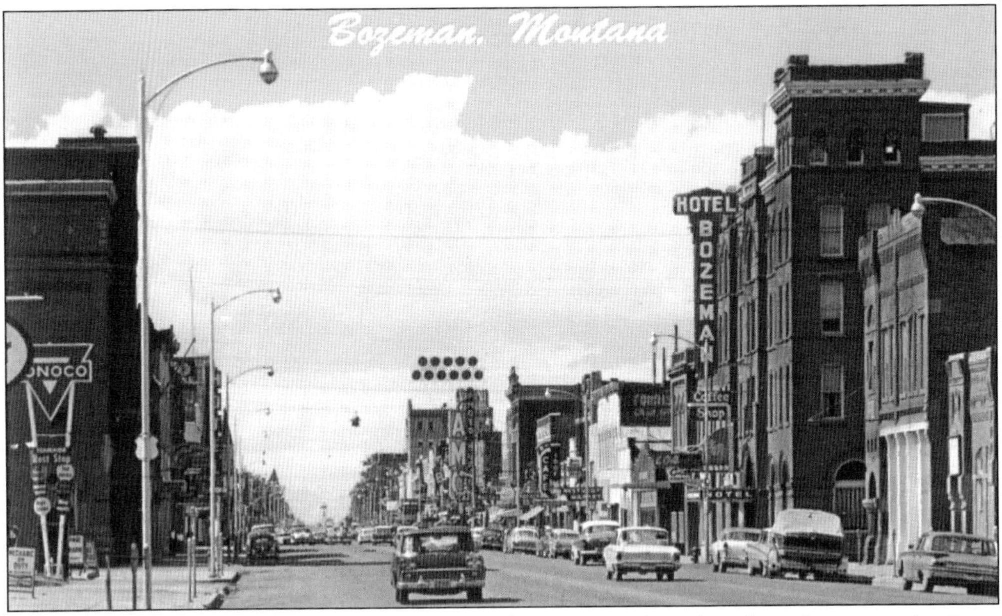

LOOKING WEST ON MAIN STREET, *c.* 1961. The Bozeman Hotel anchors the eastern business district as shown in this chrome postcard view. Bozeman's Main Street remains relatively vibrant today, despite the addition of shopping centers, the Gallatin Valley Mall, and much additional business growth on North Seventh Avenue and North Nineteenth Avenue in recent years. A tragic natural gas explosion occurred on March 5, 2009, costing one life and destroying several buildings on the north side of Main Street, just west of the Bozeman Hotel.

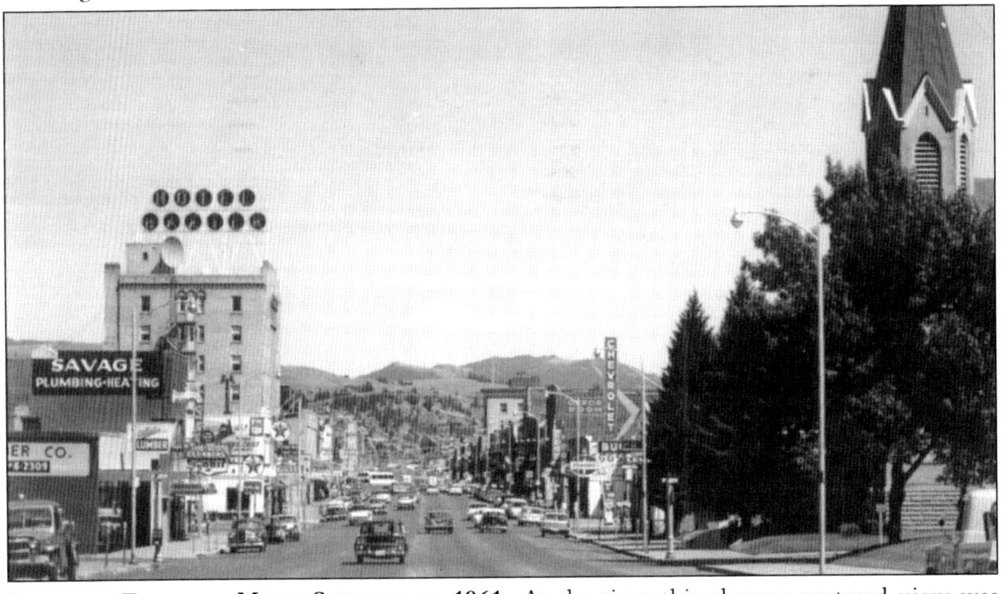

LOOKING EAST ON MAIN STREET, *c.* 1961. At the time this chrome postcard view was taken in about 1961, many changes had recently taken place about a mile to the west. The new Bozeman high school was completed in 1957. Just to the west of the new high school, Buttrey's shopping center had opened in 1960. Today, the Baxter Hotel, shown at left, remains the prominent building on Main Street, and Holy Rosary Catholic Church (steeple visible at right) continues to operate as well.

Five

Montana State University

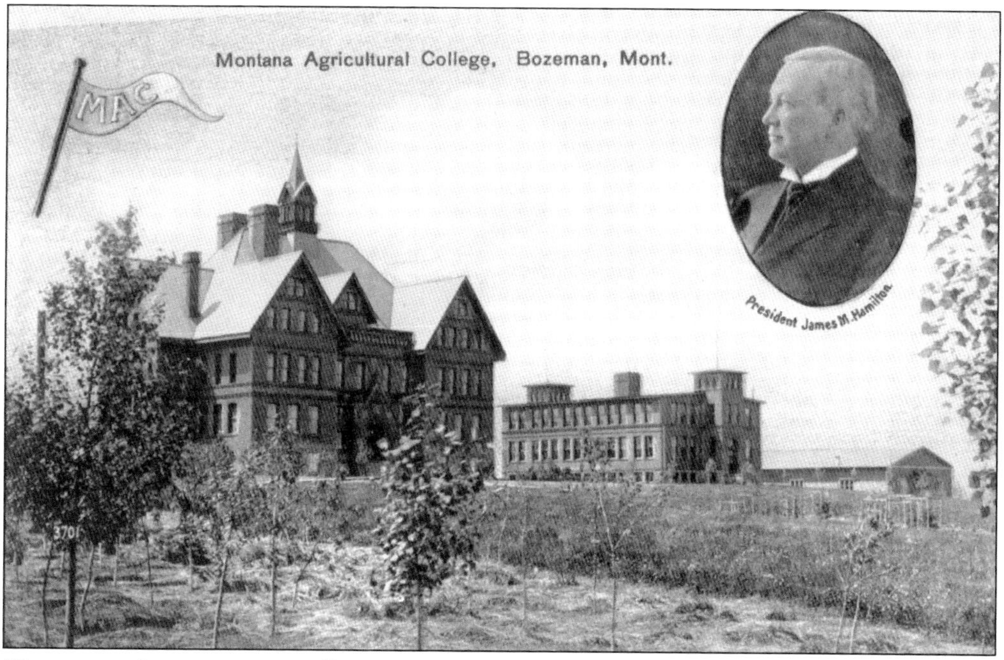

Montana Agricultural College and President Hamilton. This *c.* 1908 printed postcard image shows Montana Hall, left, and the old chemistry building on the early campus of what is now Montana State University. In 1893, the Agricultural College of the State of Montana was founded as the state's land grant college. Renamed Montana College of Agriculture and Mechanic Arts, it became better known as Montana Agricultural College, or MAC. Soon after, the institution was renamed Montana State College, and in 1965, it earned its present name, Montana State University, or MSU.

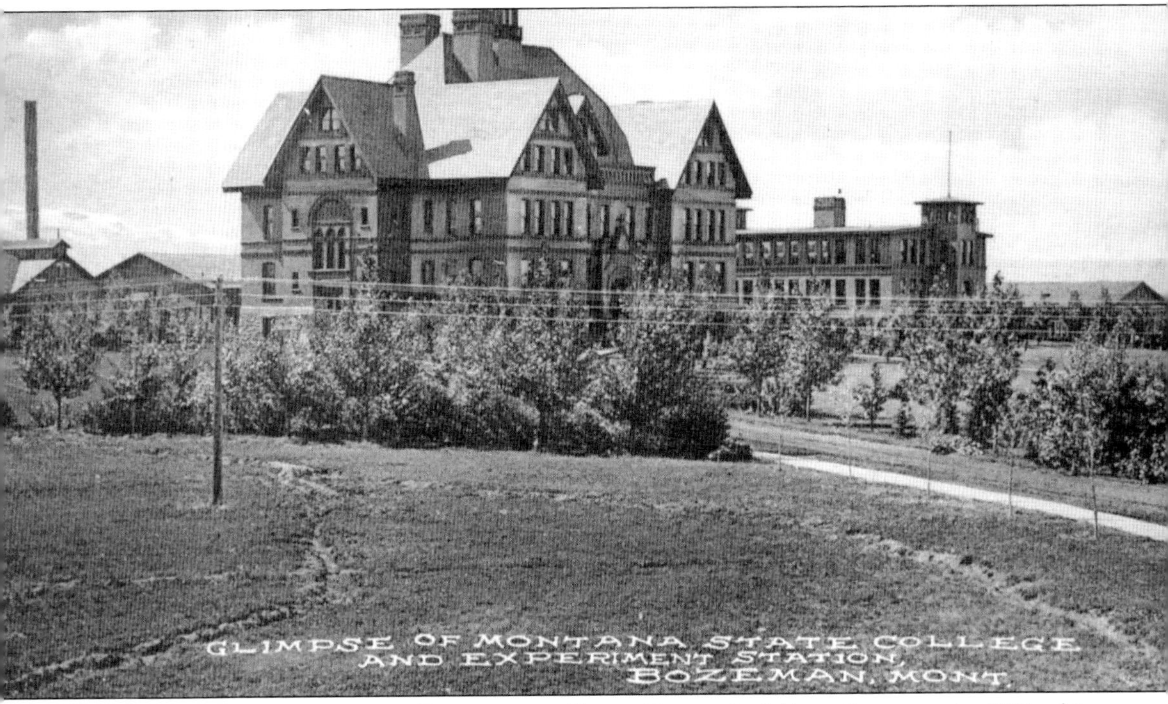

MONTANA STATE COLLEGE PANORAMIC VIEW. Postmarked from Bozeman in 1913, this double-sized postcard provides a good view of much of the early campus. Note that the institution was referred to as Montana State College and Experiment Station on the postcard. Main Hall,

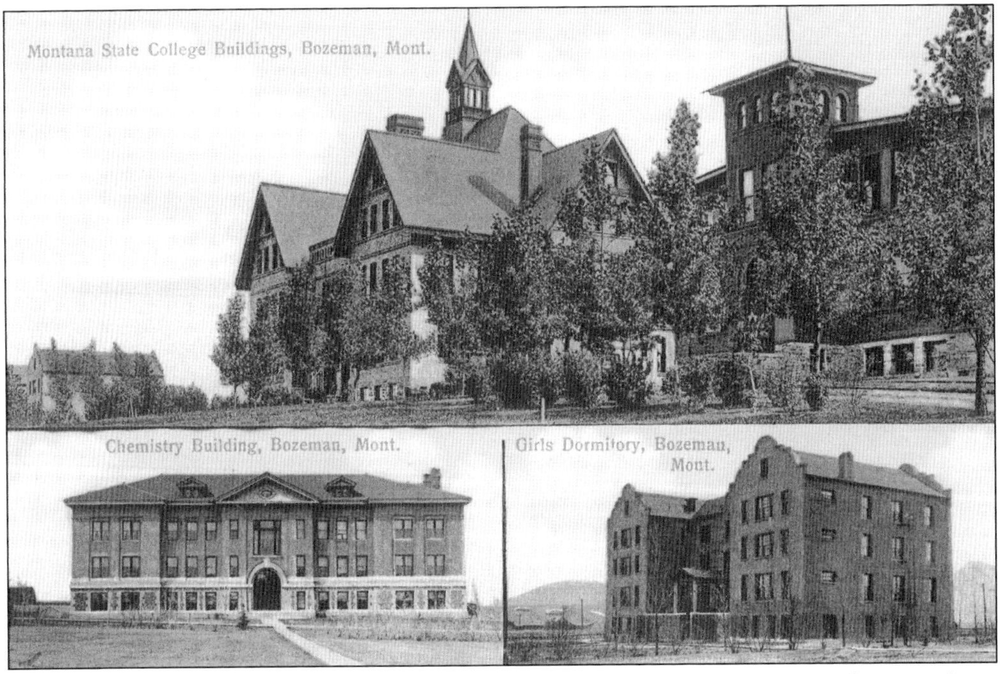

MONTANA STATE COLLEGE MULTI-VIEW. Pictured here in a *c.* 1912 printed postcard are more early campus buildings. The top view shows Main Hall, at left, and the old chemistry building is seen in the lower left view. At lower right is the girls' dormitory building.

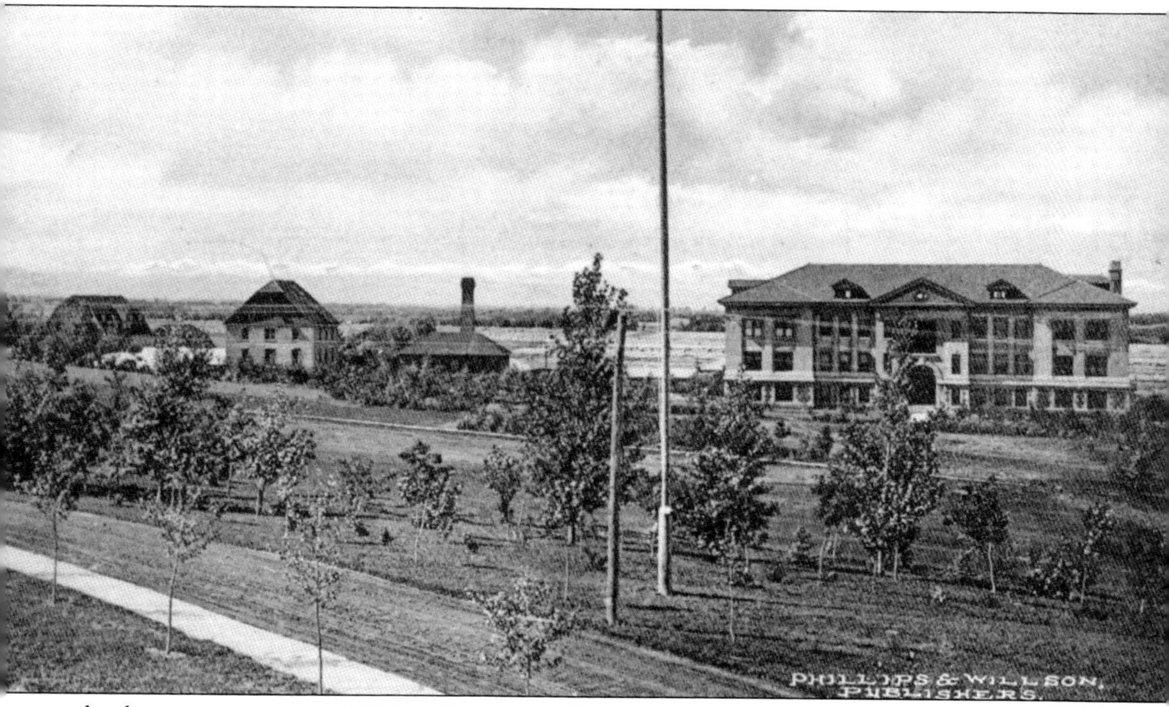

also known as Montana Hall, is the large building at left. Next to it is the old chemistry building, which burned down in 1916. The structure at the far right is Linfield Hall.

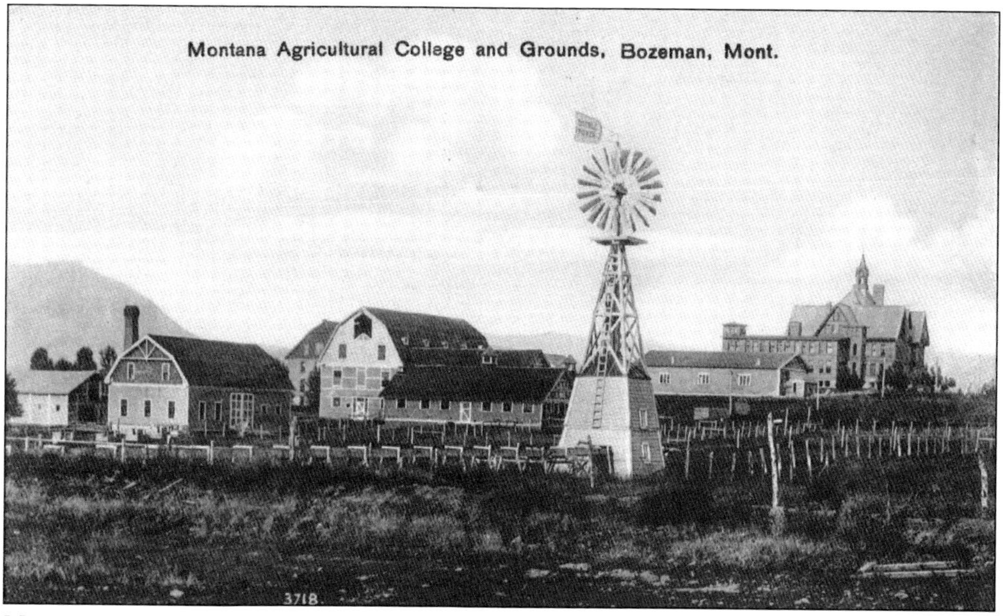

MONTANA STATE COLLEGE AGRICULTURAL BUILDINGS. A windmill set up to help supply water to livestock is prominent in the foreground of this view showing the college's barns and other agricultural structures. Visible in this *c.* 1910 printed postcard view is Main Hall, the college's administration building, at right.

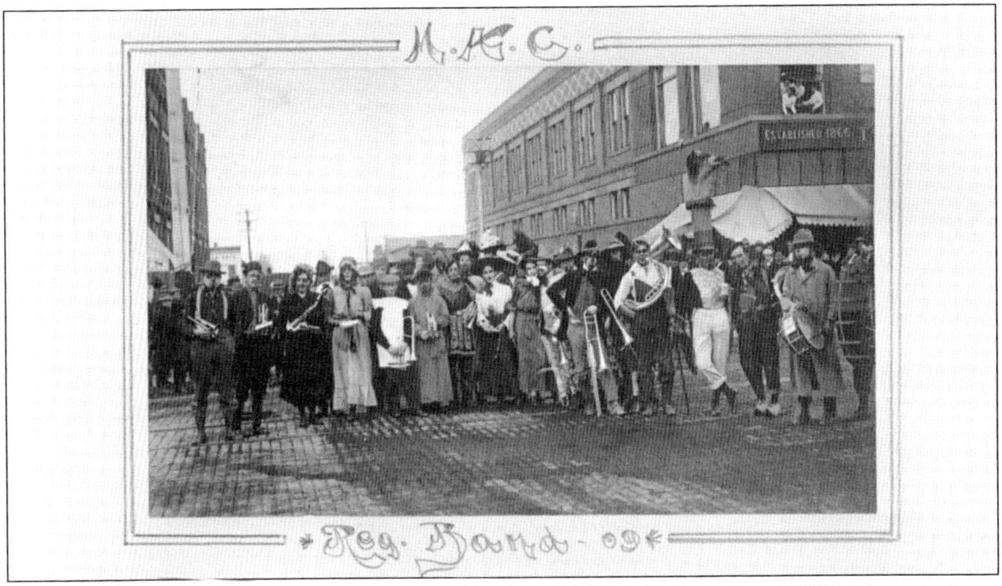

COLLEGE BAND ON MAIN STREET, 1909. Captioned "M.A.C. Reg. Band '09," this real-photo view may have been taken during the Sweet Pea Festival in August 1909. The band members are certainly dressed for fun, as many sport makeup and wear humorous costumes. MAC was short for Montana Agricultural College. (Photograph by Schlechten Studio, Bozeman, Montana.)

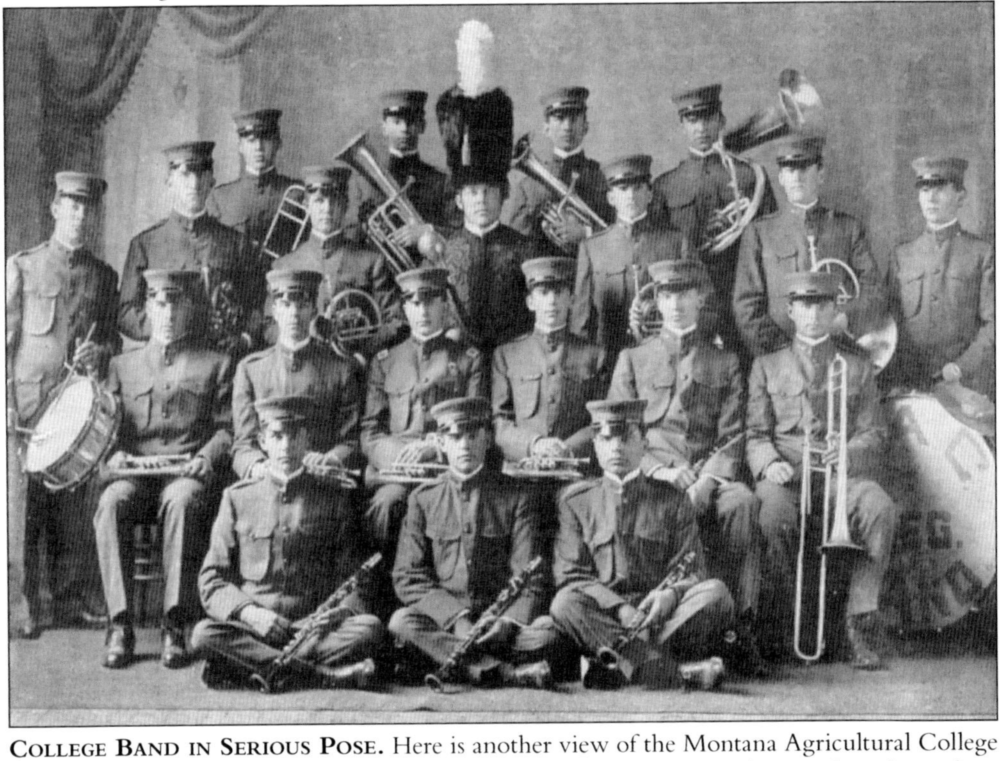

COLLEGE BAND IN SERIOUS POSE. Here is another view of the Montana Agricultural College Regimental Band. Quite a contrast to the image at the top of the page, the members shown here are dressed in their formal attire and strike a serious pose. The bandleader was Louis Howard, as noted on this *c.* 1910 printed postcard. (Courtesy of Ken Hamlin.)

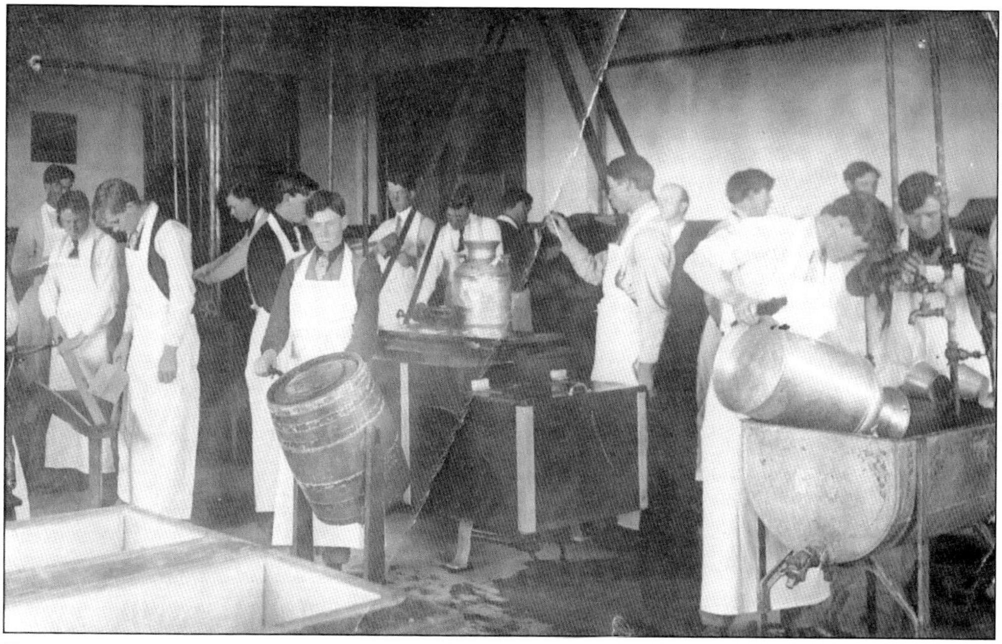

Dairy Class, *c.* 1912. Postmarked from Bozeman, a message from "Frank" penned on the back of this real-photo postcard reads, "This is a picture of the dairy class. Finished it last semester. Got an A on the exam. Taking stock judging this semester like it fine. Masquerade at the springs next Friday."

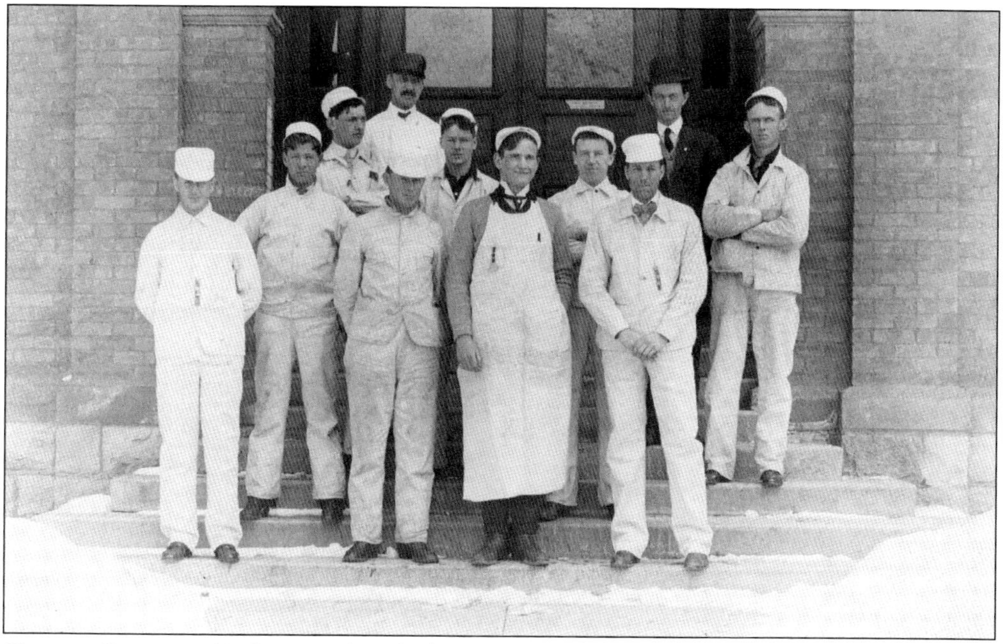

Cheese Class, *c.* 1908. Penned on the back of this *c.* 1908 real-photo postmark by presumably one of the young men in the image is, "The pict is the cheese class of '08 at the M.A.C. The man at the left in upper row with black cap is State Milk Inspector Havens. The man in the derby is Class Officer Fuserenel . . . we were looking right on to the snow and it made us squint." (Courtesy of Ken Hamlin.)

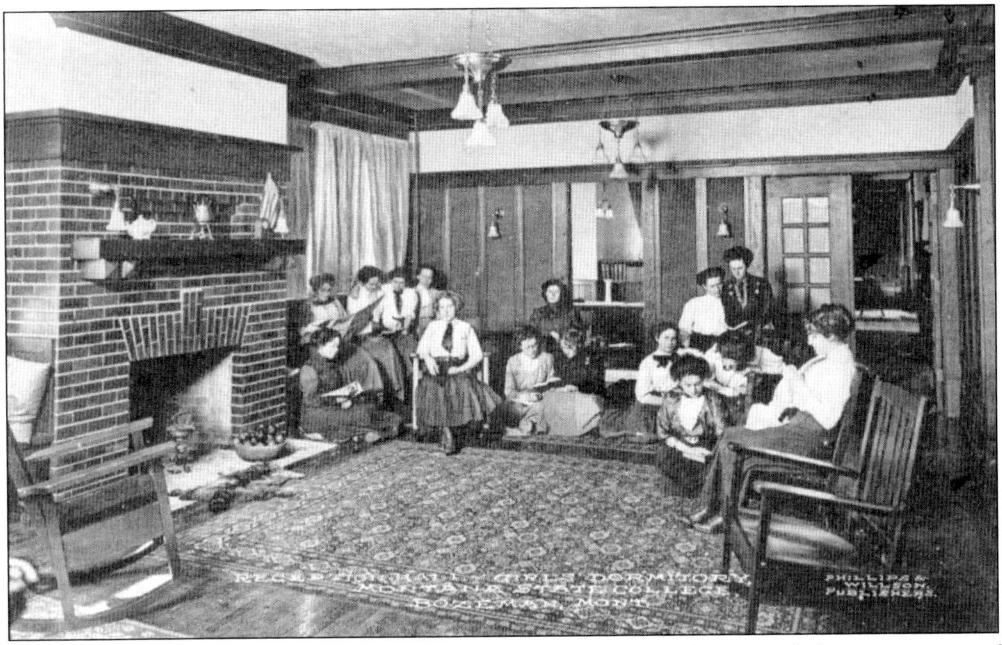

RECEPTION HALL, GIRLS DORMITORY. This *c.* 1915 printed postcard shows a group of college girls entertaining themselves with reading, sewing, and conversation. Are there boys outside just waiting for the photographer to finish so they can visit their girlfriends? (Courtesy of Ken Hamlin.)

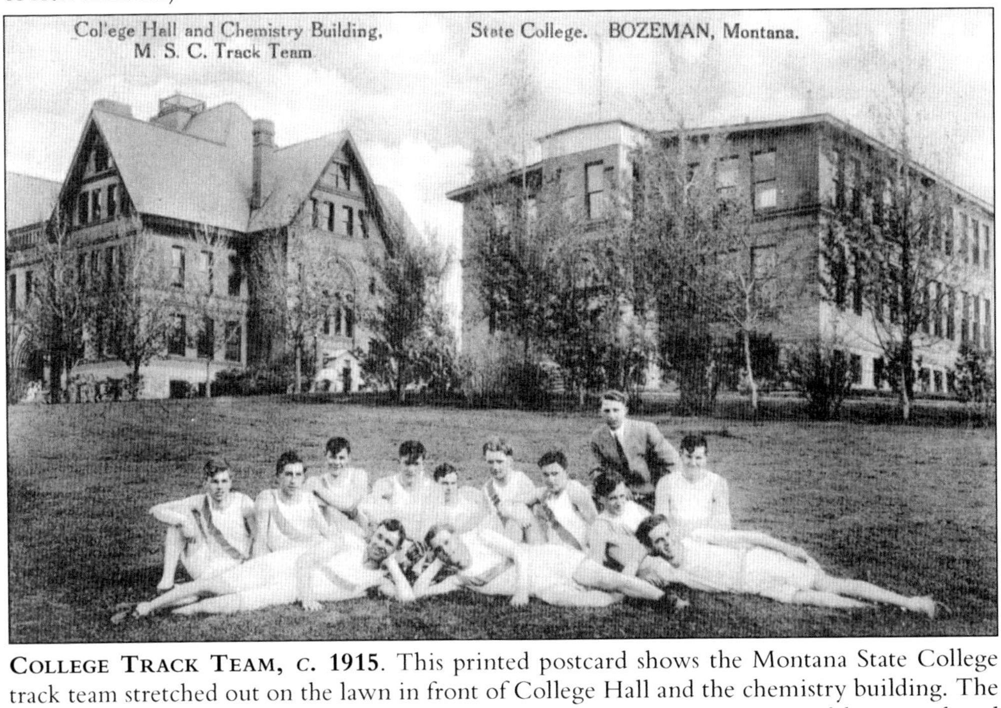

COLLEGE TRACK TEAM, *C.* 1915. This printed postcard shows the Montana State College track team stretched out on the lawn in front of College Hall and the chemistry building. The Bobcats have well-respected track and field and cross-country programs and have produced many national-caliber athletes. Coaches, in recent decades, who have been instrumental to the program include Rob Stark, Dale Kennedy, and Mike Carignan.

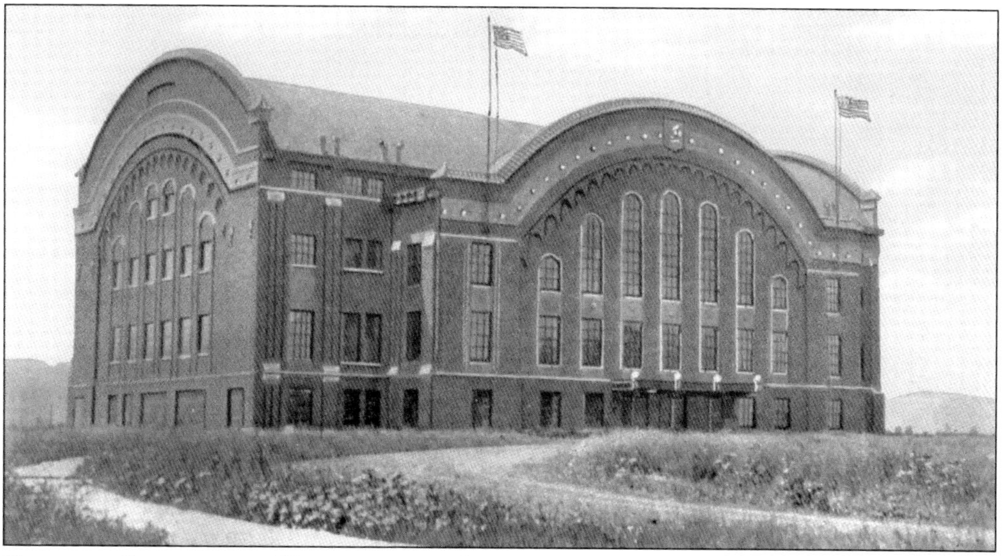

College Gymnasium, Home of the Golden Bobcats. This *c.* 1925 printed postcard shows the old gym, which served as a facility for physical education classes as well as for basketball games. Montana State boasts one of college basketball's legendary teams—the Golden Bobcats of the late 1920s. Utilizing an up-tempo style, coach Ott Romney's team, led by Cat Thompson, Frank Ward, Val Glynn, and Max Worthington, was named national champions by the Helms Foundation in 1928–1929. Cat Thompson was named one of the five greatest players in the first half of the 20th century.

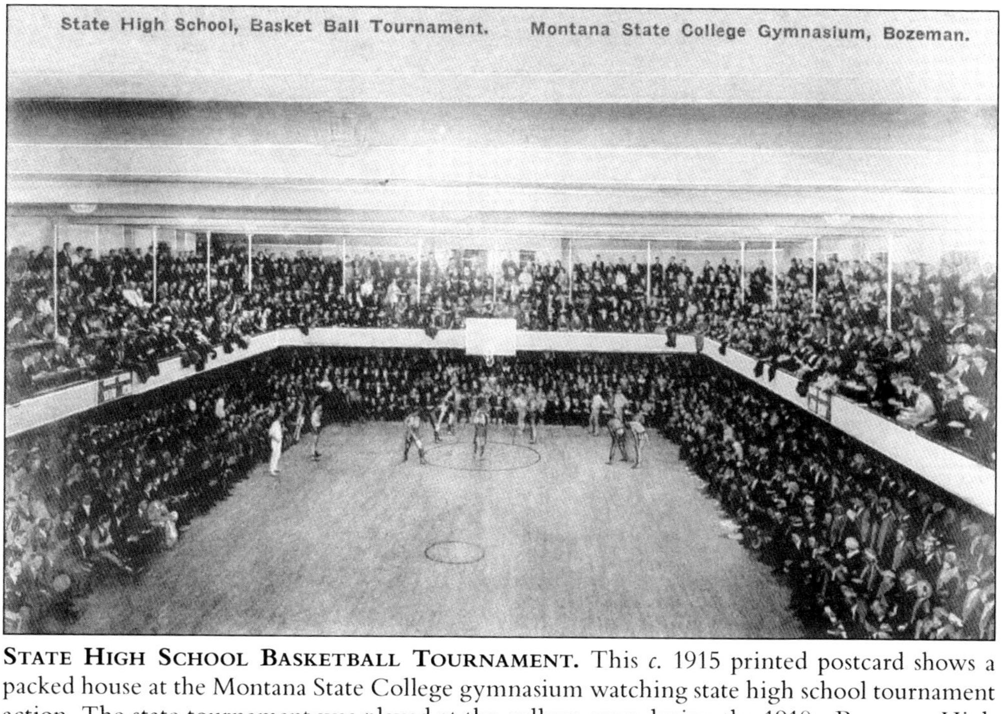

State High School Basketball Tournament. This *c.* 1915 printed postcard shows a packed house at the Montana State College gymnasium watching state high school tournament action. The state tournament was played at the college gym during the 1910s. Bozeman High School played in its first state championship game in 1917 but fell to Butte High by a score of 21-10. (Courtesy of Ken Hamlin.)

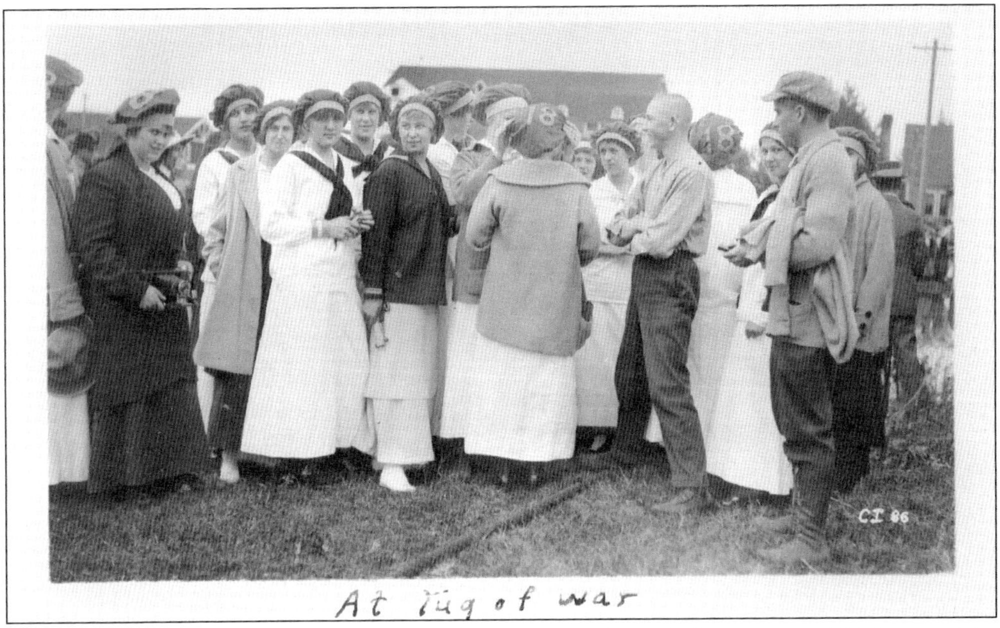

Getting Ready for Tug-of-War. The Montana State College class of 1918 assembles near the edge of a pool before the serious tug-of-war competition begins. Note that the ladies are wearing caps with "18" on them, and the lady in the dark clothing at left has her camera ready. The heavy rope sits on the ground in the center foreground of this *c.* 1920 real-photo postcard.

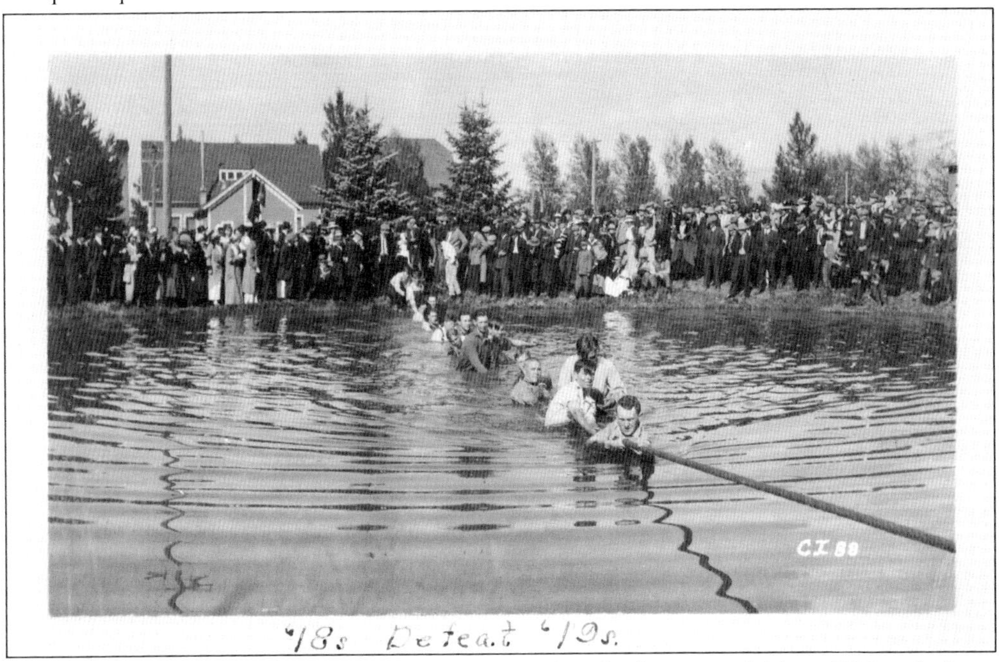

Class of 1919 in the Water. The note penned at the bottom of this *c.* 1920 real-photo postcard tells the story. The class of 1919 team was pulled into the water by their class of 1918 counterparts in this interclass tug-of-war competition. A large crowd of Montana State College students look on from water's edge.

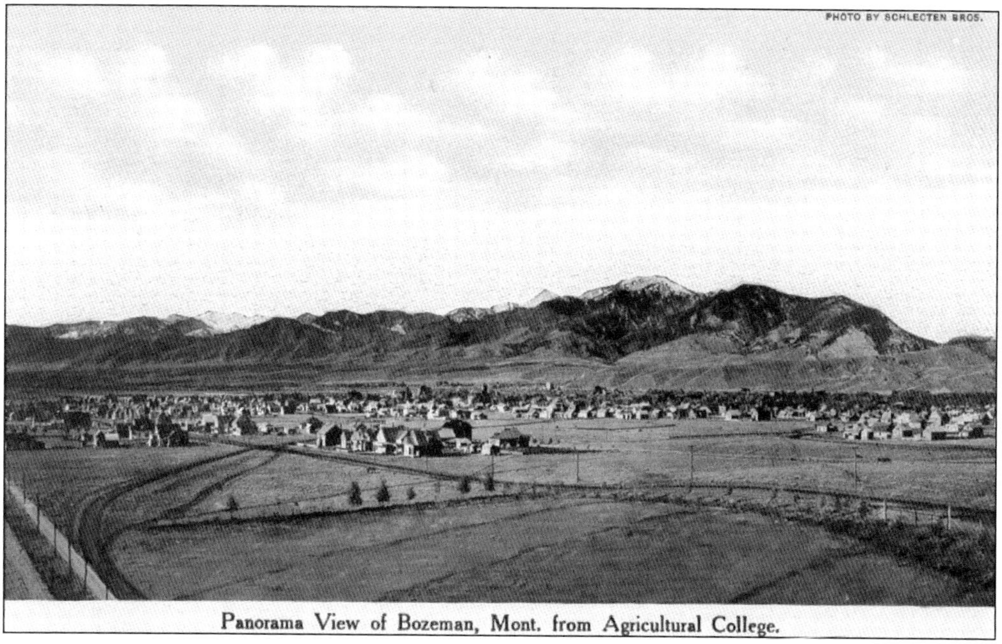

VIEW OF BOZEMAN FROM COLLEGE, *C.* 1910. This printed postcard looks north to the town of Bozeman from the college, possibly from the administration building. There was a considerable gap between the southernmost houses in Bozeman and the northern edge of campus at that time. Today there is no gap.

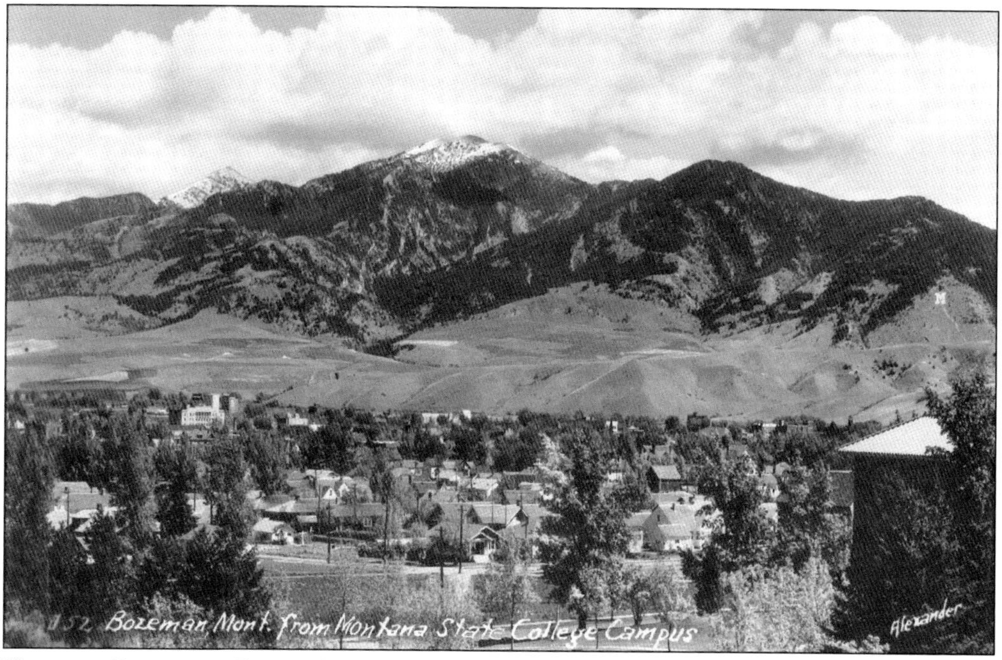

VIEW OF BOZEMAN FROM COLLEGE, *C.* 1955. By the time this real-photo postcard image was taken, the southern edge of the Bozeman community had grown to the edge of the college campus. This view looks north over the town of Bozeman to the Bridger Mountains in the background. (Photograph by Bertha Alexander, Bozeman, Montana.)

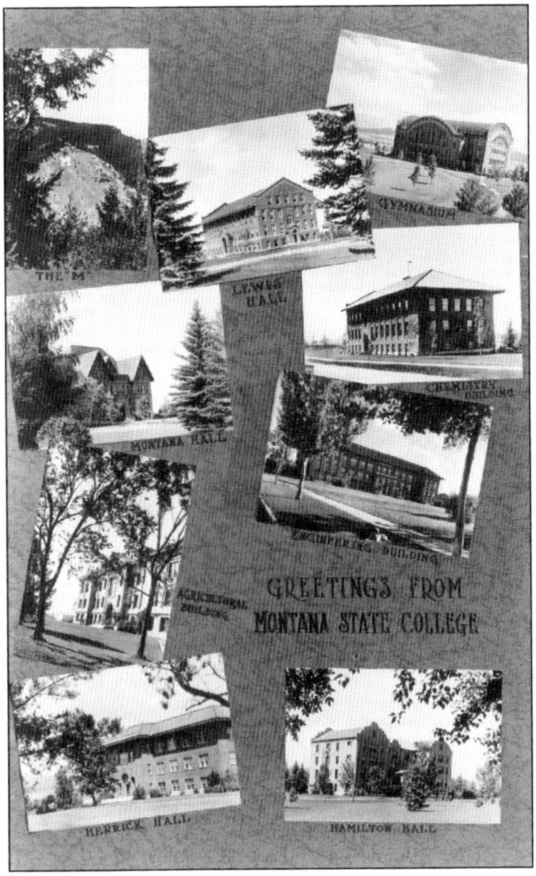

Greetings from Montana State College. This *c.* 1940 real-photo postcard multi-view features, from top left, Big M, Lewis Hall, gymnasium, chemistry building, engineering building, Hamilton Hall, Herrick Hall, agricultural building, and Montana Hall.

Women's Campus Dormitories, c. 1945. This real-photo postcard shows the Alfred Atkinson Quadrangle. Probably the only major construction done on campus during the 1930s, this group of buildings was completed in 1935. These dormitories were a desirable commodity for female students who wished to live on campus. Known as the Quads, these Tudor-style buildings each house about 20 students who live like family with a common kitchen and dining room. (Photograph by Sanborn Souvenir Company, Denver, Colorado.)

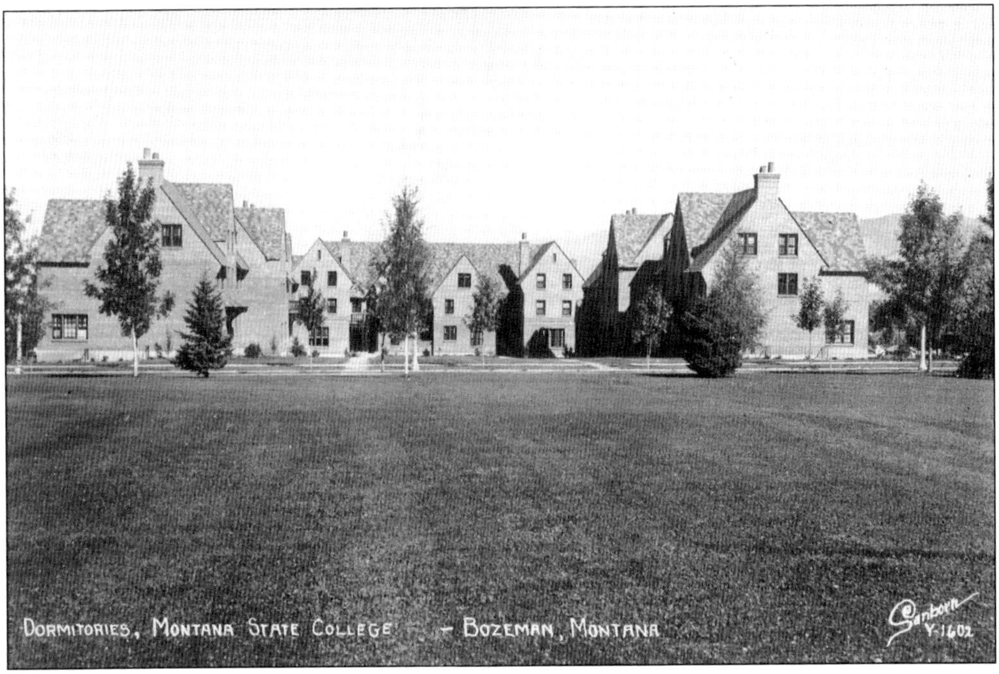

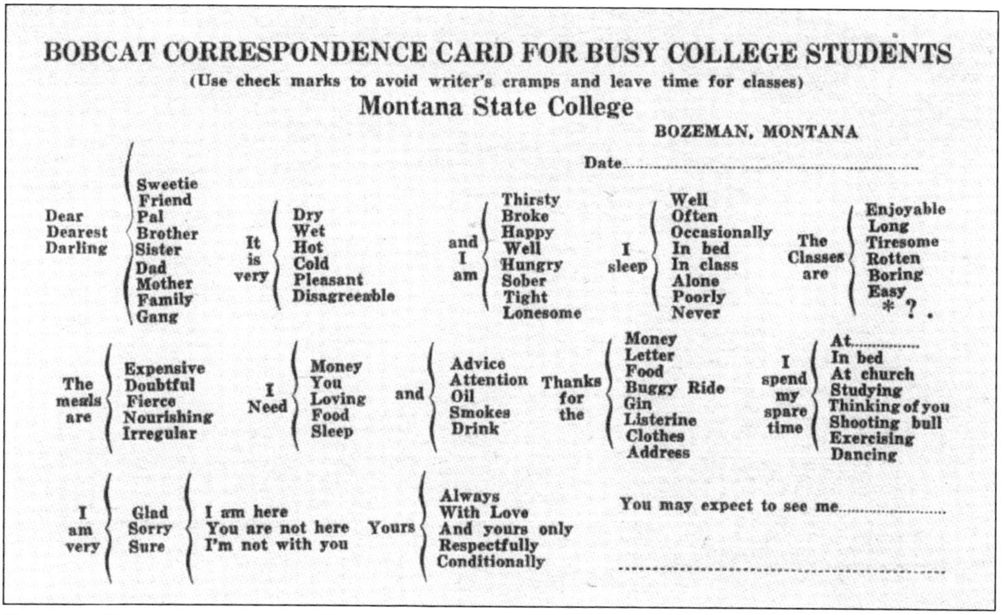

BOBCAT CORRESPONDENCE CARD FOR BUSY COLLEGE STUDENTS

(Use check marks to avoid writer's cramps and leave time for classes)

Montana State College

BOZEMAN, MONTANA

Date..

Dear / Dearest / Darling { Sweetie / Friend / Pal / Brother / Sister / Dad / Mother / Family / Gang }

It is very { Dry / Wet / Hot / Cold / Pleasant / Disagreeable }

and I am { Thirsty / Broke / Happy / Well / Hungry / Sober / Tight / Lonesome }

I sleep { Well / Often / Occasionally / In bed / In class / Alone / Poorly / Never }

The Classes are { Enjoyable / Long / Tiresome / Rotten / Boring / Easy / * ? . }

The meals are { Expensive / Doubtful / Fierce / Nourishing / Irregular }

I Need { Money / You / Loving / Food / Sleep }

and { Advice / Attention / Oil / Smokes / Drink }

Thanks for the { Money / Letter / Food / Buggy Ride / Gin / Listerine / Clothes / Address }

I spend my spare time { At.............. / In bed / At church / Studying / Thinking of you / Shooting bull / Exercising / Dancing }

I am very { Glad / Sorry / Sure }

{ I am here / You are not here / I'm not with you }

Yours { Always / With Love / And yours only / Respectfully / Conditionally }

You may expect to see me........................

....

BOBCAT CORRESPONDENCE CARD, c. 1955. This printed postcard made it easy for the super-busy student to fill out the basic information about campus life and needs. The instructions include, "Use check marks to avoid writer's cramps and leave time for classes." The Montana State College notation indicates that this card dates prior to 1965, when the Montana legislature changed the school name to Montana State University.

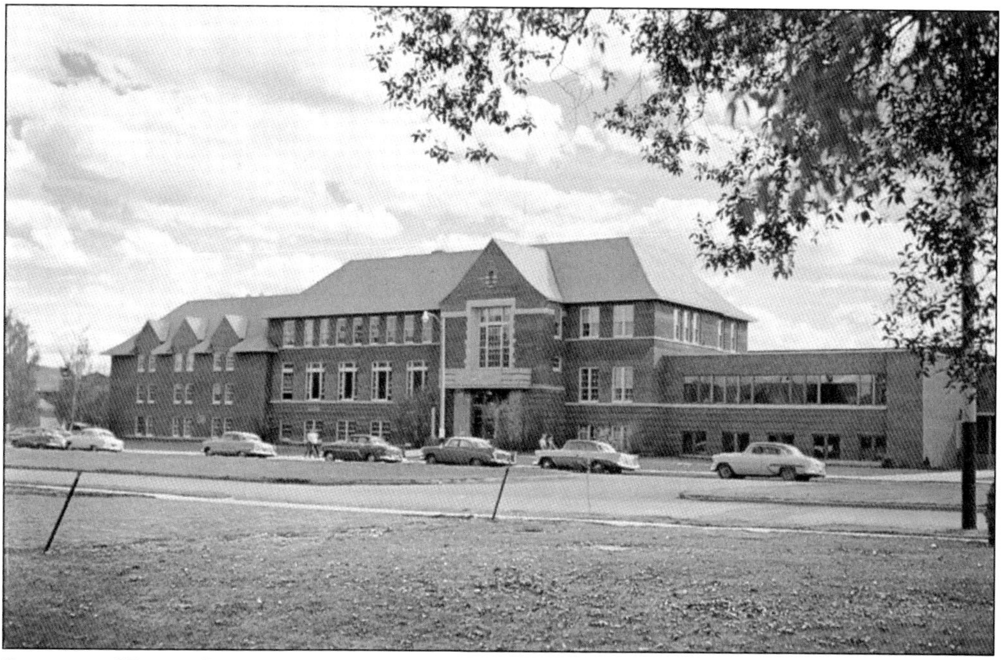

STUDENT UNION BUILDING (SUB), c. 1960. This chrome postcard shows the ever-popular SUB, which featured a large lounge, dining facilities for almost 1,000, a theater, store, meeting rooms, bowling alleys, and a ballroom. It also housed student government and publication offices. The Associated Students Store at Montana State College published this card.

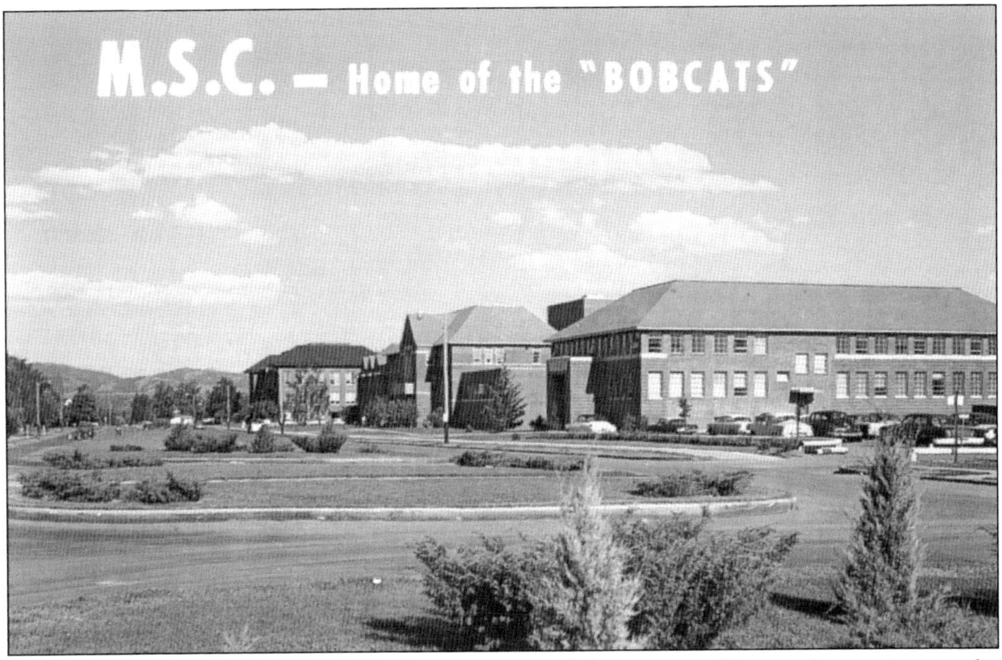

CAMPUS BUILDINGS C. 1956. This chrome postcard shows, according to the caption on the back, "the many new and modern buildings on the M. S. C. campus." The cars at right date mostly from the early 1950s. The SUB is at center.

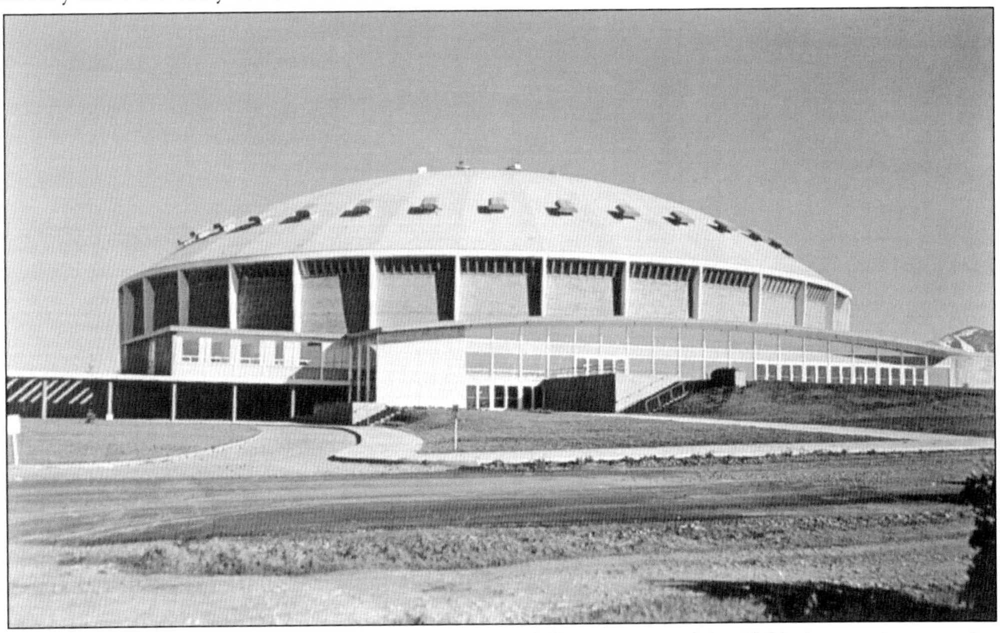

THE FIELDHOUSE, C. 1960. When the MSC Fieldhouse opened in 1956, it was the premier college basketball and all-purpose facility in the Northwest. It was the largest domed structure in the western hemisphere without a center support. Now renamed the Brick Breeden Fieldhouse/Worthington Arena, it regularly hosts volleyball, indoor track and field events, concerts, and of course, Bobcat and Lady Cats basketball. National college rodeo finals and a world middleweight championship boxing match have also taken place at this venue.

Six

Bozeman Miscellaneous Views

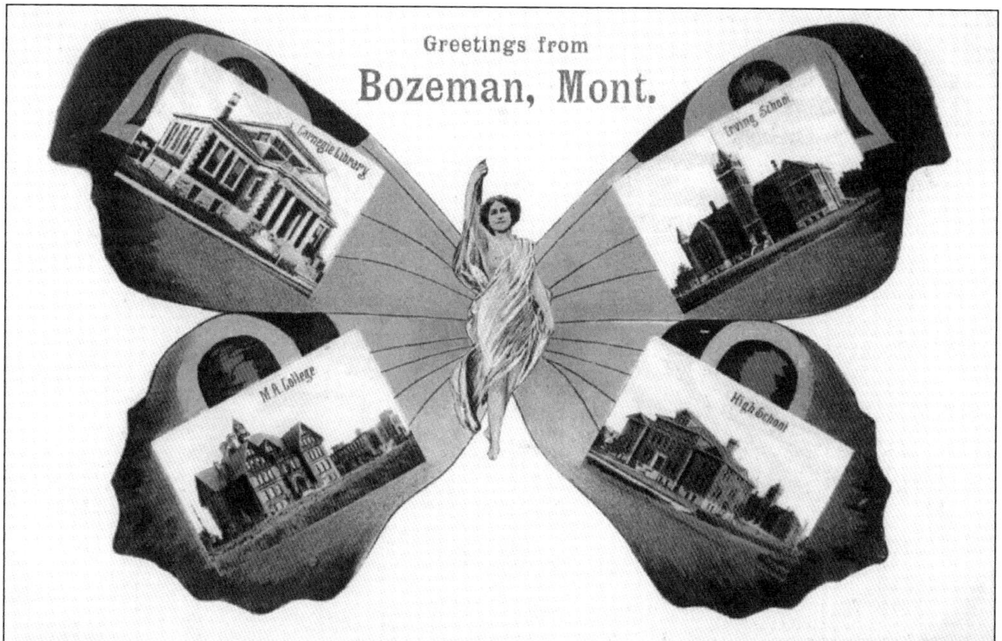

Fantasy Butterfly Greetings. Art nouveau and fantasy were in vogue at the time this *c.* 1910 printed postcard was produced. Four local buildings are pictured in the wings of a butterfly. From top left are the Carnegie Library, Irving School, Gallatin County High School, and Montana Hall at the Montana Agricultural College.

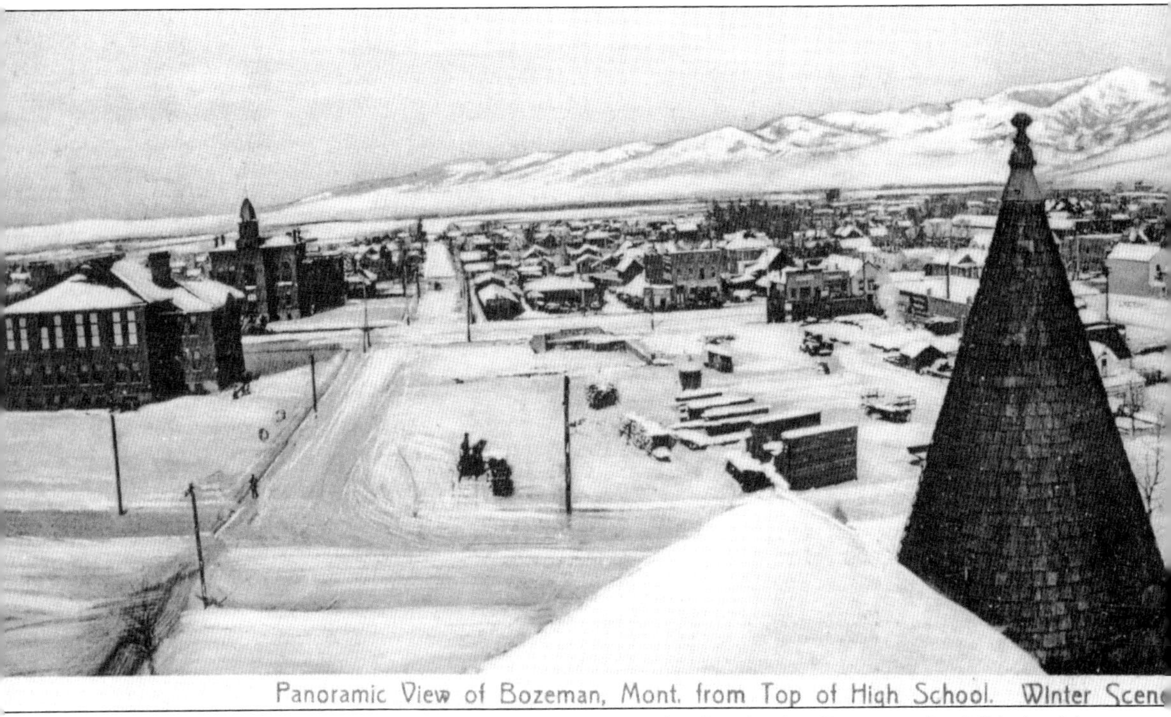

PANORAMIC VIEW FROM OLD HIGH SCHOOL. Much of early-day Bozeman is visible in this wintertime panoramic view taken from a high spot at the West Side School, looking northeast.

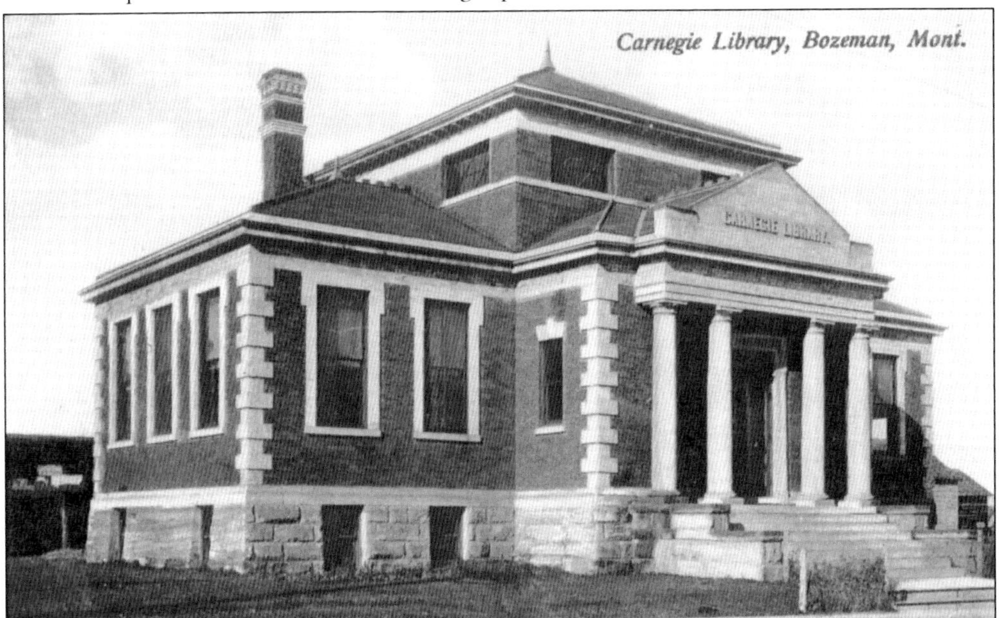

CARNEGIE LIBRARY. This printed postcard, postmarked from Bozeman in 1908, shows the newly constructed Carnegie Library. This building was located at the southwest corner of Mendenhall Street and Bozeman Avenue. Bozeman now has a beautiful new library, located at 626 East Main Street, which opened in 2006.

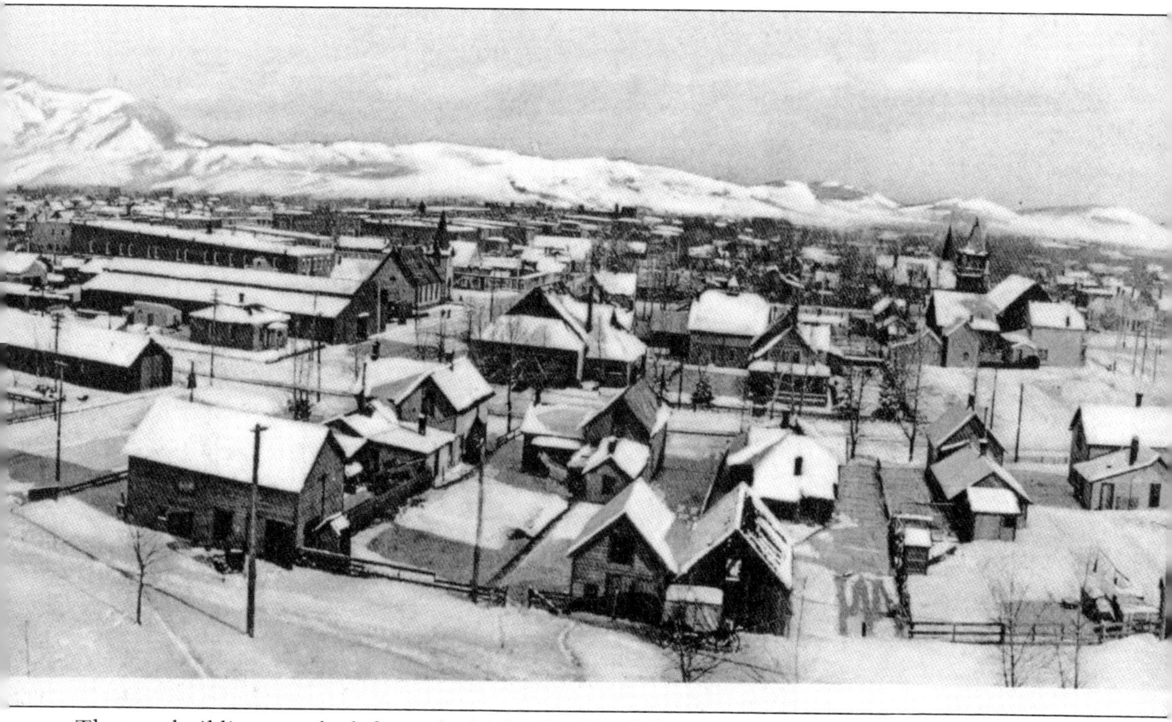

The two buildings on the left are the high school and the county courthouse (with the tower). This printed postcard was mailed from Bozeman to Helena in 1907.

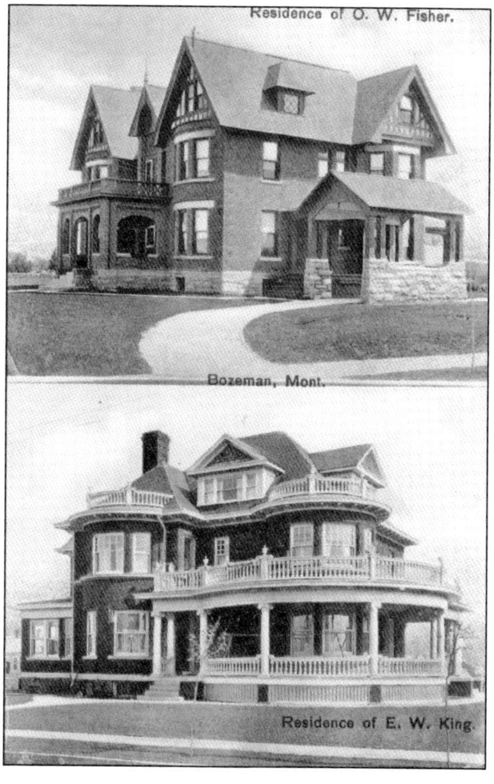

TWO FANCY EARLY HOMES. This *c.* 1908 printed postcard shows two of Bozeman's finer residences. The home above right was the residence of O. W. Fisher and was located at 712 South Willson Avenue. The residence of E. W. King was across the street at 725 South Willson Avenue. Both homes are included in the historic neighborhood walking tour provided by the Bozeman City Planning Office.

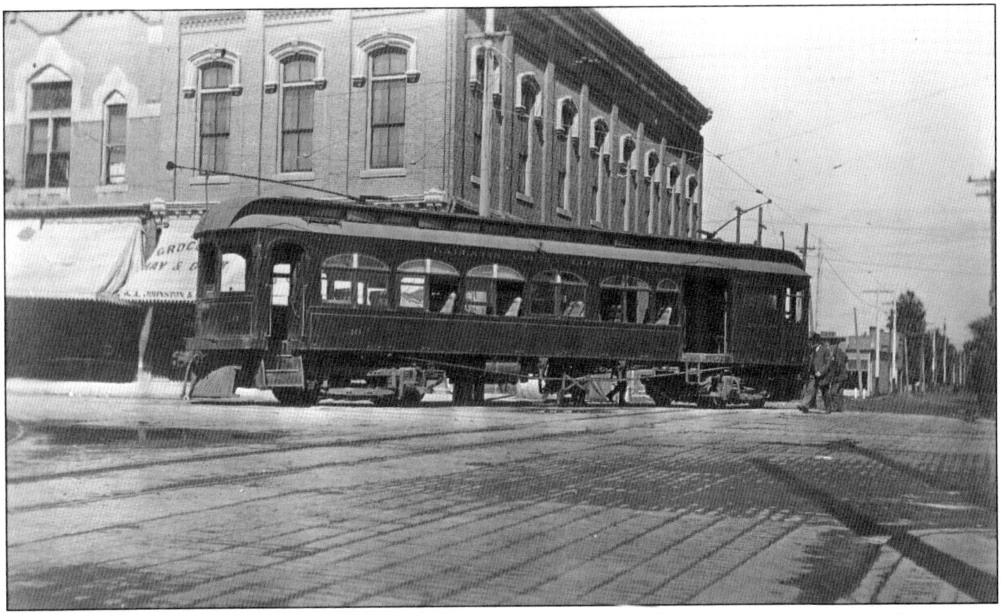

Gallatin Valley Electric Railway. Known as an electric streetcar and also as an interurban, this car is passing in front of the J. A. Johnston Grocery Store on Main Street. This real-photo postcard was postmarked from Bozeman in 1910. The Gallatin Valley Electric Railway was established in 1909 and covered a 17-mile trek between Salesville (now Gallatin Gateway) and Bozeman.

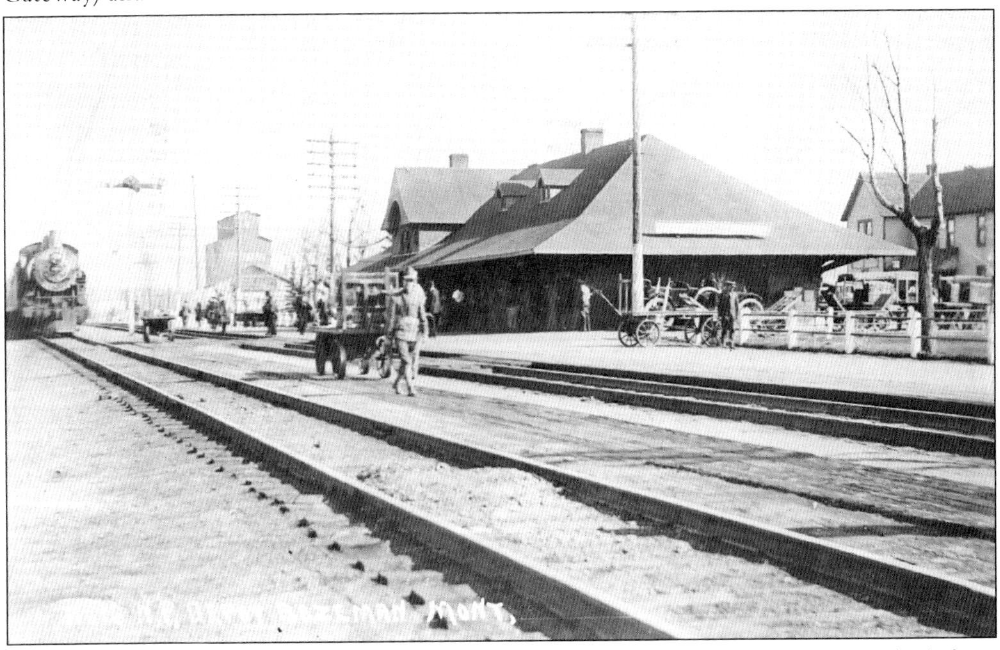

Northern Pacific Train and Depot. This real-photo postcard, postmarked from Bozeman in 1919, shows a train pulling into the NP depot. The arrival of the Northern Pacific Railroad into the Gallatin Valley in 1883 was a major factor in ensuring the valley's prosperity. Products and people could now be readily transported to and from the area. (Courtesy of Ken Hamlin.)

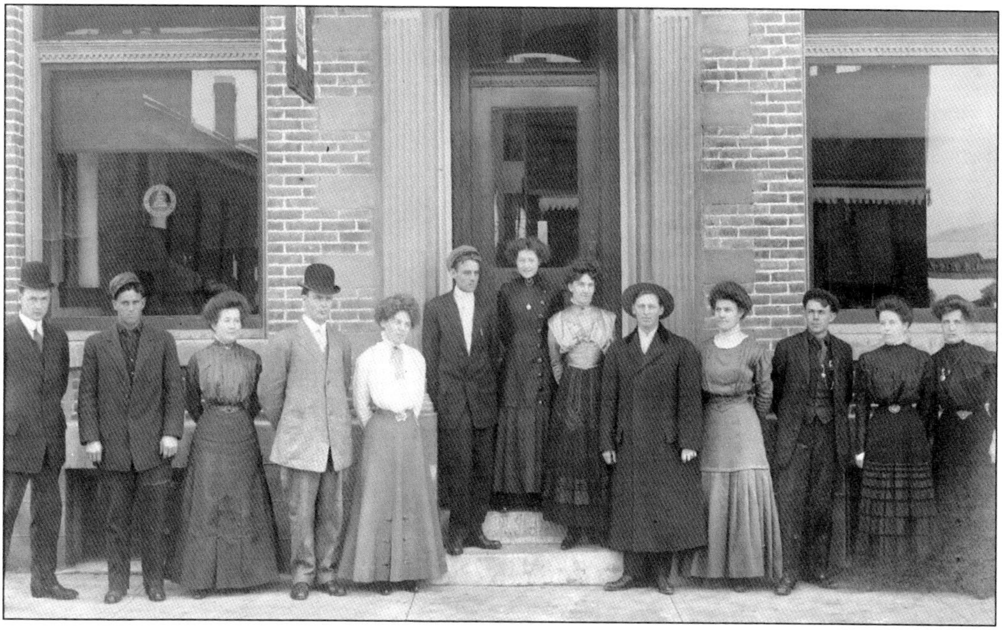

TELEPHONE WORKERS IN FRONT OF OFFICE. A somewhat humorous message is found on the back of this real-photo postcard, postmarked from Bozeman in 1910. "I just now received your card so thought I would send you a picture of our Tel. Bunch, what do you think of it? I doubt it is very good though, but is as good as can be expected considering who is in it." The window at left has bell symbol imprint and the wording "Rocky Mountain Bell Telephone." (Photograph by Schlechten Studio, Bozeman, Montana.)

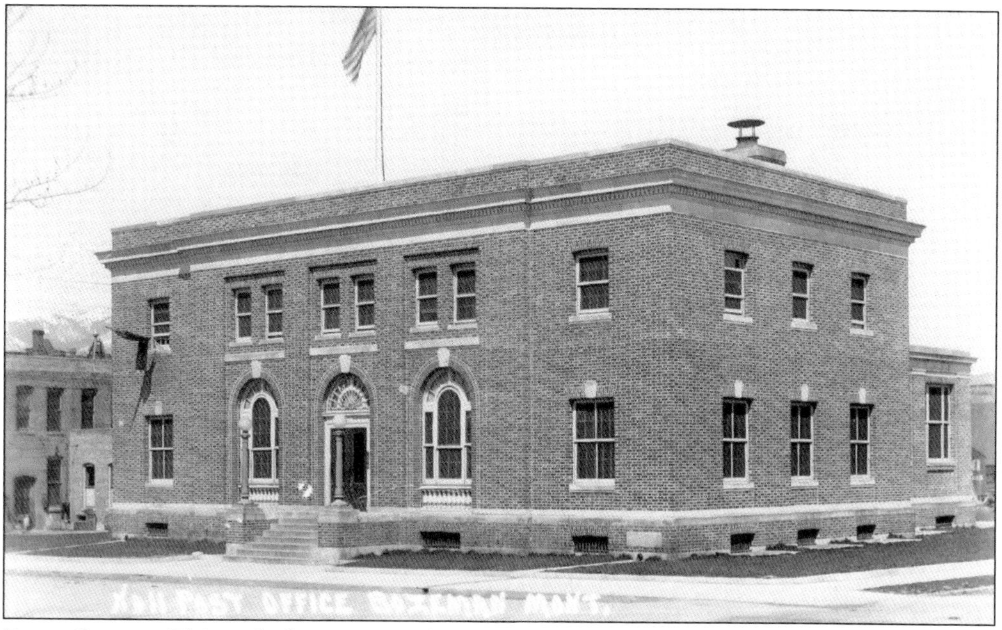

POST OFFICE. This real-photo postcard, postmarked from Bozeman in 1919, shows the post office that served the city from 1915 to 1966 from its location on the corner of Babcock Street and South Tracy Avenue. Prior to 1915, the post office was on Main Street. Today the new Federal Building and post office are located at 32 East Babcock Street.

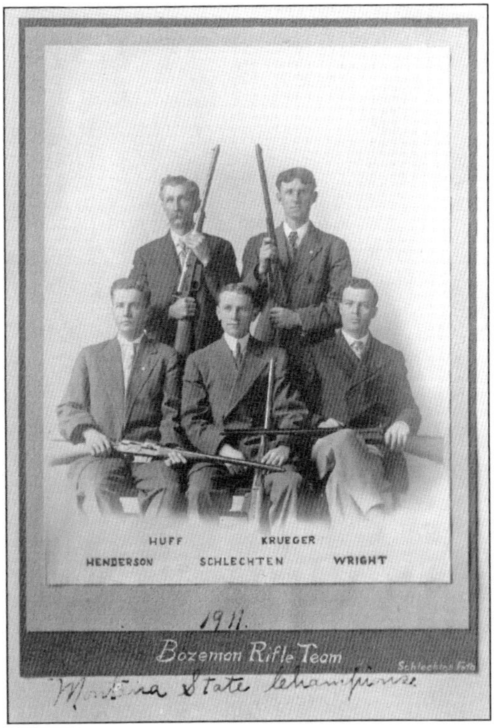

BOZEMAN RIFLE TEAM. These five sharpshooters were "1911 Montana State Champions," going by the penned caption at bottom. The text on the back expounds: "We beat Butte (Indoor Champions of the United States) at 200 yds. offhand with large rifles and a target with 8 in. bullseye." Identified on this *c.* 1911 real-photo postcard are, from left to right, Henderson, Huff, Schlechten, Krueger, and Wright. (Photograph by Schlechten Studio, Bozeman, Montana.)

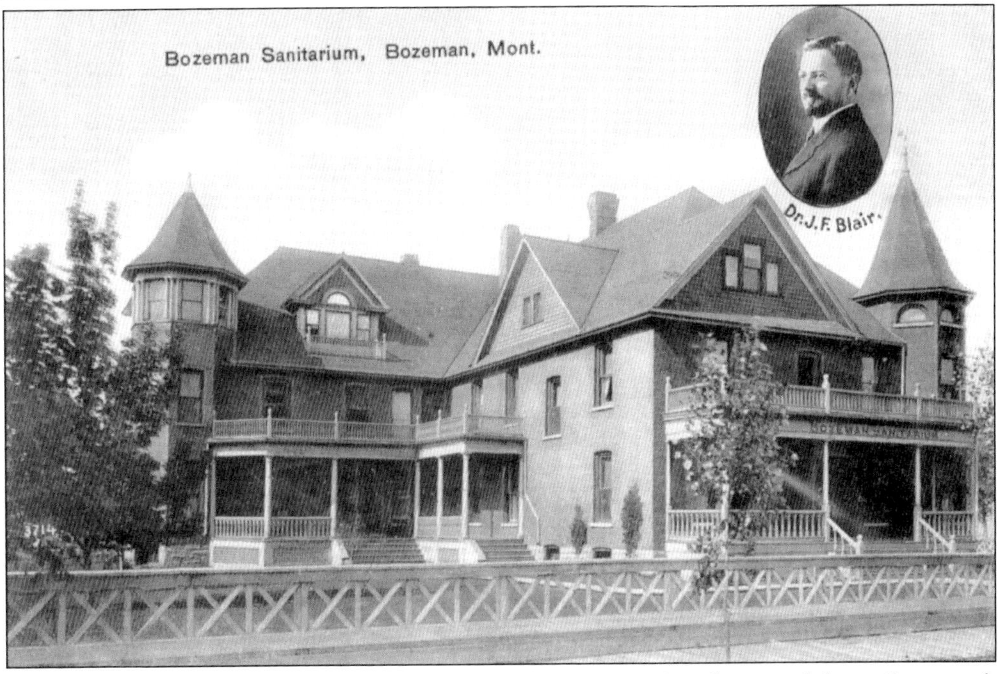

BOZEMAN SANITARIUM AND DR. J. F. BLAIR. This *c.* 1908 printed postcard shows Bozeman's original sanitarium, which was built by Dr. and Mrs. Henry Foster in 1896. This three-story brick structure stood on the corner of Lamme Street and Tracy Avenue and was built at a cost of about $20,000. This 20-bed hospital was apparently under the auspices of Dr. J. F. Blair at the time this postcard was made.

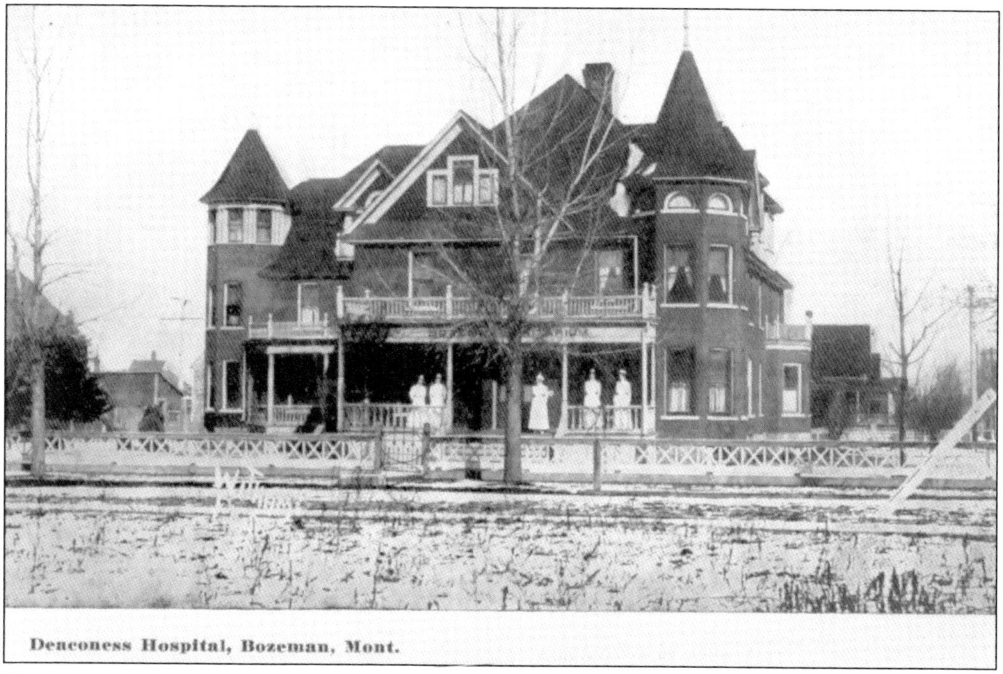

DEACONESS HOSPITAL IN 1912. Five nurses pose on the porch of this newly purchased hospital, as shown in this *c.* 1912 printed postcard view. The Bozeman community and the Methodist Church combined to purchase the Bozeman Sanitarium in 1911, and the hospital was soon incorporated. The growing community would necessitate the construction of a larger hospital eight years later.

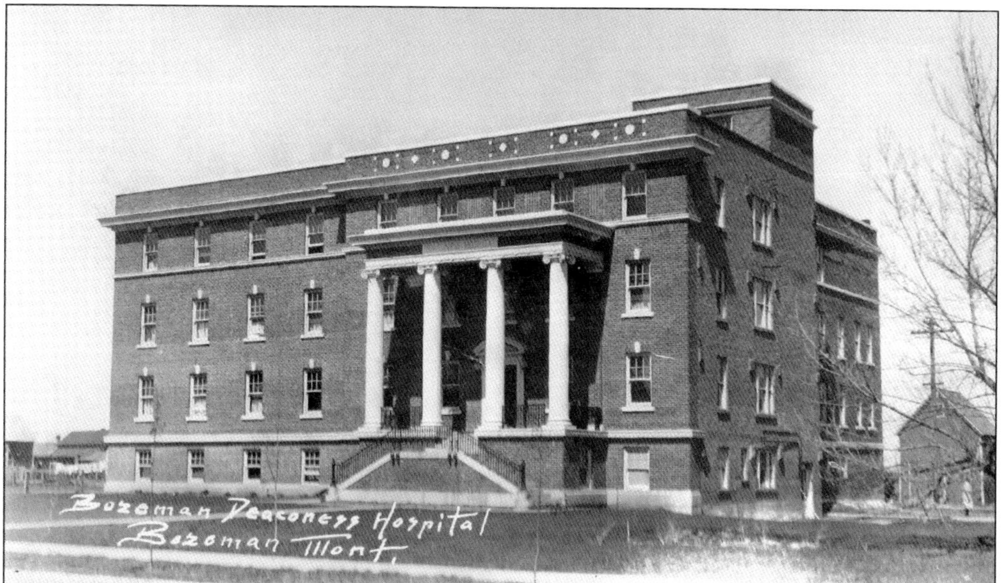

DEACONESS HOSPITAL IN 1935. This real-photo postcard shows the new 50-bed hospital that was completed in 1920. It was expanded over the years, including a west wing addition in 1944 and an intensive care unit in 1969. In 1986, the current Deaconess Hospital, located on Highland Boulevard, was constructed. (Courtesy of Ken Hamlin.)

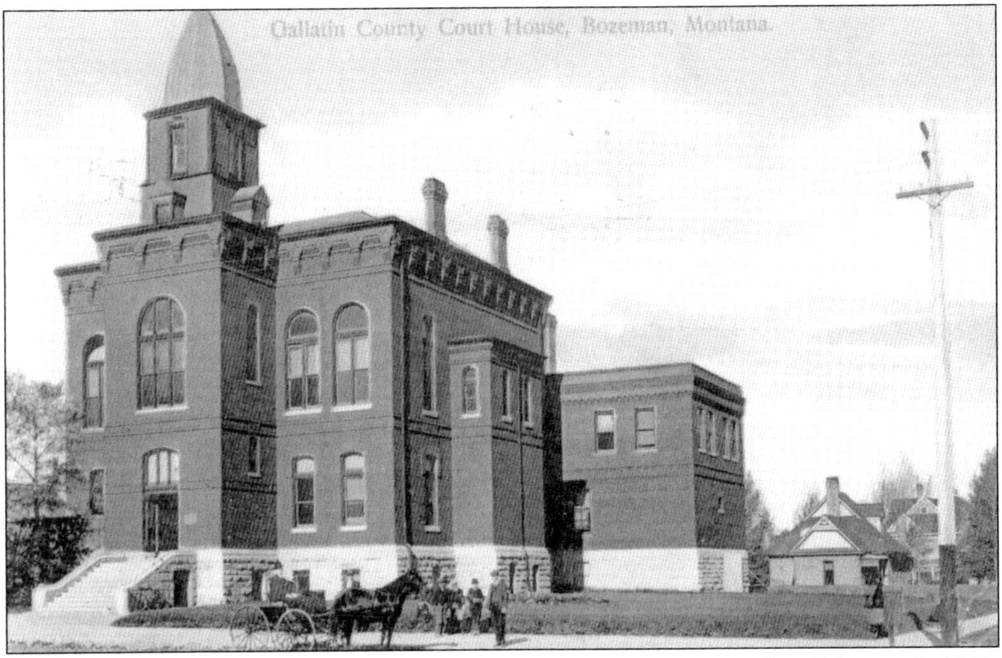

OLD GALLATIN COUNTY COURT HOUSE. Gallatin County was created on February 2, 1865, as an original county in Montana Territory with Bozeman named the county seat. This printed postcard, postmarked in 1908, shows the old county courthouse, which was constructed in 1880. Its address was listed as 511 West Main Street. This courthouse was demolished in 1935 to make way for the new courthouse (below) at the same site.

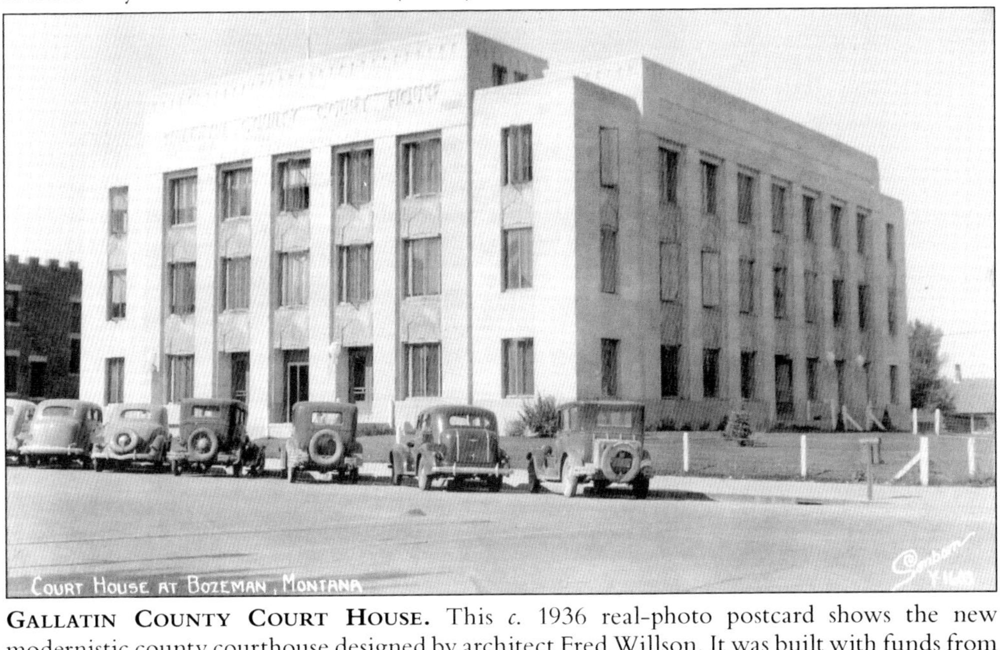

GALLATIN COUNTY COURT HOUSE. This *c.* 1936 real-photo postcard shows the new modernistic county courthouse designed by architect Fred Willson. It was built with funds from the WPA (Works Progress Administration), a federal program under Pres. Franklin Roosevelt's New Deal. It is located at 311 West Main Street, next to the Pioneer Museum. (Photograph by Sanborn Souvenir Company, Denver, Colorado; courtesy of R. Dale Beland.)

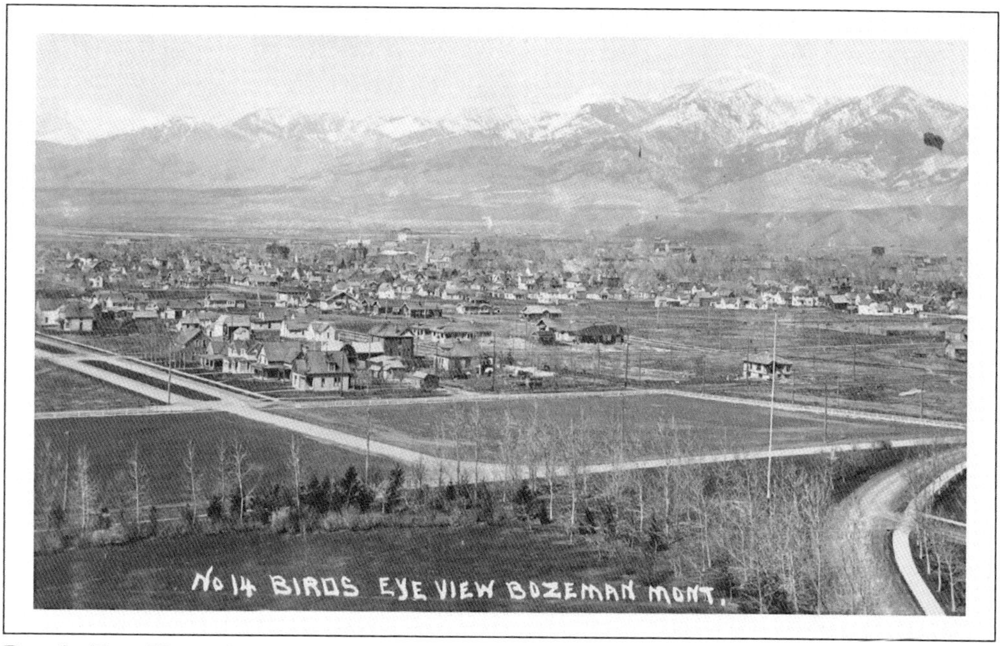

Bird's-Eye View Around 1918. This real-photo postcard shows much of the Bozeman community looking to the northeast from the vantage point of Montana State College. The southern part of the Bozeman residential district was closing in on the college campus grounds, but there were still many empty lots at this time.

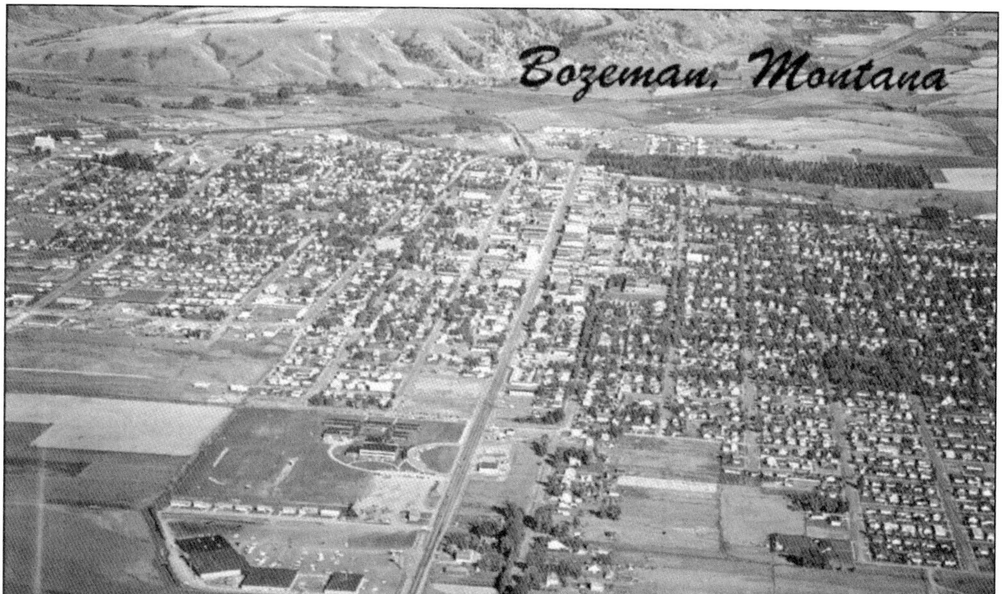

Bird's-Eye View Around 1961. This chrome postcard shows an aerial view of the growing Bozeman area looking to the east. Main Street runs from the left-center bottom toward the top of this view. The new high school and the new Buttrey's shopping center are located at lower left, on the western outskirts of Bozeman at the time. The town was on the verge of heavy expansion in a westward direction.

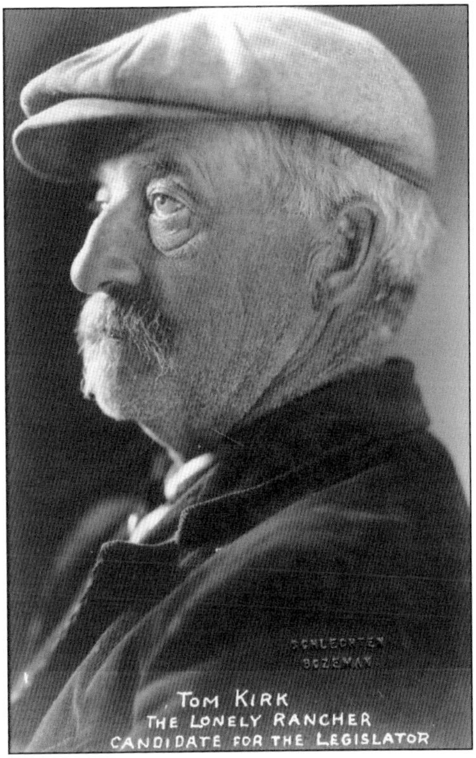

TED KIRK RUNNING FOR LEGISLATURE. This fellow looks like the "working man's candidate." The side profile of Tom Kirk, "the lonely rancher," is shown in this *c.* 1910 real-photo political advertising postcard. Kirk was listed as a rancher in the 1912 Polk city directory. He was unsuccessful in his legislative bid. Hopefully, one of his postcards touched the heart of a Bozeman area maiden and Mr. Kirk's loneliness issues were solved. (Photograph by Schlechten Studio, Bozeman, Montana.)

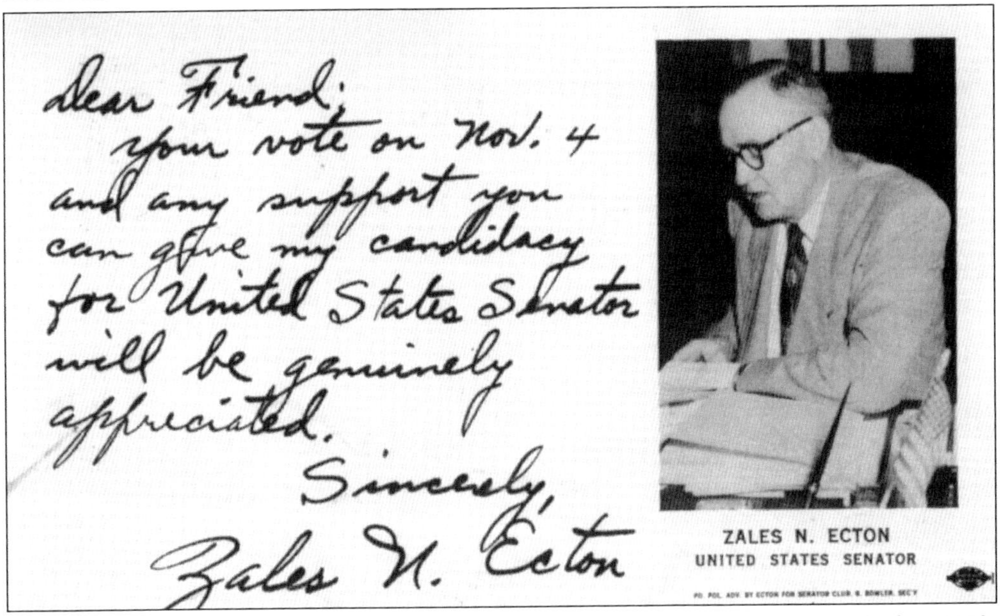

ZALES ECTON RUNNING FOR U.S. SENATOR. This printed postcard, postmarked in 1952, promotes the reelection bid of Zales Ecton, a Bozeman-area rancher, for a U.S. Senate seat from Montana. He had won election in 1946 to become the first Republican senator to represent Montana in many years. After Mike Mansfield narrowly defeated him in the 1952 campaign, Ecton resumed his ranching business in the Gallatin Valley. He died in Bozeman in 1961. (Courtesy of Ken Hamlin.)

Seven

Belgrade

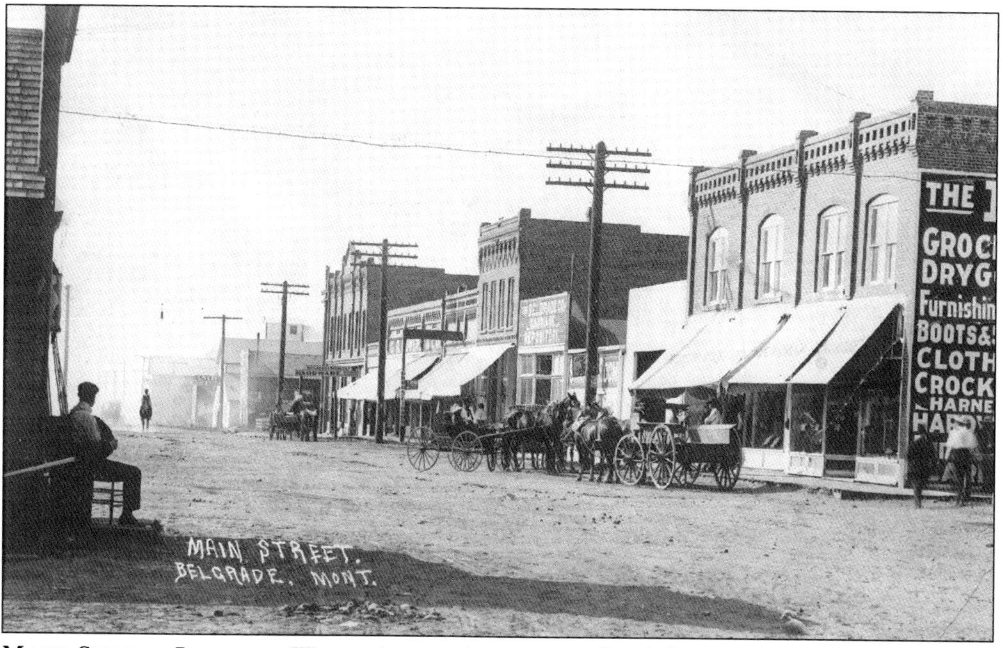

Main Street Looking West. A man sits on a stool at left and observes Main Street in Belgrade in this 1908 real-photo image. The Belgrade Company Grocery and Dry Goods store is at right. Several horse-drawn carriages are parked near the entrance to the Belgrade Company Carriage Depository at the center of the image. The G. R. Power Company and Rutledge and Schultz Hardware Company are visible farther down the street. (Photograph by C. A. Kinsey, Belgrade, Montana; courtesy of Ron Iverson.)

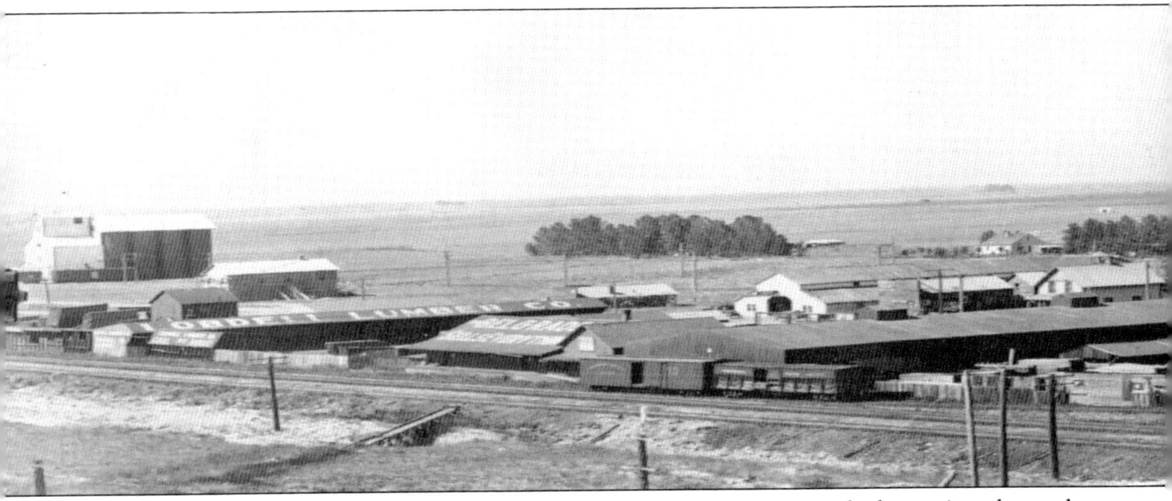

Panoramic View of Western Business District. This *c.* 1910 real-photo view shows the lumberyards that were constructed on the south side of Main Street with access to the Northern Pacific Railroad. The Belgrade Company dominated the area with a large yard and several structures. The sign on the side of the building at right reads, "The Belgrade Co., Ltd. Sells

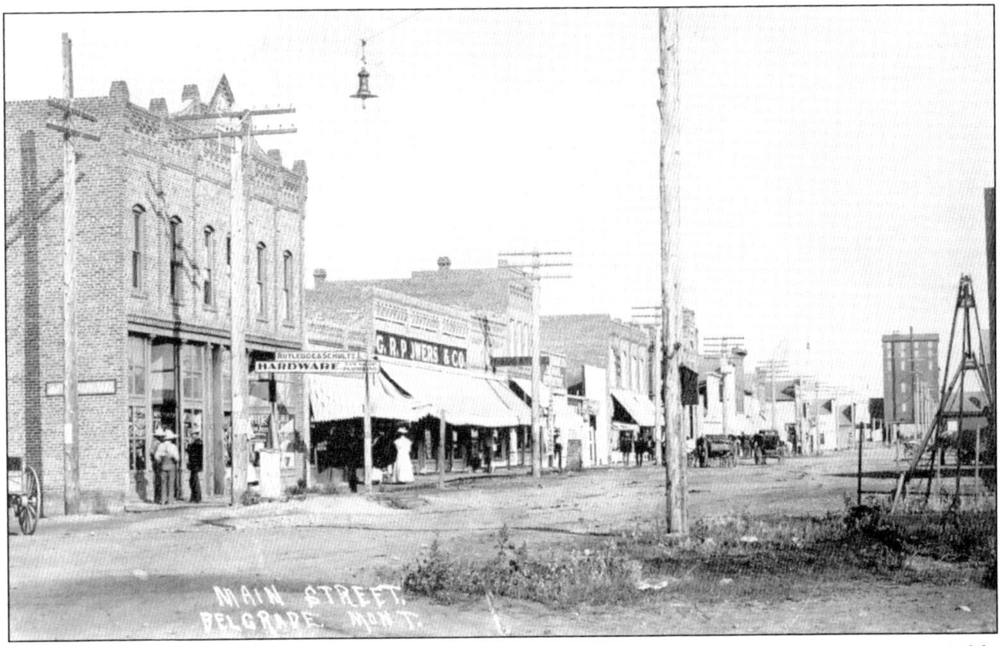

Main Street Looking West. Most of the north side of Belgrade's Main Street is visible in this *c.* 1908 real-photo view. Rutledge and Schultz Hardware anchors the west end of the business district at left. The G. R. Powers and Company store and a drug and cigar store are also visible. Although the photographer is not identified, it was probably C. A. Kinsey of Belgrade, Montana, who took the image. (Courtesy of Ken Hamlin.)

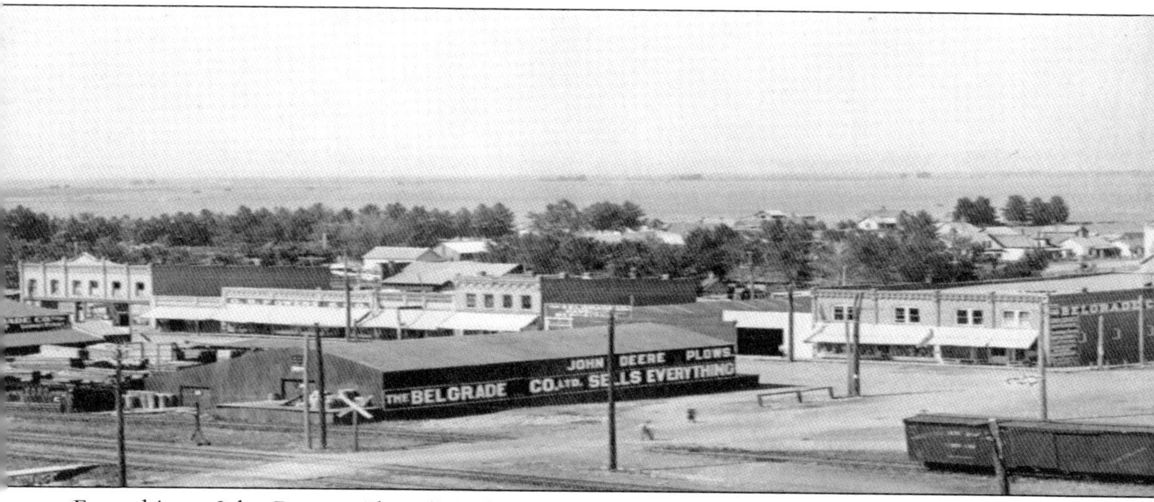

Everything—John Deere—Plows." At far left is the Obdell Lumber Company, and Broadway Avenue intersects Main Street at far right. The western end of Main Street and part of the town's residential district are in the background.

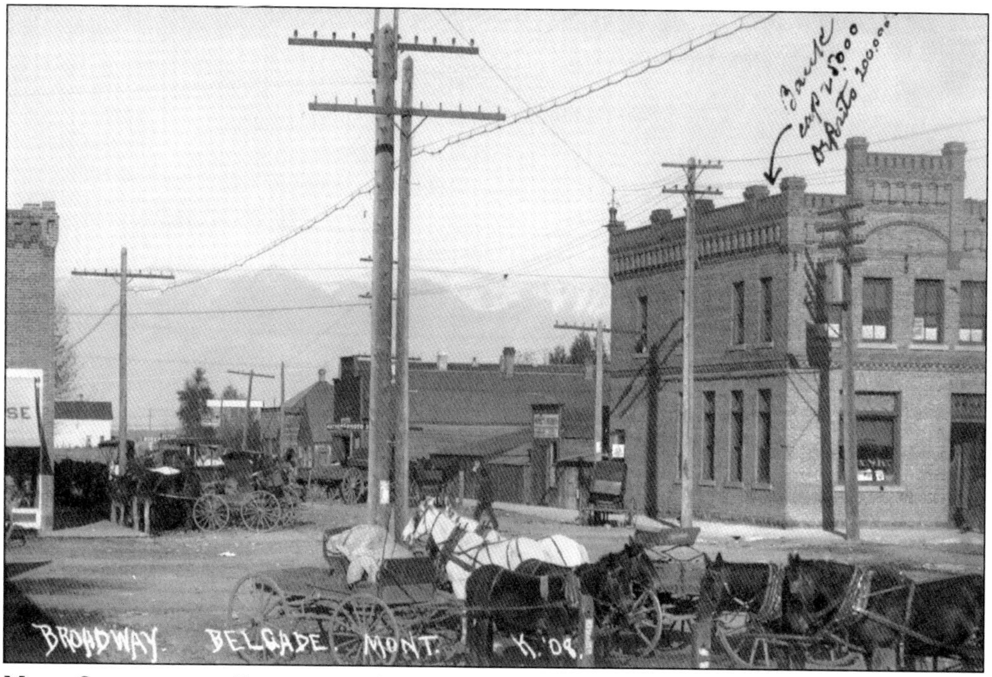

MAIN STREET AND BROADWAY AVENUE LOOKING NORTH. The Belgrade State Bank is the large brick building at right in this *c.* 1908 real-photo view. Someone penned, "Bank cap. $25,000 Deposits $200,000," above the image of the bank. A Bell Telephone sign on the side of the bank indicates the telephone office was likely set up there. Mathews Photo Studio can be seen near the center of the image, and several horse-drawn carriages are visible in both the foreground and background. Automobiles were soon to make an appearance in Belgrade, but not yet. (Photograph by C. A. Kinsey, Belgrade, Montana.)

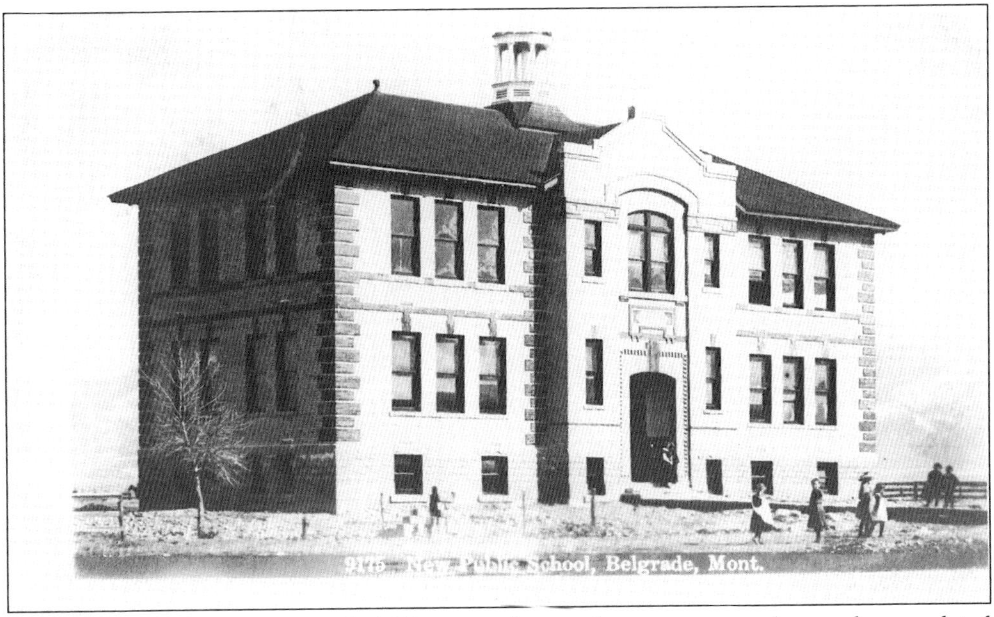

New Public School. Several children stand near the entrance to the newly completed Belgrade public school pictured in this vintage real-photo view. The school opened in 1909, and landscaping was still in progress. This new school replaced an older one that was located on the northwestern outskirts of Belgrade. (Photograph by M. L. Zercher, Topeka, Kansas.)

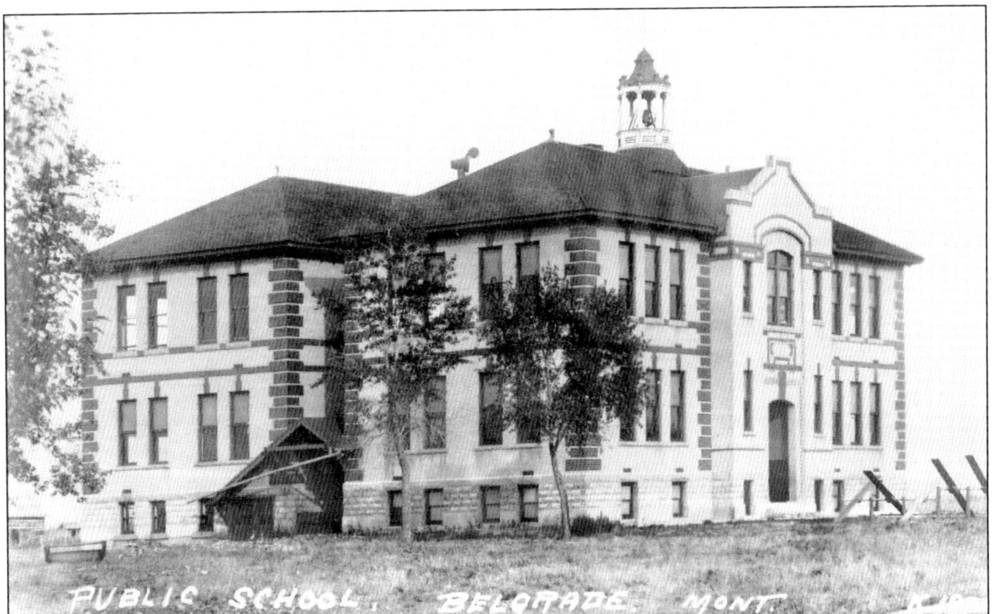

School With New Addition. This *c.* 1920 real-photo view shows the new addition at the back of the Belgrade public school. Note the teeter-totters at far right. The trees have grown considerably when compared with the earlier view at the top of this page. (Photograph by C. A. Kinsey, Belgrade, Montana.)

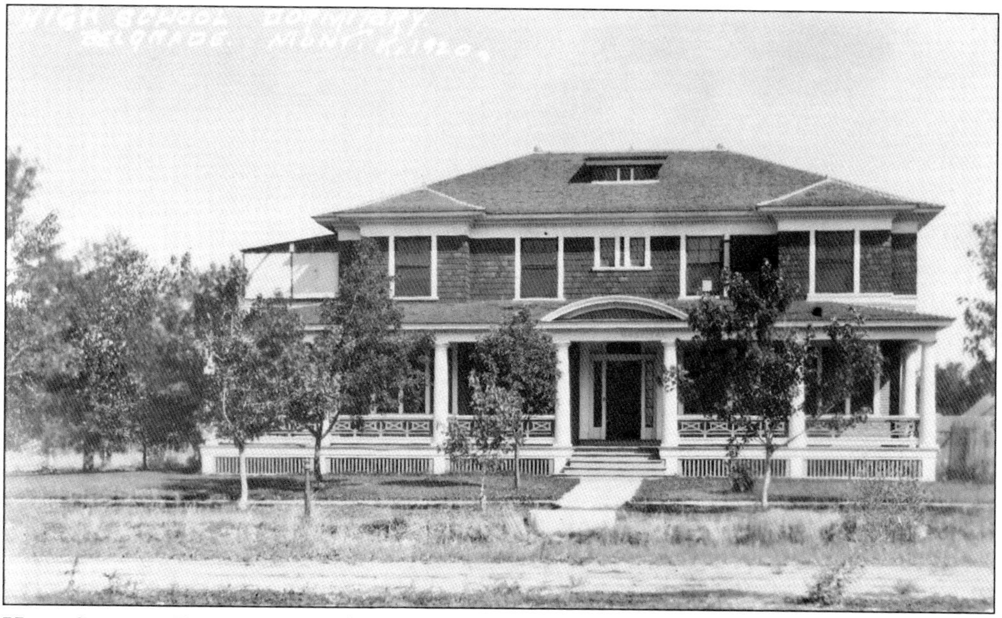

HIGH SCHOOL DORMITORY. This *c.* 1920 real-photo view shows the dormitory constructed for out-of-town high school students. Before the advent of school bus transportation and good roads, students who lived in outlying farms and ranches stayed in this building during the week in order to attend high school. (Photograph by C. A. Kinsey, Belgrade, Montana.)

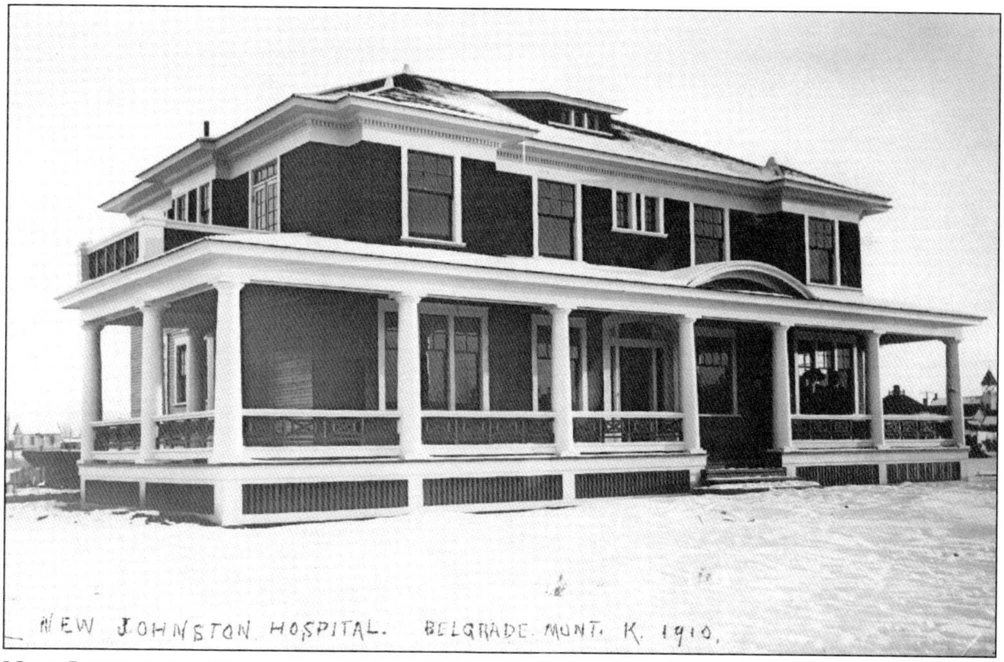

NEW JOHNSTONE HOSPITAL. This *c.* 1910 real-photo view shows the town's new hospital, which had just opened. It was located on Quaw Boulevard. This hospital closed many years ago, and area residents now use the Bozeman Deaconess Hospital, located about 10 miles to the west. (Photograph by C. A. Kinsey, Belgrade, Montana.)

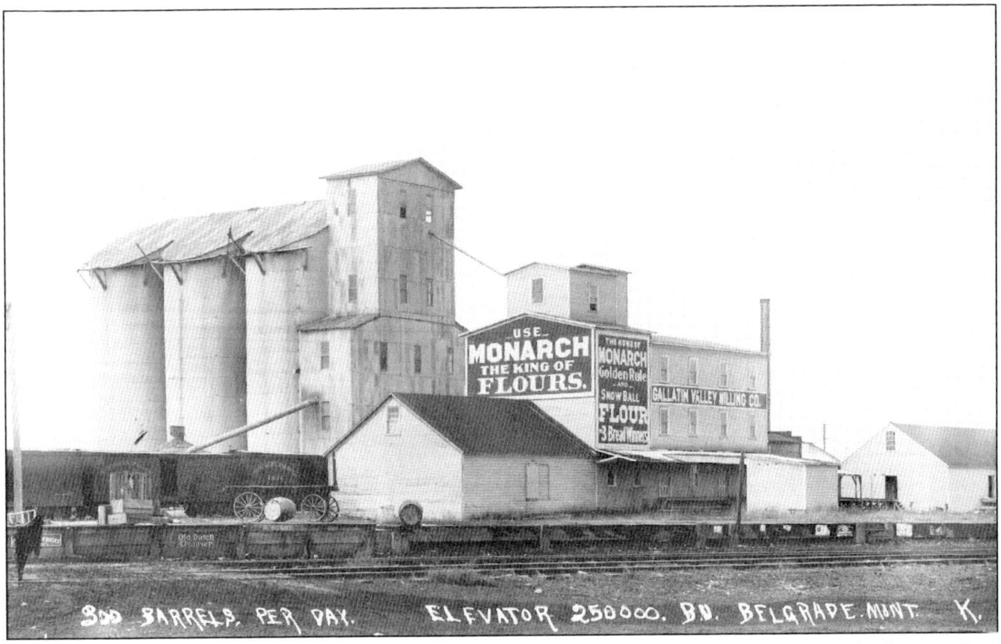

GALLATIN VALLEY MILLING COMPANY AND ELEVATORS. This *c.* 1910 real-photo view shows one of the largest milling and elevator businesses in Belgrade at the time. Note the large advertising signage painted on the wall of the mill: "Monarch—the King of Flours." The capacity of the elevators is listed in the caption as 250,000 bushels. (Photograph by C. A. Kinsey, Belgrade, Montana.)

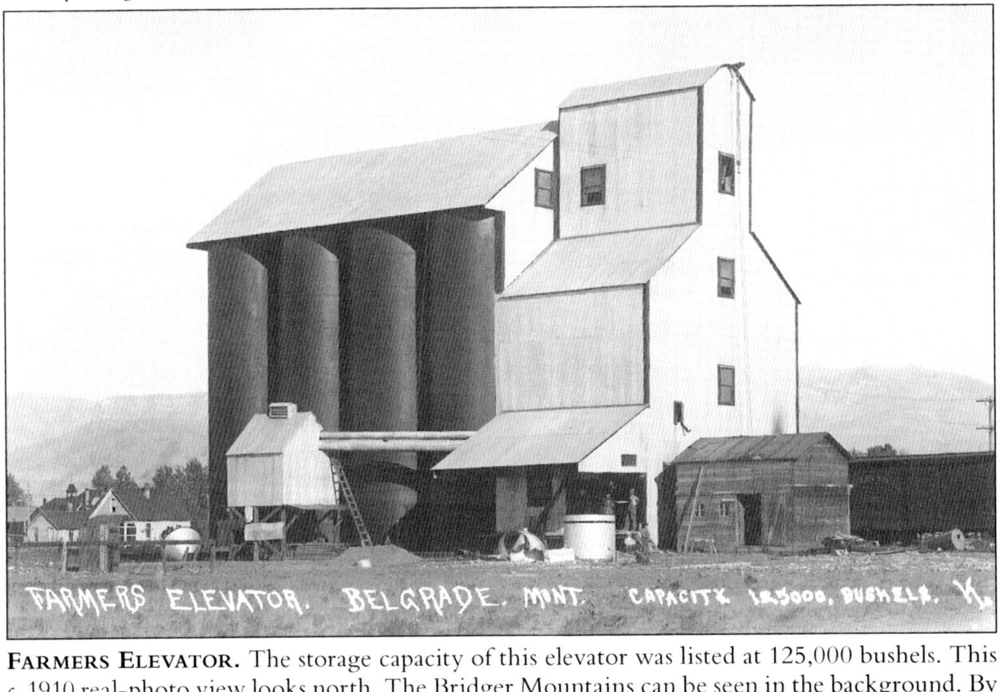

FARMERS ELEVATOR. The storage capacity of this elevator was listed at 125,000 bushels. This *c.* 1910 real-photo view looks north. The Bridger Mountains can be seen in the background. By the time this card was made, Belgrade had installed a water system (1906) and electricity (1907). (Photograph by C. A. Kinsey, Belgrade, Montana.)

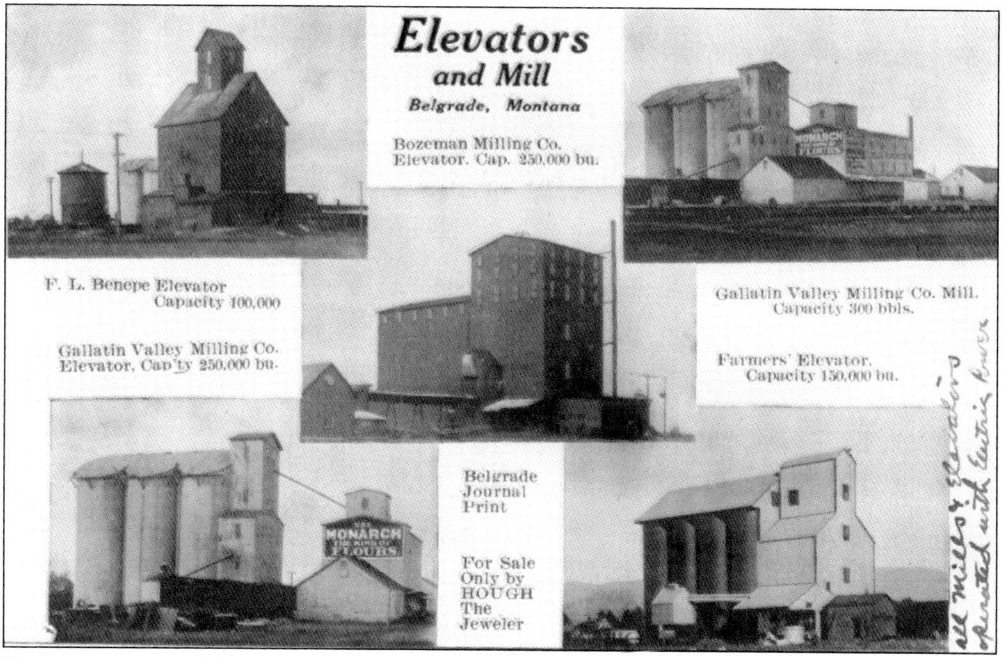

Elevators and Mill Multi-View. This *c.* 1910 printed postcard was published by Hough Jeweler and shows most of the town's prominent mills and grain elevators and their capacity. Known as the "Hub of the Gallatin Valley," Belgrade was incorporated in 1906. The town's name came about as a way to show appreciation to railroad investors from Belgrade, Serbia, who helped finance the Northern Pacific Railroad's excursion into Montana in 1883.

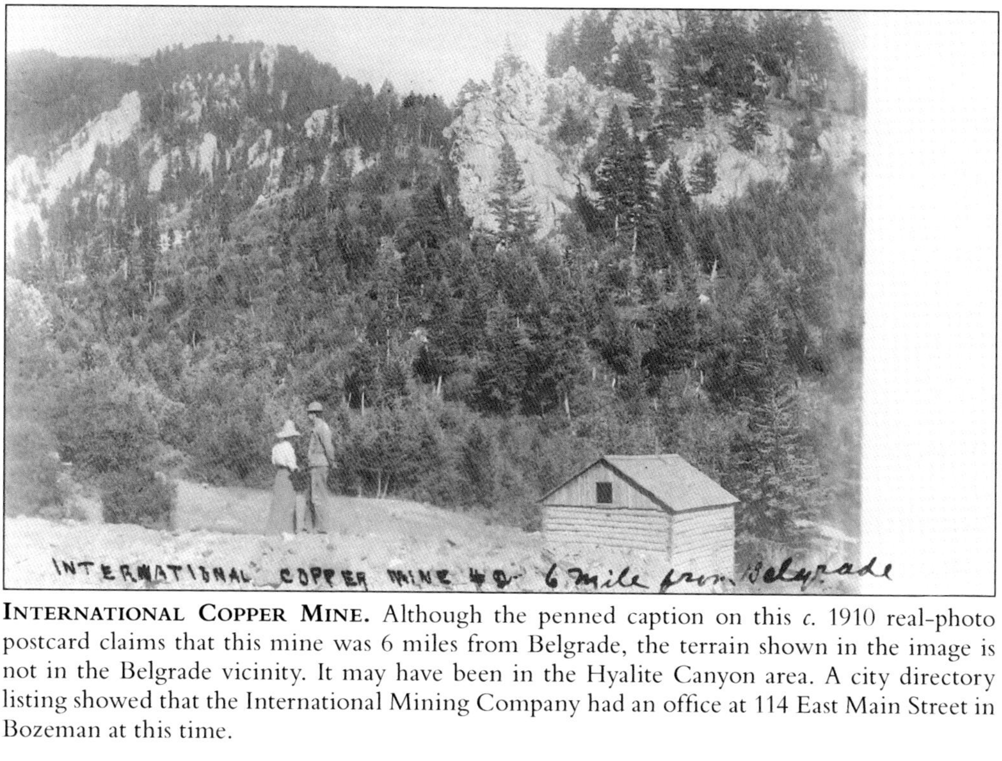

International Copper Mine. Although the penned caption on this *c.* 1910 real-photo postcard claims that this mine was 6 miles from Belgrade, the terrain shown in the image is not in the Belgrade vicinity. It may have been in the Hyalite Canyon area. A city directory listing showed that the International Mining Company had an office at 114 East Main Street in Bozeman at this time.

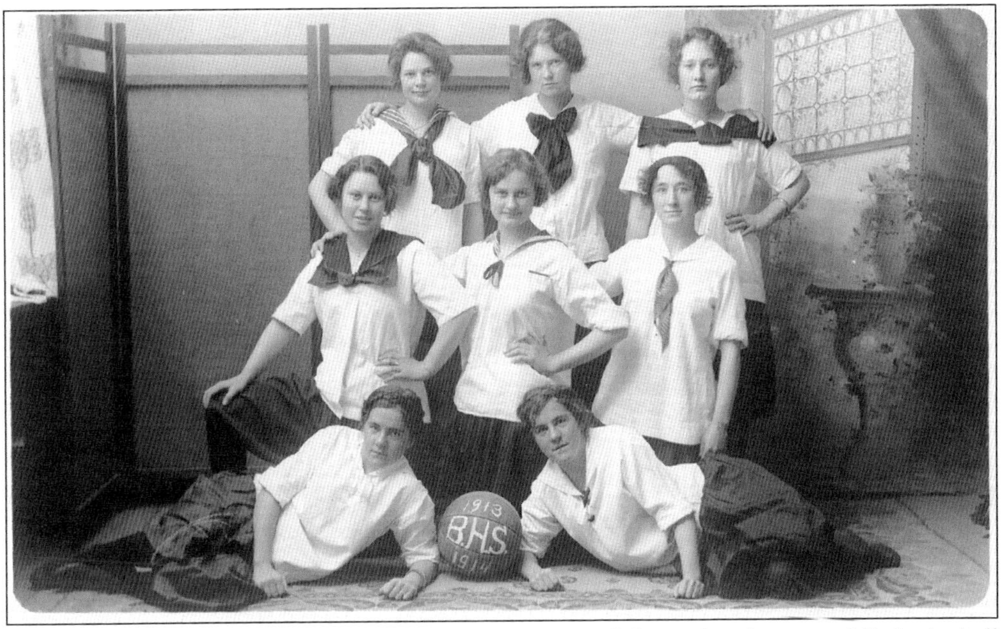

GIRL'S BASKETBALL TEAM. The 1913–1914 version of the Belgrade prep girl's basketball team poses in this vintage real-photo image. Players, as identified on the back card, included Della Barnard, Bessie Stimpson, Susie Kurtzmen, Hazel Mack, Elsie Kremer, Laurie Ballard, Edith Ballard, and Eva Ballard. Message written on back of card concludes, "How's that for a team?"

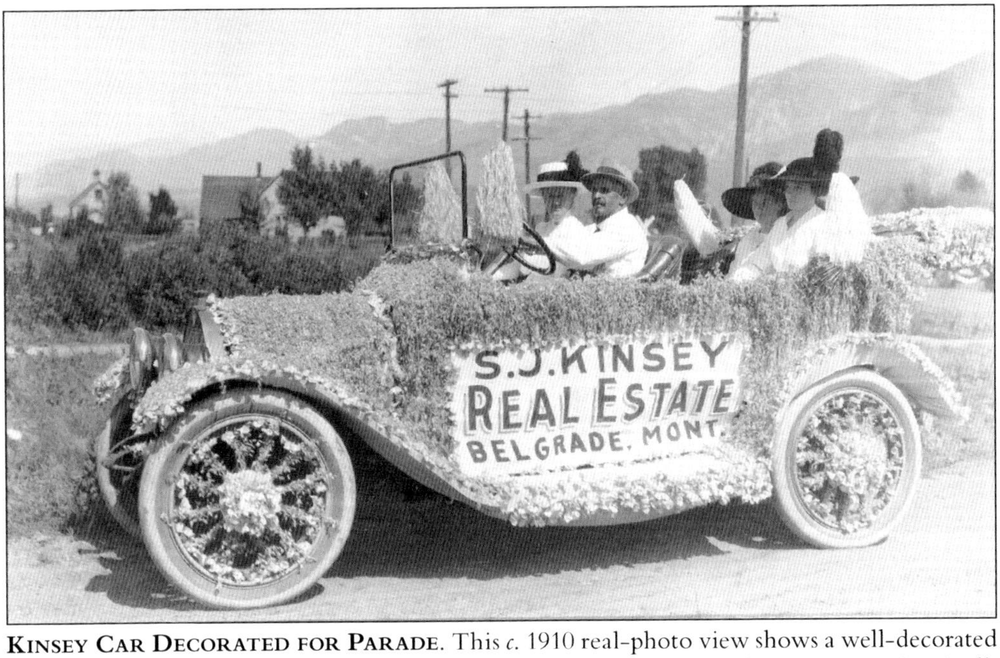

KINSEY CAR DECORATED FOR PARADE. This *c.* 1910 real-photo view shows a well-decorated car ready for the Bozeman Sweet Pea Carnival parade. In later years, the Sweet Pea Carnival's name was changed to the Sweet Pea Festival. Printed on the side of the card is "S. J. Kinsey—Real Estate—Belgrade, Mont." Sanford Kinsey was partner in a Belgrade real estate business and may have been the father of prominent Belgrade photographer Charles Kinsey.

PRESBYTERIAN CHURCH UNDER CONSTRUCTION. Postmarked 1911 from Belgrade, this real-photo view shows the Presbyterian church nearing completion. This church was completed and dedicated in the same year and has been in use ever since. Today it is known as the Belgrade Community Church.

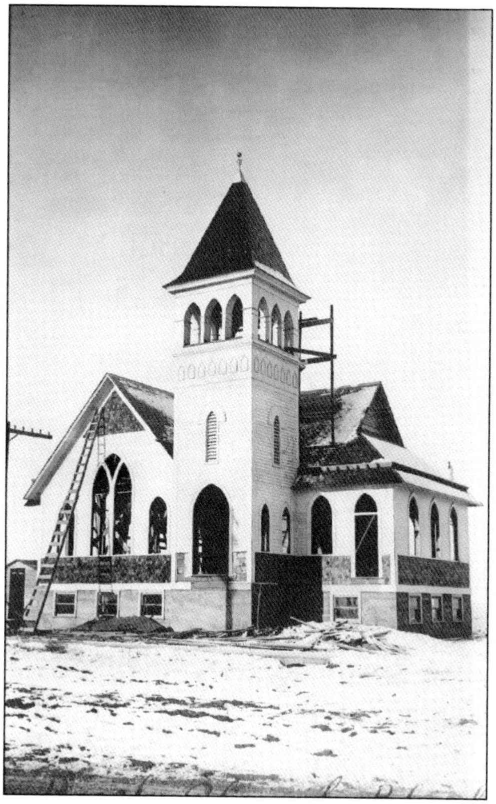

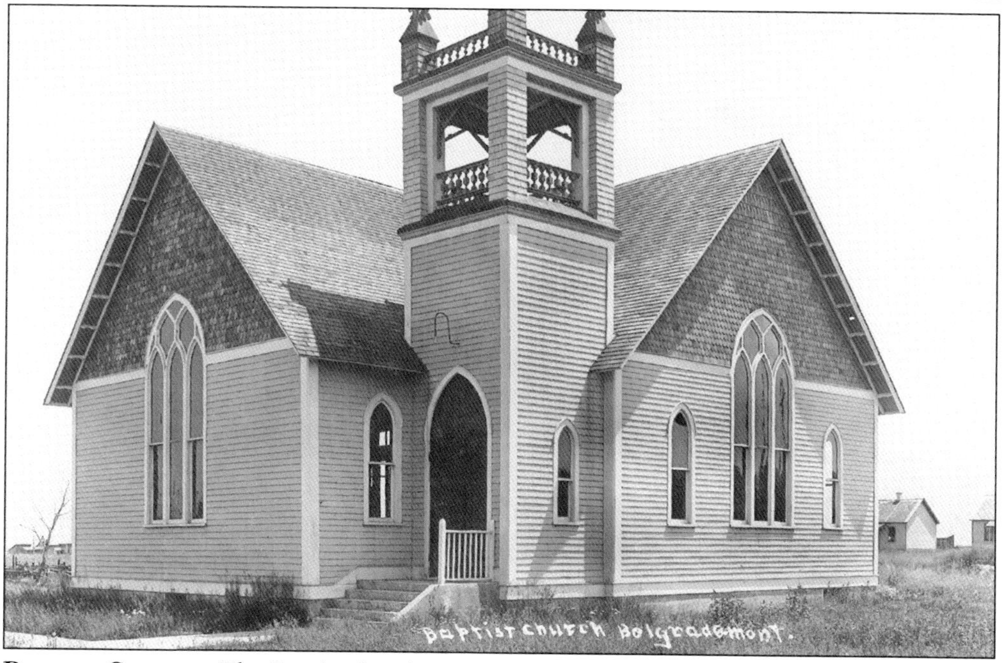

BAPTIST CHURCH. The Baptist church was an early arrival in the Gallatin Valley, forming in 1883. It organized in the Belgrade and Manhattan areas. This new Baptist church had recently been completed in the Belgrade area when this *c.* 1910 real-photo view was made.

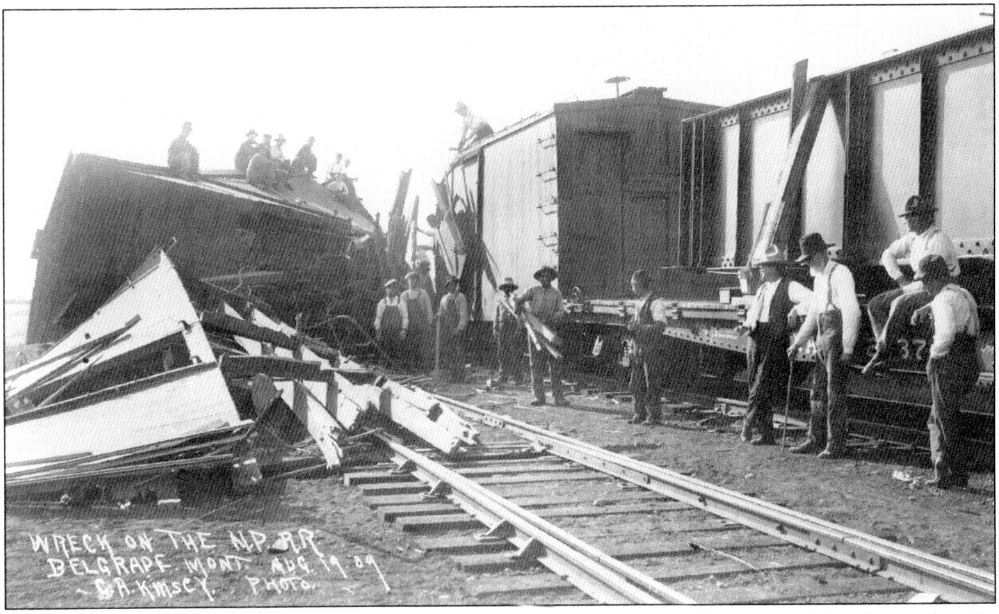

TRAIN WRECK. This vintage real-photo image shows a wreck on the Northern Pacific Railroad near Belgrade on August 19, 1909. Workers and bystanders inspect the damage from the ground and from atop the overturned car at left. With local photographer Charles Kinsey on hand to take photographs of the disaster, why not get in the picture? (Photograph by C. A. Kinsey, Belgrade, Montana.)

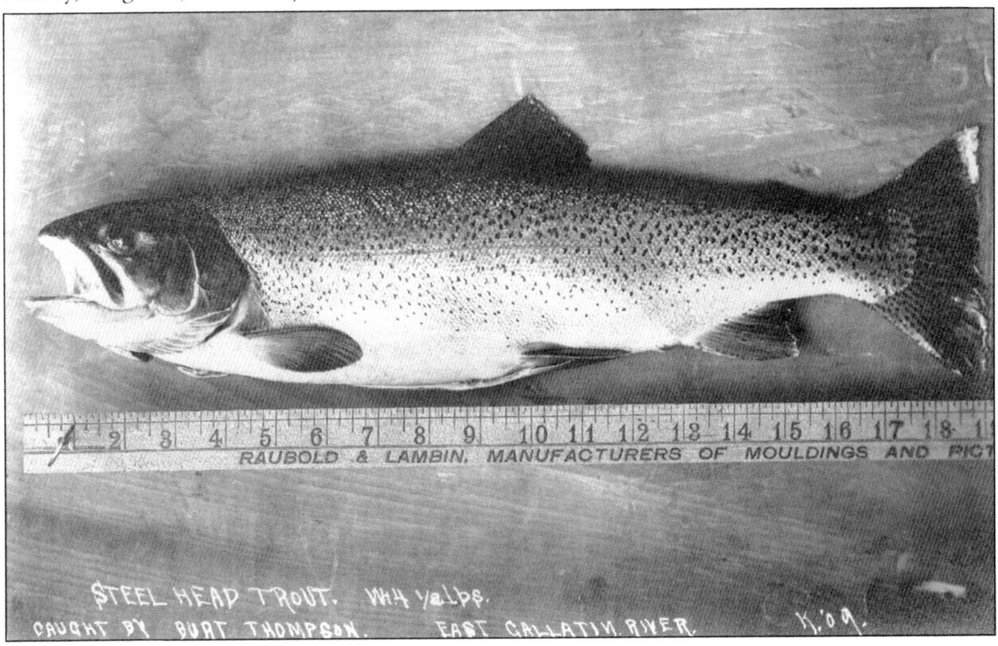

WHAT A CATCH! This *c.* 1909 real-photo image shows a steelhead trout, weighing in at 4.5 pounds and stretching to 19 inches in length based on the yardstick shown. Burt Thompson caught this fish on the East Gallatin River. This river begins about 1 mile east of Bozeman and runs west, flowing near Belgrade before joining the main Gallatin River just north of Manhattan. (Photograph by C. A. Kinsey, Belgrade, Montana.)

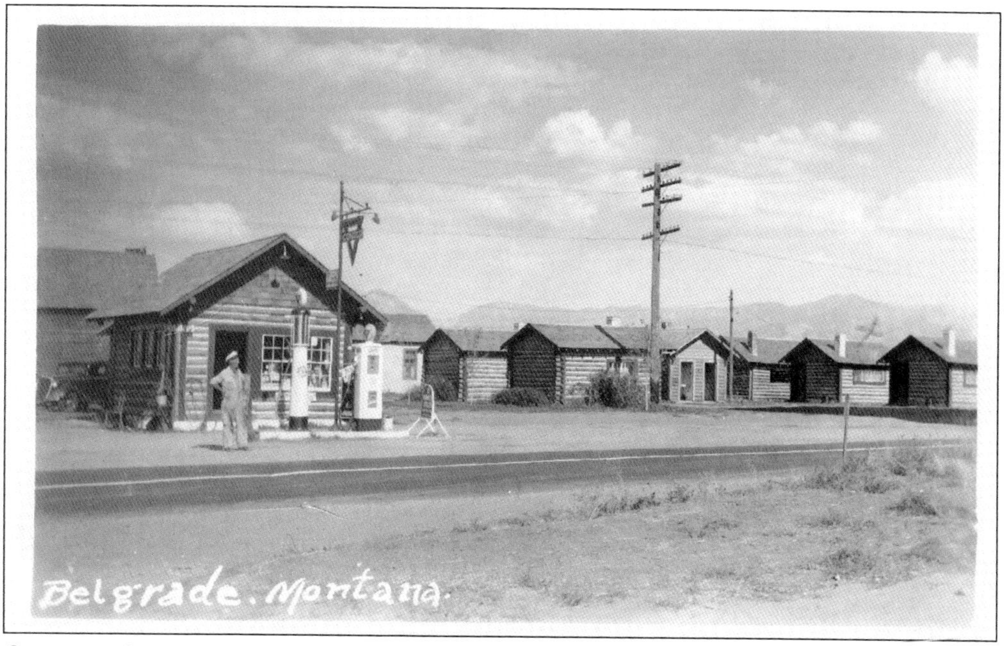

CONOCO GAS STATION AND CABINS. Postmarked 1941, this real-photo image shows a combination gas station and lodging business. It was located on the north side of West Main Street, when the main highway ran through Belgrade. When the interstate highway opened in the valley around 1972, many roadside operations like this one were forced out of business.

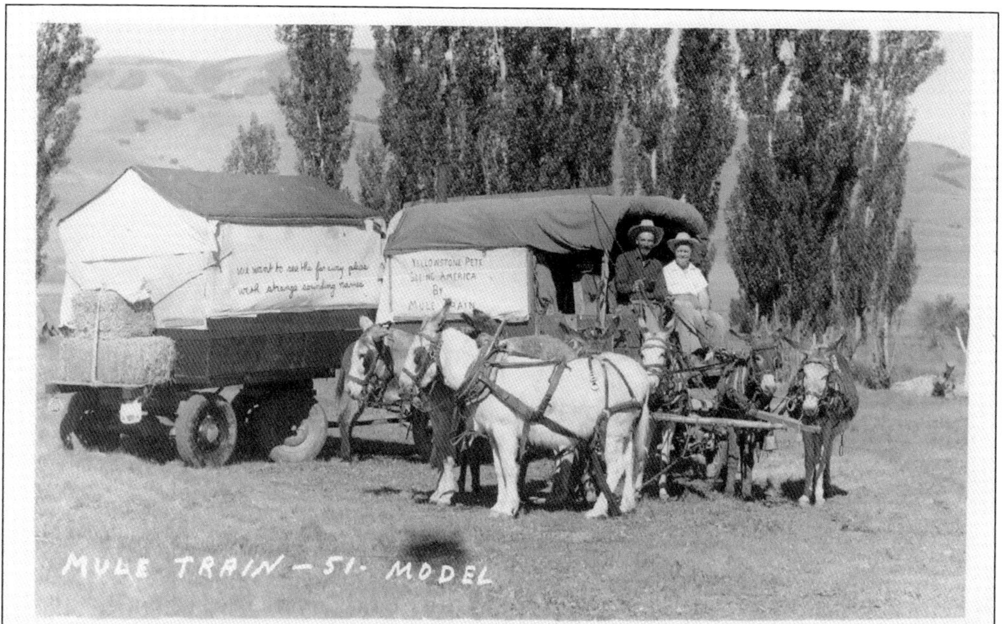

YELLOWSTONE PETE AND HIS WIFE. Pictured in this *c.* 1950 real-photo image is Pete Robbins and his wife. Nicknamed Yellowstone Pete, he made a series of postcards and sold them to help finance his travels. He and his wife and their team of wagons and donkeys once made a 90-mile trek to West Yellowstone via the Gallatin Canyon. He continued on another 20 miles to Island Park, Idaho.

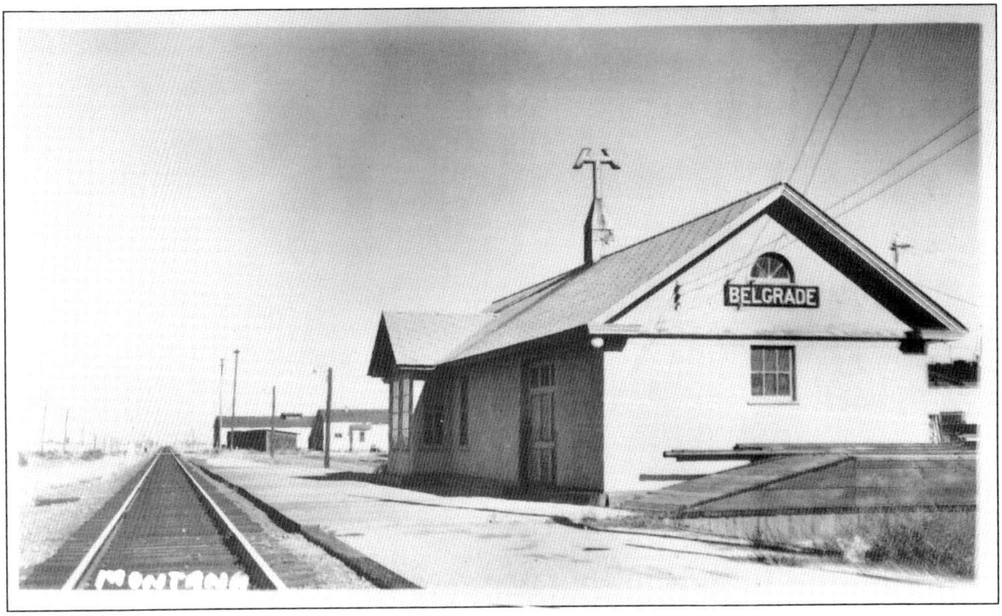

RAILROAD DEPOT. This *c.* 1950 real-photo image shows the Northern Pacific Railroad station. It was constructed in 1935 and was located near the back entrances of the Bozeman Chamber of Commerce and Montana Camp, two neighboring buildings on Main Street. Northern Pacific closed its service about 1970. This building was sold and moved intact in 2006.

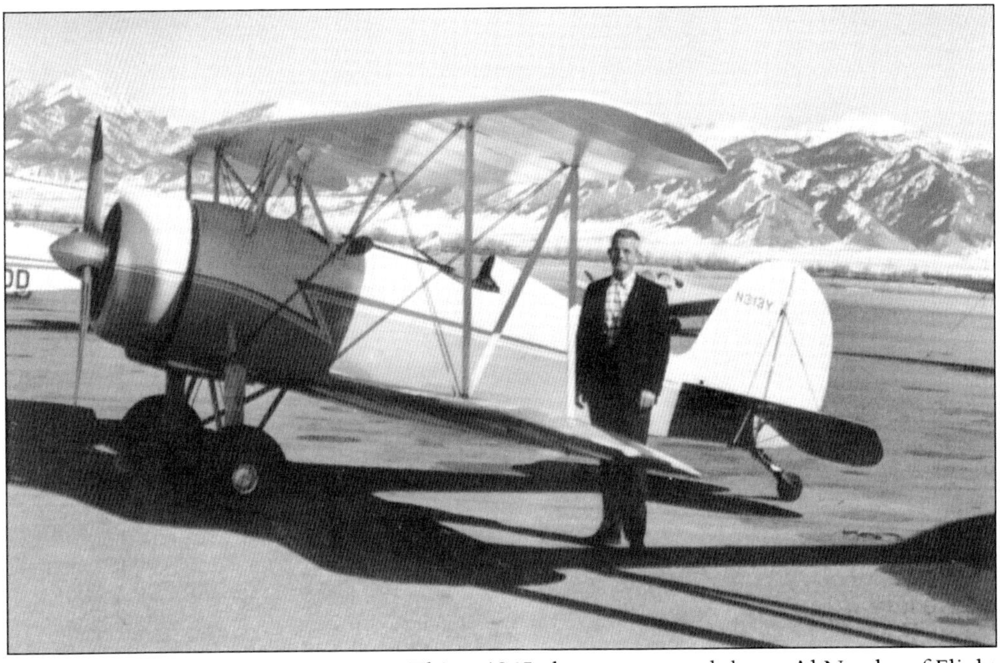

AL NEWBY, AIR SHOW PROMOTER. This *c.* 1965 chrome postcard shows Al Newby of Flight Line, Inc. of Belgrade and his 1932 Great Lakes 2T-1A. Newby used this aircraft to put on air shows in Montana and the Northwest. Sadly, Newby died while performing aerial maneuvers just north of Bozeman. (Photograph by Duncan MacNab; courtesy of Ken Hamlin.)

Eight

South to Gallatin Canyon

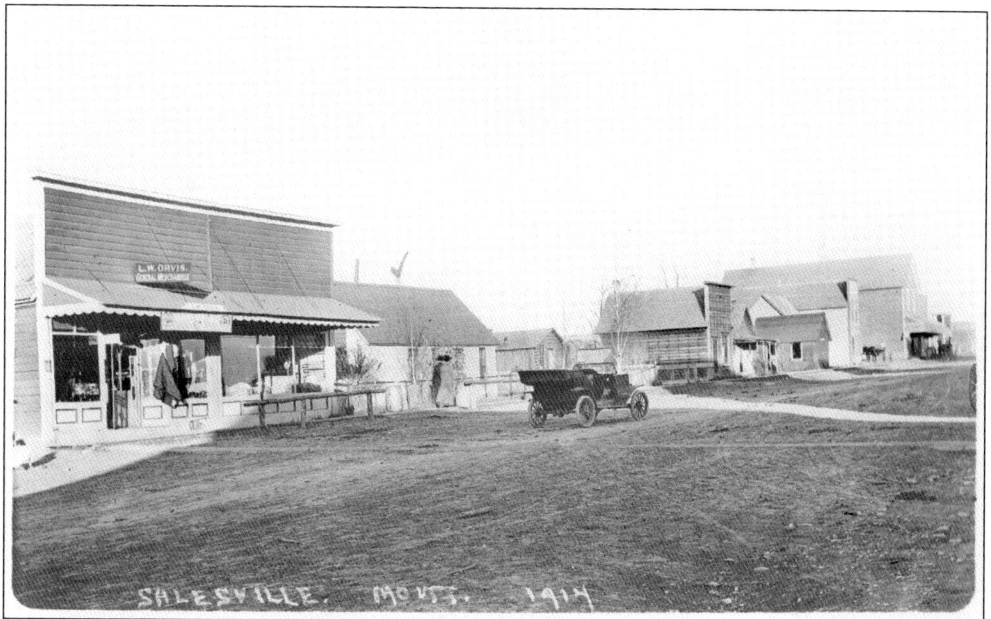

Salesville Street View. Postmarked from Salesville in 1914, this real-photo image shows a single auto in front of L. W. Orvis's General Merchandise store. Located about 15 miles southwest of Bozeman, Salesville would later be renamed Gallatin Gateway when the Milwaukee Road—a nickname for the railroad known before 1928 as the Chicago, Milwaukee, and St. Paul Railroad and afterwards as the Chicago, Milwaukee, St. Paul, and Pacific (CMStP&P) Railroad, also called the Milwaukee Railroad—constructed the Gallatin Gateway Inn. The town's original name, prior to 1883, was Slabtown.

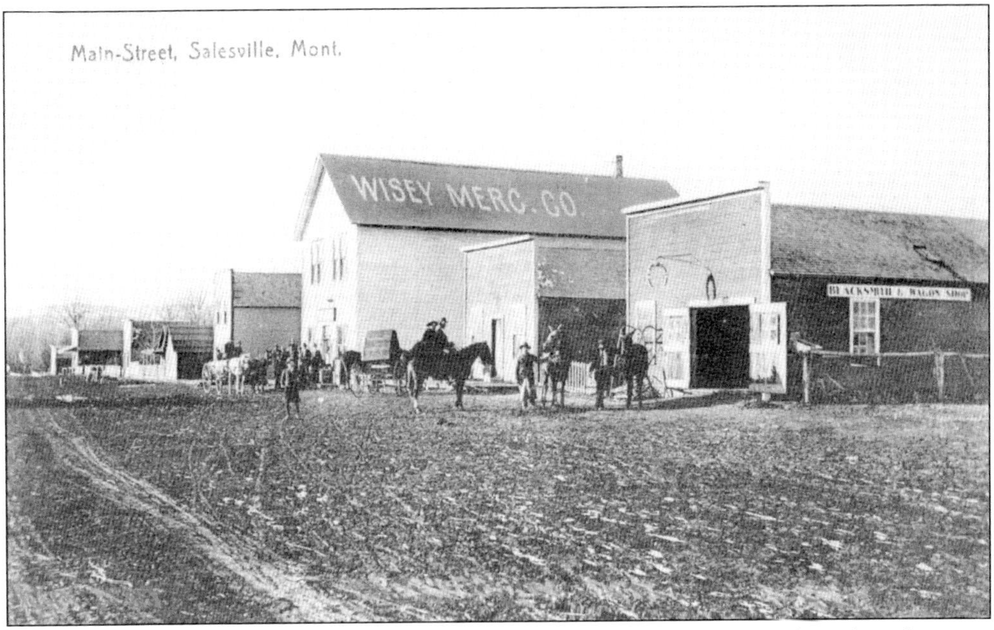

SALESVILLE MAIN STREET. This *c.* 1910 printed postcard shows the blacksmith and wagon shop at right. The larger building at center is the Wisey Mercantile Company store. Salesville was named after the early settler and sawmill operator Zachariah Sales, who came with his family via wagon train into the Gallatin Valley in 1865. (Courtesy of Ken Hamlin.)

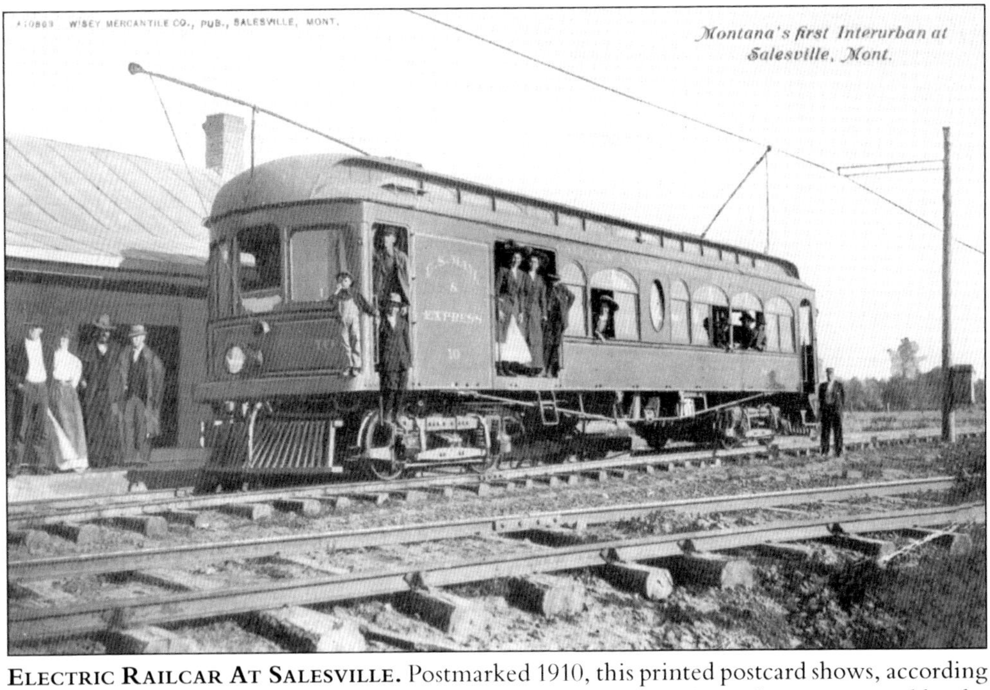

ELECTRIC RAILCAR AT SALESVILLE. Postmarked 1910, this printed postcard shows, according to the caption, "Montana's first interurban at Salesville, Mont." This railcar was owned by the Gallatin Valley Electric Railway Company and motored between Salesville and Bozeman. It opened for service in 1909.

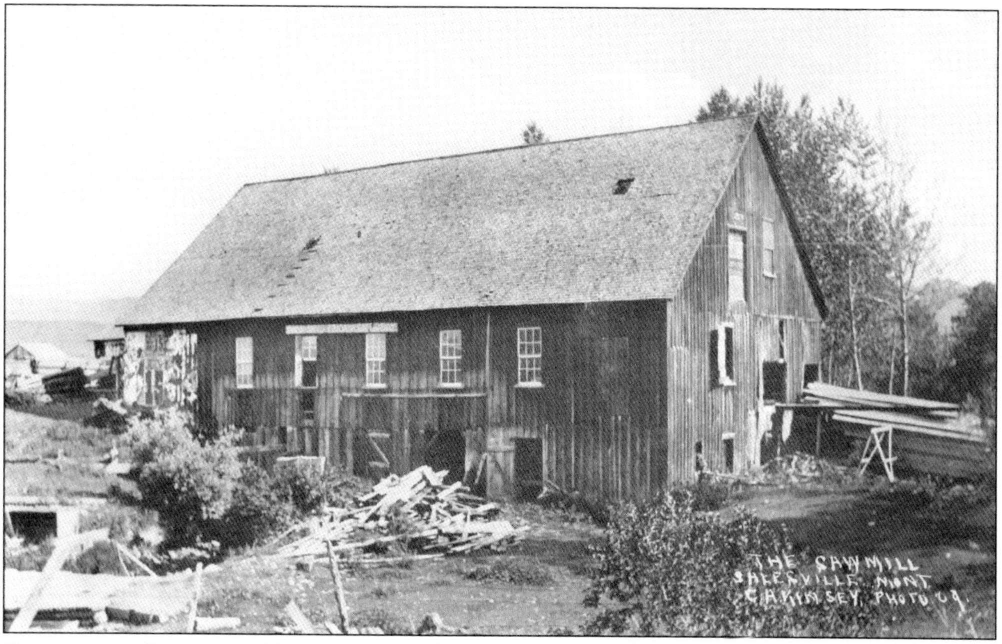

SALESVILLE SAWMILL. This *c.* 1909 real-photo image shows an old sawmill near Salesville. Logging camps in the Gallatin Canyon to the south floated logs down the Gallatin River during spring's high water to this sawmill and others in the area, including a mill at Central Park. (Photograph by C. A. Kinsey, Belgrade, Montana.)

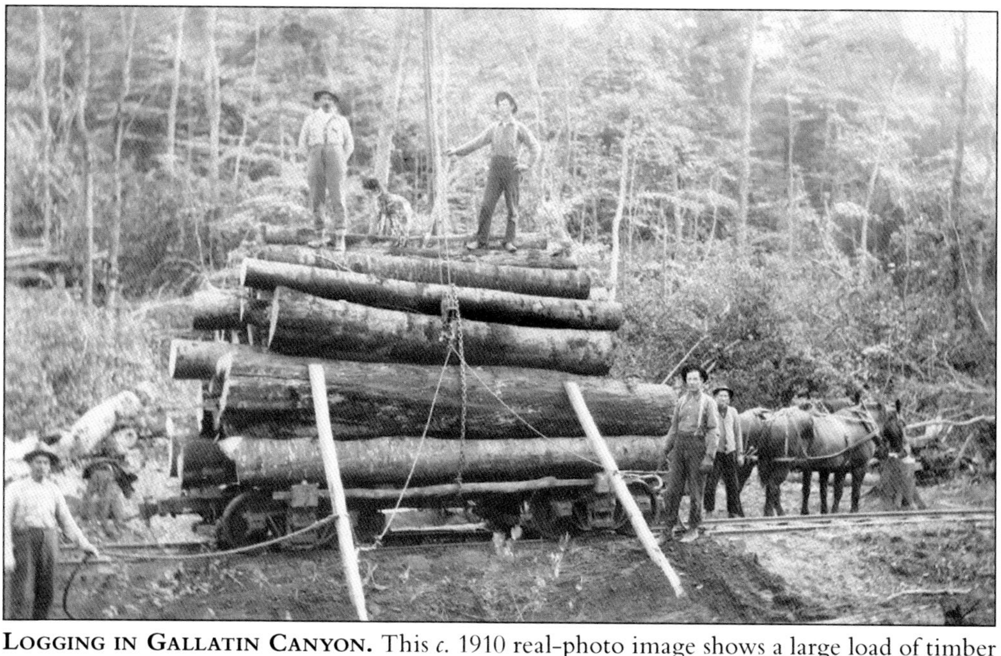

LOGGING IN GALLATIN CANYON. This *c.* 1910 real-photo image shows a large load of timber being prepared for hauling by railroad. This timber may have been transported to Salesville, some 20 miles to the north, for cutting and processing. (Courtesy of Ron Iverson.)

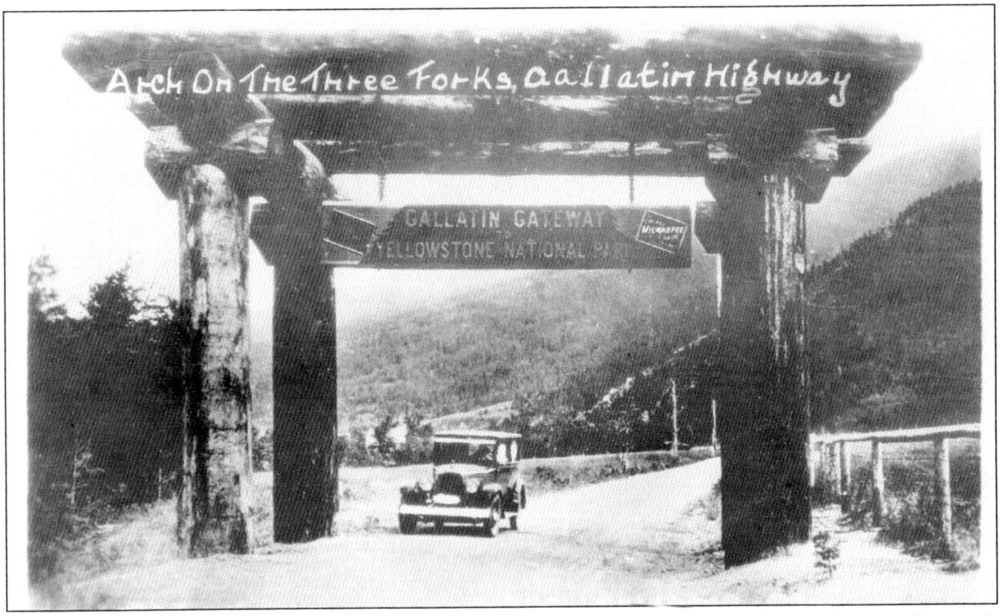

GALLATIN GATEWAY ARCH. Postmarked 1937, this real-photo image shows the wooden arch that signified the entrance to Yellowstone National Park through the Gallatin Valley and beyond. It was located about 6 miles south of Gallatin Gateway and was a promotion of the CMSt&P Railroad encouraging travel to Yellowstone Park. About 40 years later, the arch was removed to allow for the widening of Highway 191. (Courtesy of Steve and Robin Hamilton.)

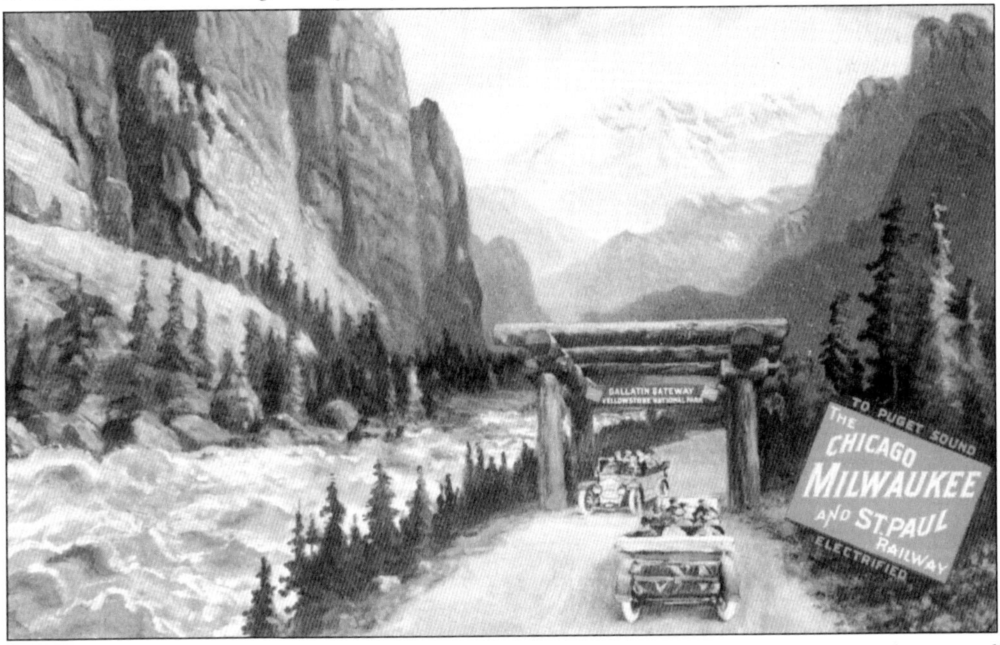

GALLATIN GATEWAY RAILROAD PROMOTION. Postmarked in 1927, this printed postcard was published by the CMSt&P railroad to promote travel to Yellowstone Park. Text printed on the back includes: "Cutting through the virgin wilderness of the Gallatin National Forest and the spectacular canyon of the Gallatin River, Gallatin Gateway is the wonder entrance to Yellowstone Park and 'The Greatest Gateway to the Greatest National Park.'"

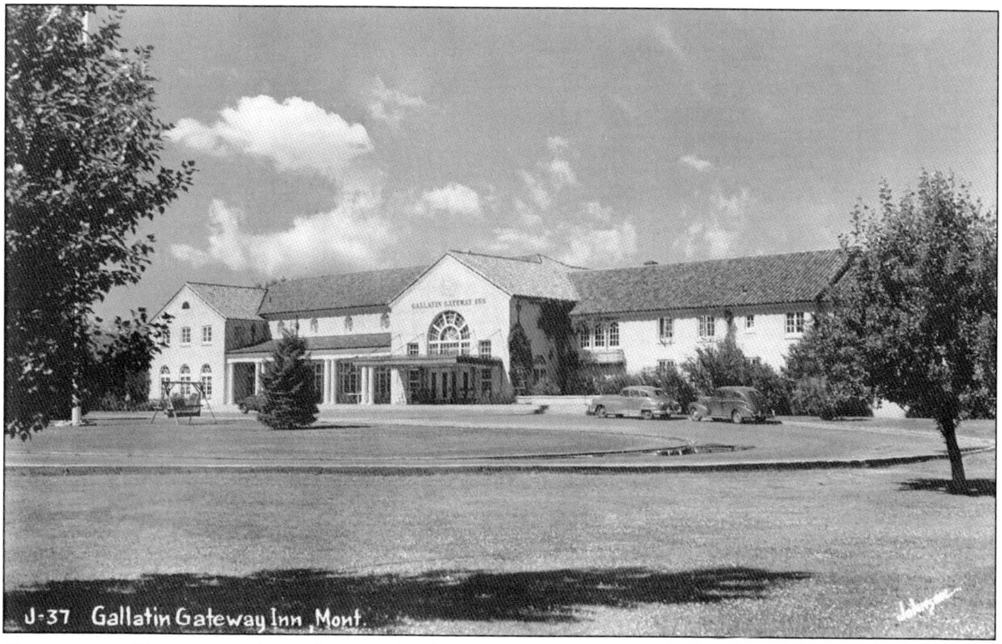

Gallatin Gateway Inn. Postmarked 1950, this real photograph shows the elegant inn, which still operates today. It was built in 1927 by the CMSt&P Railroad to promote travel to Yellowstone Park. Large, comfortable motor coaches traveled daily in the summertime between the inn and the park, an 85-mile trip. (Photograph by Johnson.)

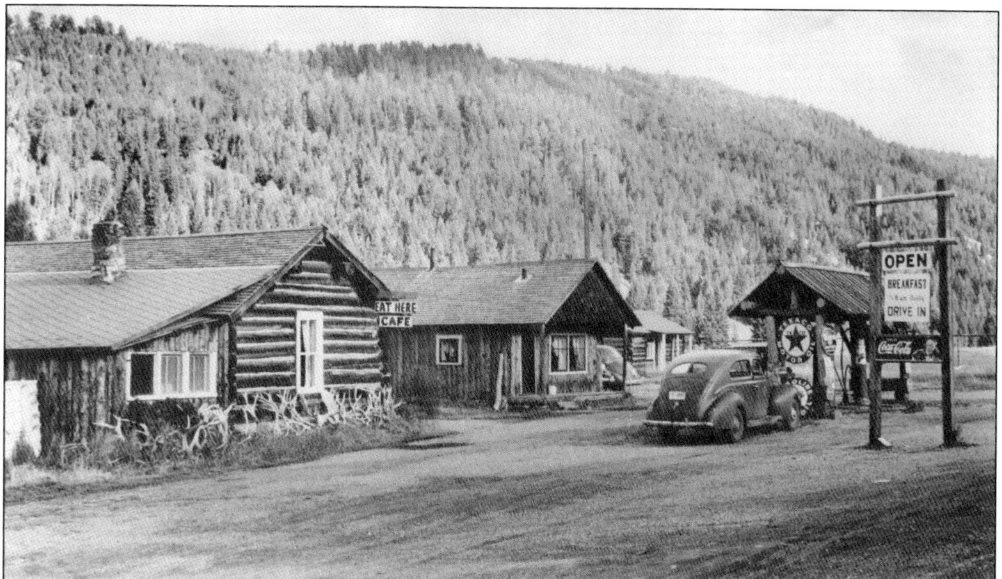

Rainbow Ranch in Gallatin Canyon. This *c.* 1940 real-photo image shows another of the dude ranches that sprang up in the Gallatin Valley. The building at left is a café and bears a homemade sign stating, "Eat Here—Café." The car at right is parked near sheltered gas pumps and Texaco advertising signs; a Coca-Cola sign is visible at the right. As the caption notes, Fran and Walt Cottrell were the owners of this business located about 50 miles south of Bozeman.

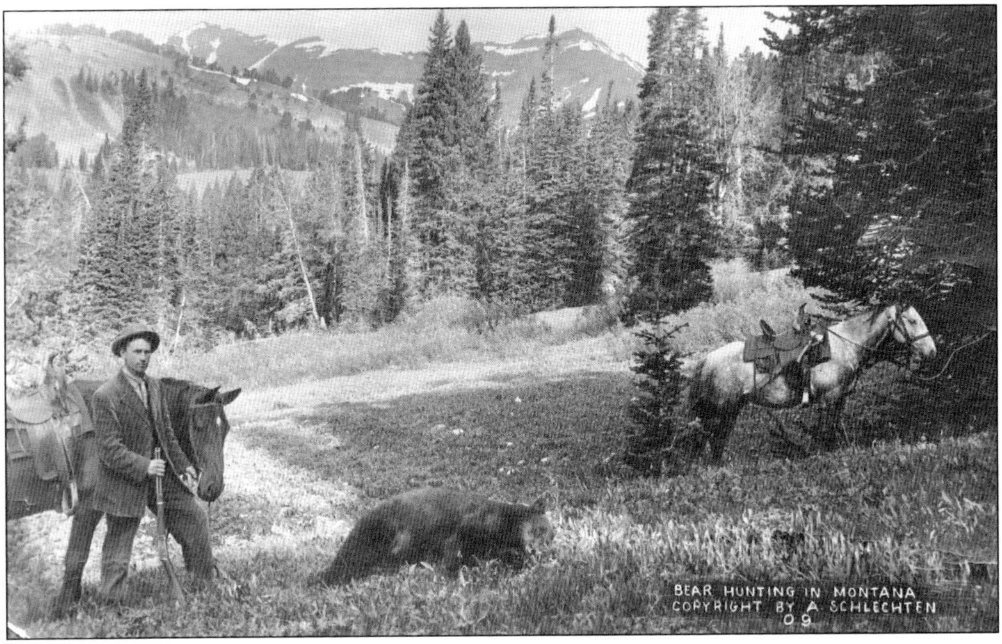

Bear Hunting Near Bozeman. This *c.* 1909 real-photo image shows a well-dressed man posed with his rifle and horse and standing next to a downed bear. The area is not identified but may have been in the Spanish Peaks area, south of Bozeman. (Photograph by A. Schlechten, Bozeman, Montana; courtesy of Ken Hamlin.)

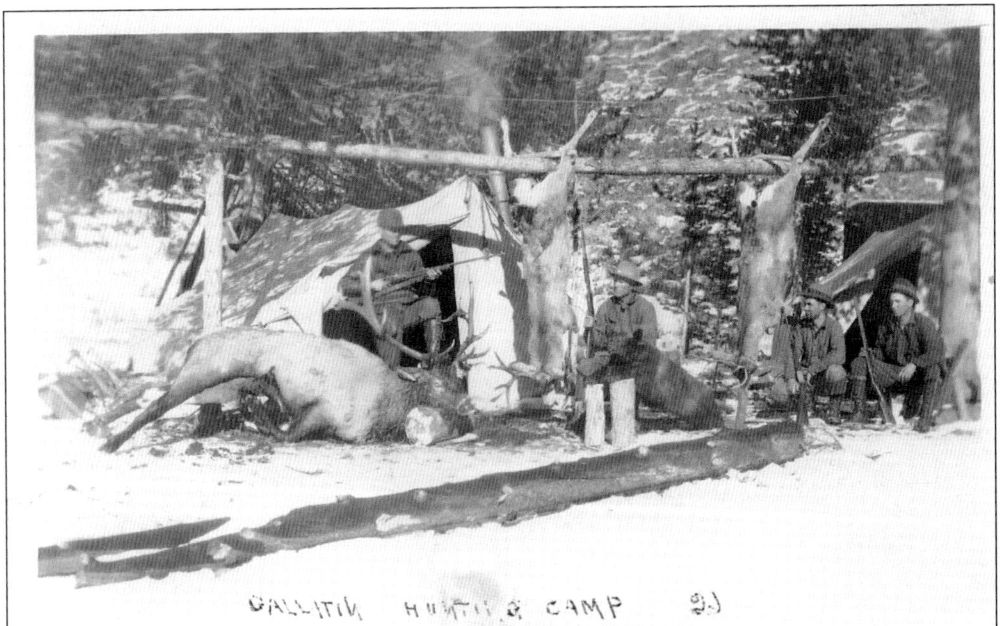

Gallatin Hunting Camp. This *c.* 1925 real-photo image shows a winter hunting camp set up in Gallatin Canyon. These four hunters pose with their rifles in front of two tents. These men will be taking home an elk and a bear. Although the photographer was not identified, C. A. Kinsey of Belgrade, Montana, likely took this image.

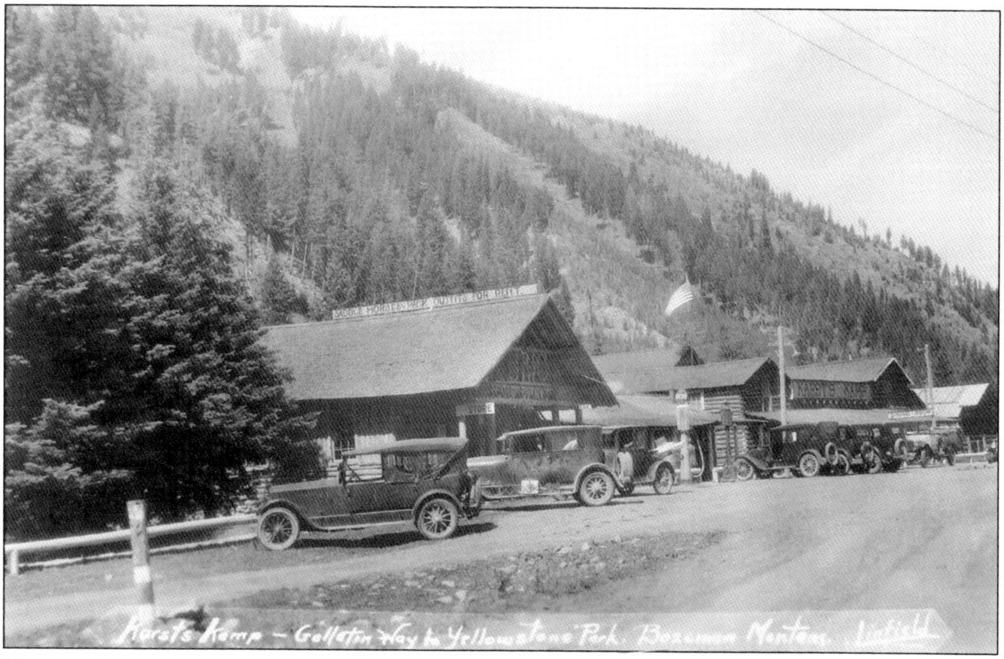

KARSTS KAMP. Located in the Gallatin Canyon about 40 miles south of Bozeman, this was one of the first dude ranches in Montana, and the first of a half dozen such operations that would develop in the Gallatin Canyon area. Founded in 1901 as Karst's Cold Springs Resort by Pete Karst, the business had greatly expanded by the time this *c.* 1928 real-photo image was taken. The sign on the roof of the building at left advertises "Saddle Horses and Pack Outfits for Rent." (Photograph by B. F. Linfield, Bozeman, Montana.)

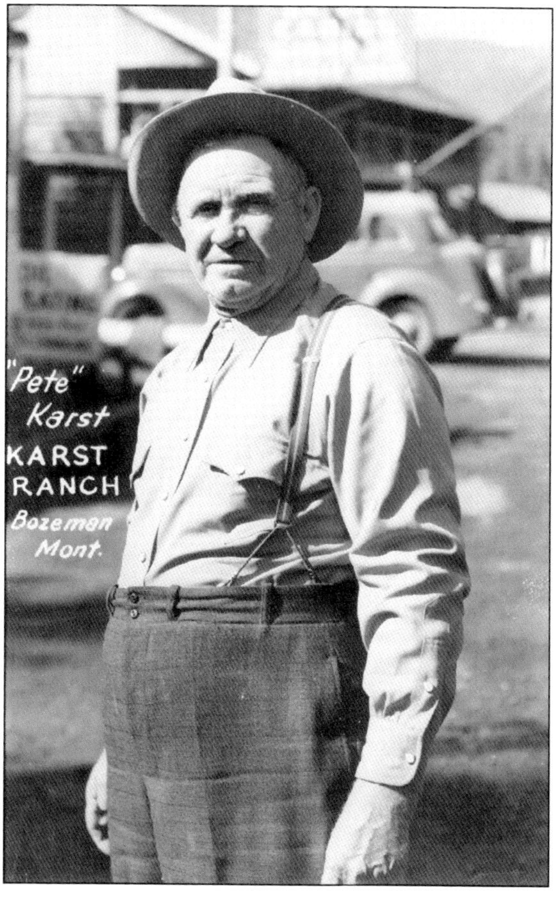

PETE KARST. This *c.* 1940 real-photo portrait shows the congenial and hardworking founder of the Karst dude ranch. Karst worked to develop his operation over a 50-year period. He also operated a profitable bus line, which transported tourists from Salesville (Gallatin Gateway) to West Yellowstone, the northwestern gateway city to Yellowstone National Park.

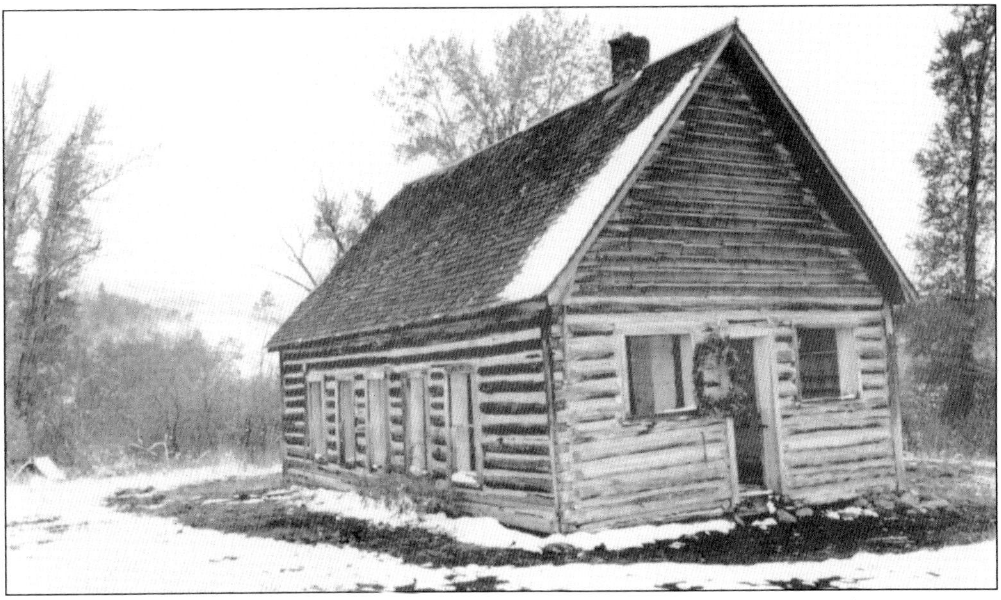

LITTLE BEAR SCHOOL HOUSE MUSEUM. This *c.* 1990 chrome postcard image shows a winter view of this little school after it was closed but before it was converted into a museum. The school was built in 1912, and classes were held there until 1950, when a larger school was built. The local community banded together to save the school and make it into a museum. It is open four days a week between Memorial Day and Labor Day and located near the Gallatin Gateway area. (Courtesy of Sandy Hart.)

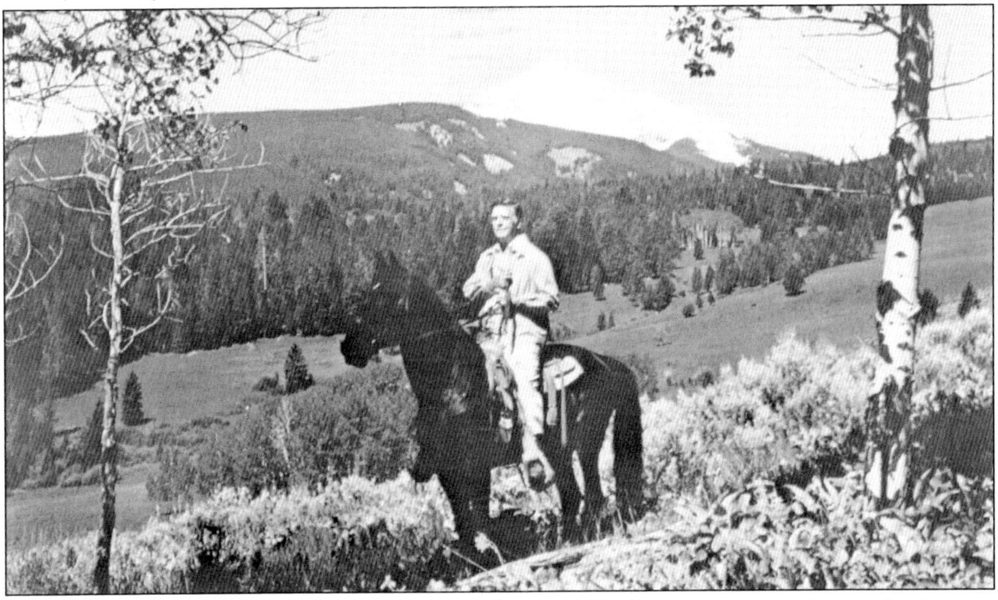

CHET HUNTLEY, FOUNDER OF BIG SKY. This *c.* 1970 chrome postcard shows the famous television newscaster Chet Huntley on horseback in a meadow near a new residential site in the Big Sky area. Lone Peak, famous for its fabulous skiing, is in the background. Huntley, who passed away at Big Sky in 1974, was chairman of the board of the early Big Sky development project. Today the area has two major villages, in addition to the highway establishment, and many expensive homes in the surrounding area. A high school will open there in fall 2009.

Nine

Western Gallatin Valley Views

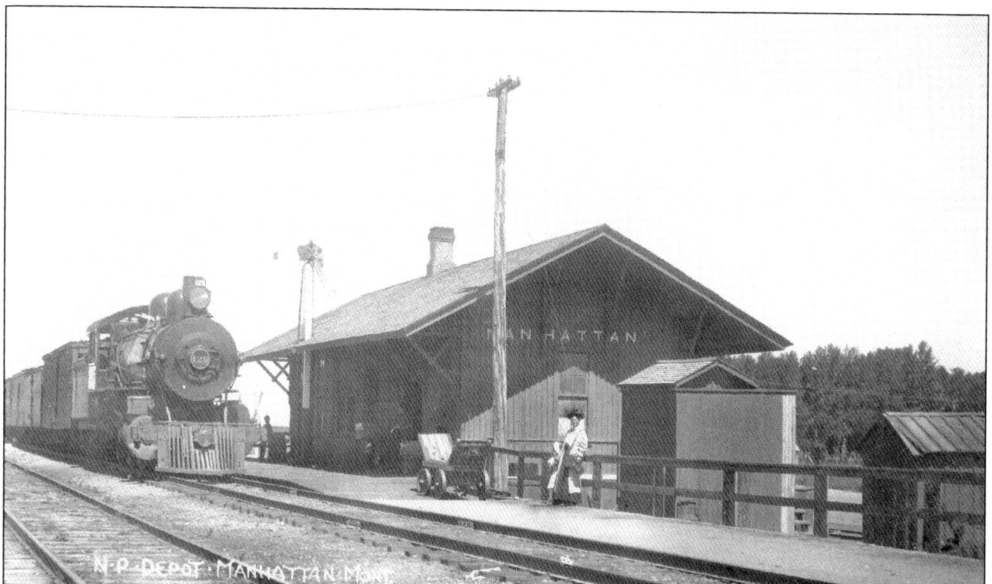

Manhattan Train Depot. This *c.* 1912 real-photo postcard shows a train pulling into the station at Manhattan. The Northern Pacific Railroad reached Manhattan and the Gallatin Valley in 1883, bringing with it the capability for local area businesses to transport grain, livestock, and wood products to markets outside their immediate area. Located 19 miles west of Bozeman, Manhattan was first called Moreland when it was founded in 1890. The next year the town's name was changed to Manhattan. (Courtesy of the Pioneer Museum, Bozeman.)

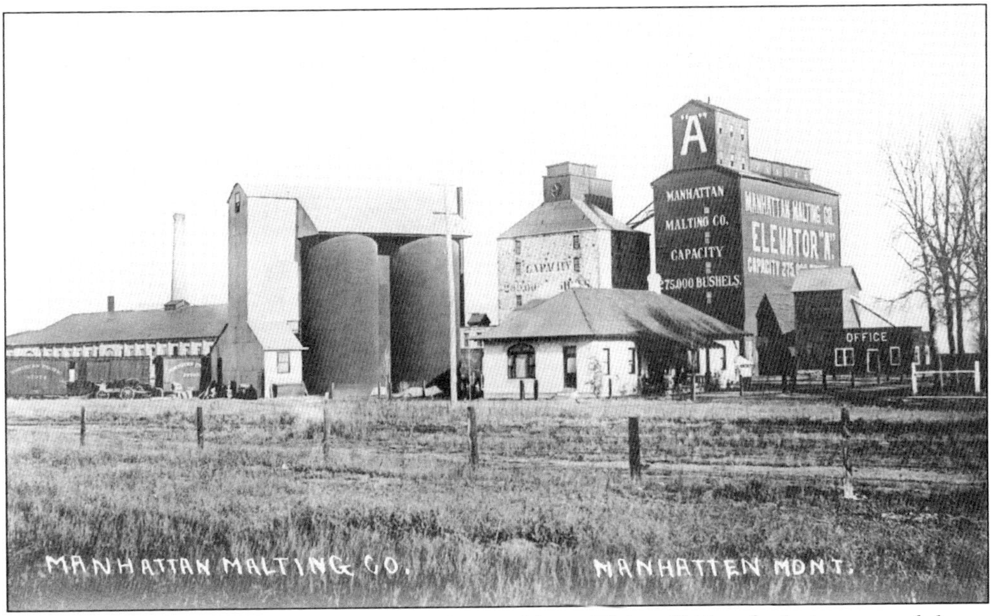

Manhattan Malting Company and Paper Mill. This *c.* 1915 real-photo postcard shows the center of one of Manhattan's biggest early-day manufacturing operations. The building at the far left was a paper mill. The elevator in the center was built in 1905 and used to store wheat. The tall stone building was the malting plant. At the right is Elevator A, which was used to store barley. The company's home office was on Manhattan Island in New York, a probable source for the town's name.

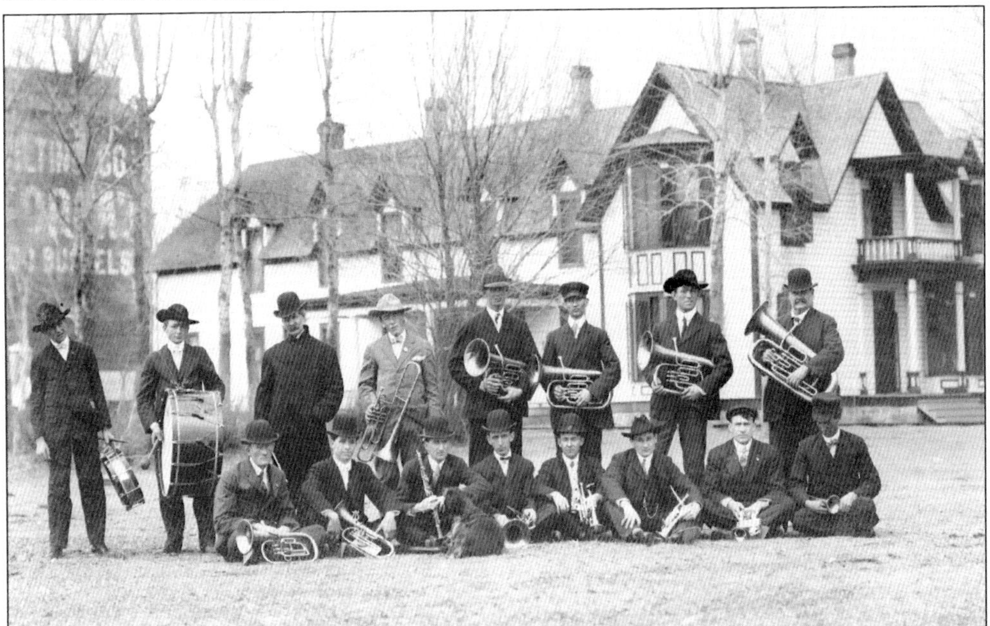

Band in Front of Manhattan Hotel. Known as the Manhattan Cornet Band, this newly formed group of mostly young men pose for a picture in front of the Manhattan Hotel, as shown in this *c.* 1910 real-photo postcard. George Kellogg was chosen as the band's first president. Elevator A of the Manhattan Malting Company is visible at far left.

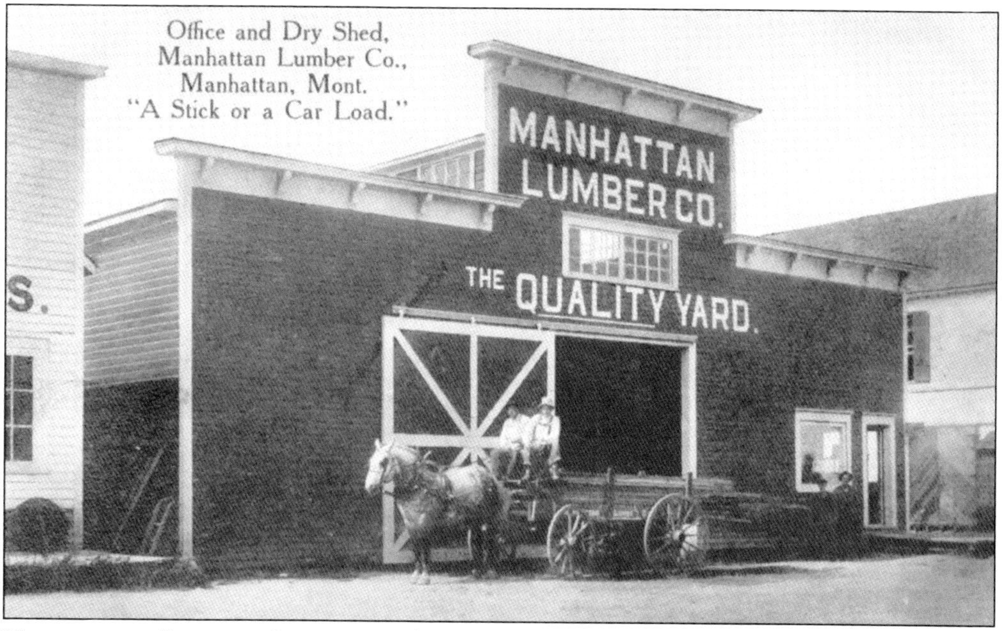

MANHATTAN LUMBER COMPANY. The advertising signage on this *c.* 1910 printed postcard advertises, "The Manhattan Lumber Co.—The Quality Yard." The caption advertises that the company will sell the consumer "a stick or a Car Load." A horse-drawn delivery wagon is shown at the entrance. (Published by Charles E. Morris Company, Great Falls, Montana.)

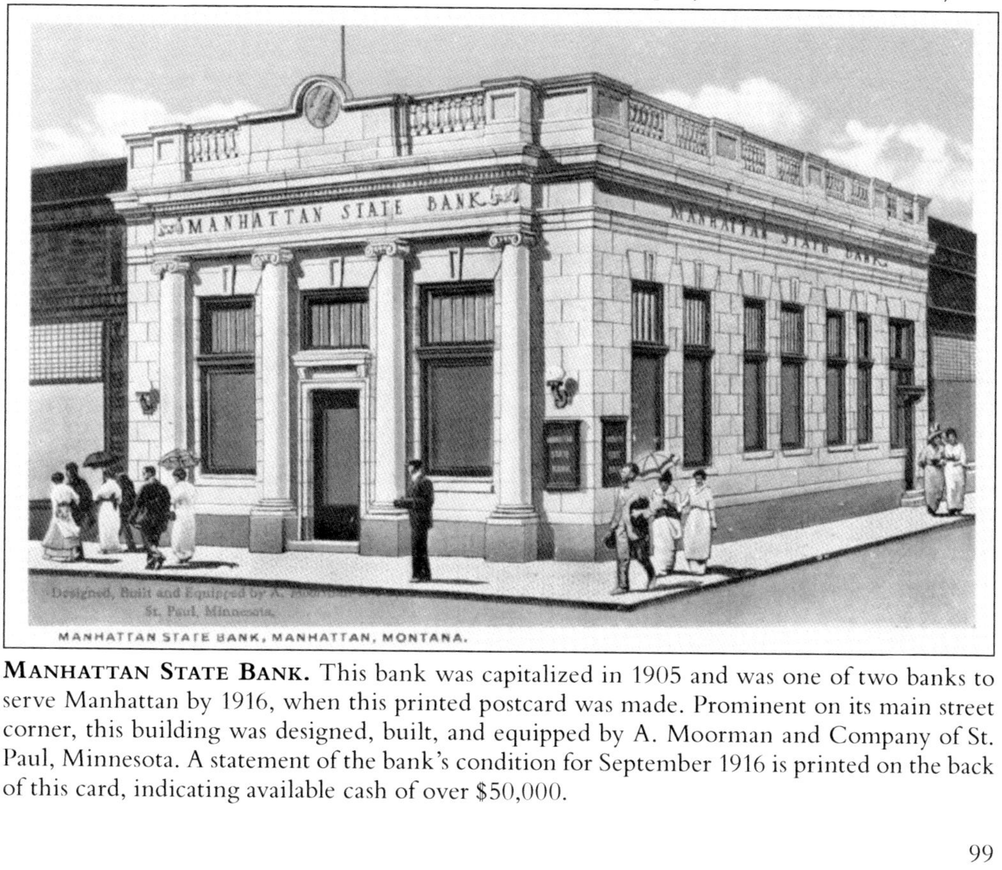

MANHATTAN STATE BANK. This bank was capitalized in 1905 and was one of two banks to serve Manhattan by 1916, when this printed postcard was made. Prominent on its main street corner, this building was designed, built, and equipped by A. Moorman and Company of St. Paul, Minnesota. A statement of the bank's condition for September 1916 is printed on the back of this card, indicating available cash of over $50,000.

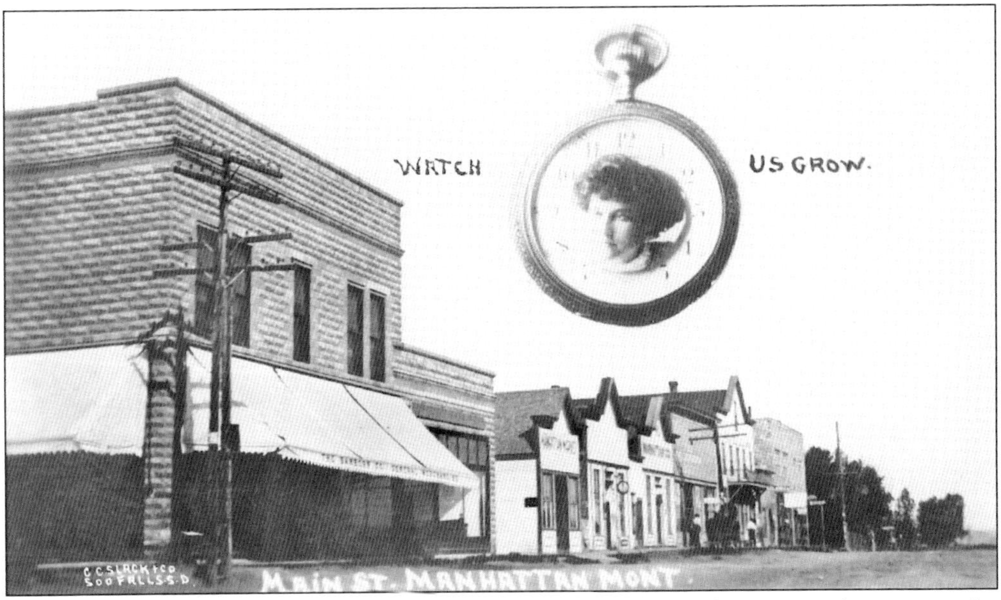

MANHATTAN, "WATCH US GROW." Clever creative photography was used to create the image shown in this *c.* 1910 real-photo postcard. The face of a pretty lady has been placed inside a pocket watch overlooking Manhattan's Main Street to go with the caption of "Watch Us Grow." This sentiment expressed the optimism for the town's stability and promise for the future. Manhattan, with a population of about 1,400, remains a prosperous town in the north-central Gallatin Valley today. (Photograph by C. C. Slack and Company, Sioux Falls, South Dakota.)

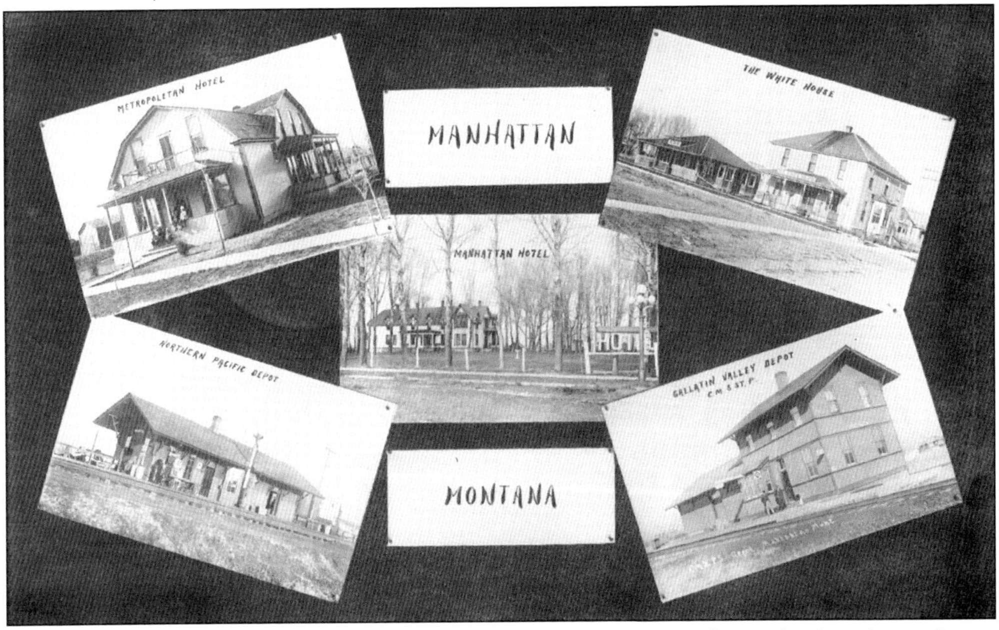

MANHATTAN MULTI-VIEW. Five miniature views of important Manhattan landmarks are shown in this real-photo postcard, postmarked 1914. From left to right are (top) the Metropolitan Hotel and the White House; (center) Manhattan Hotel; (bottom) the Northern Pacific depot and the Gallatin Valley CMStP&P Railroad depot. (Photograph by M. L. Zercher, Topeka, Kansas.)

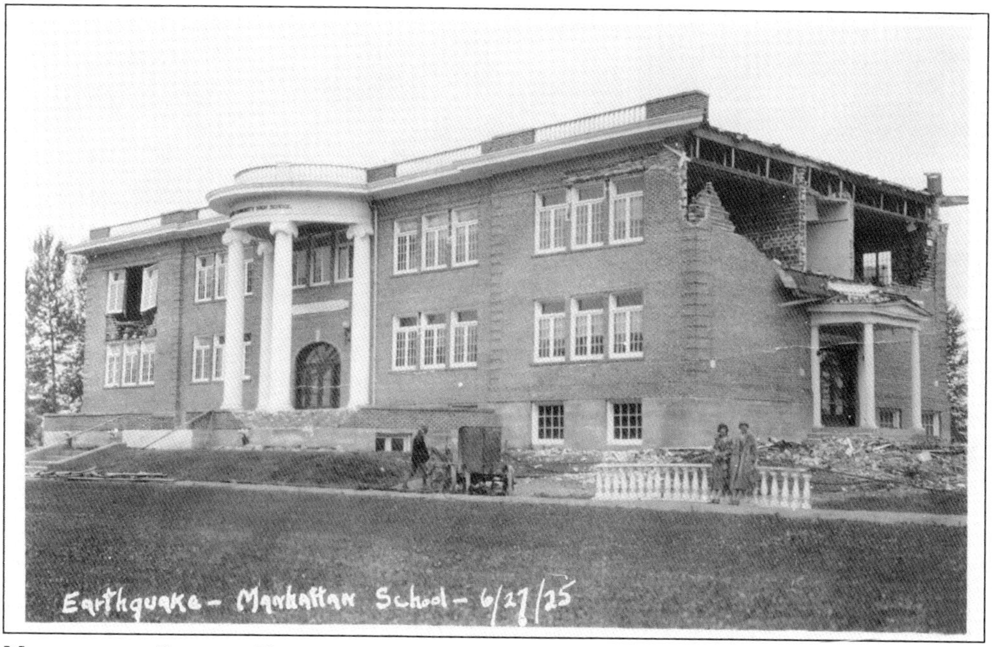

MANHATTAN SCHOOL DAMAGED BY EARTHQUAKE. On June 27, 1925, a major earthquake measuring 6.7 on the Richter scale struck the Gallatin Valley. The epicenter was close to Manhattan and the neighboring towns of Three Forks and Logan. School and church buildings were badly damaged, as exemplified in this vintage real-photo postcard showing the devastated Manhattan school.

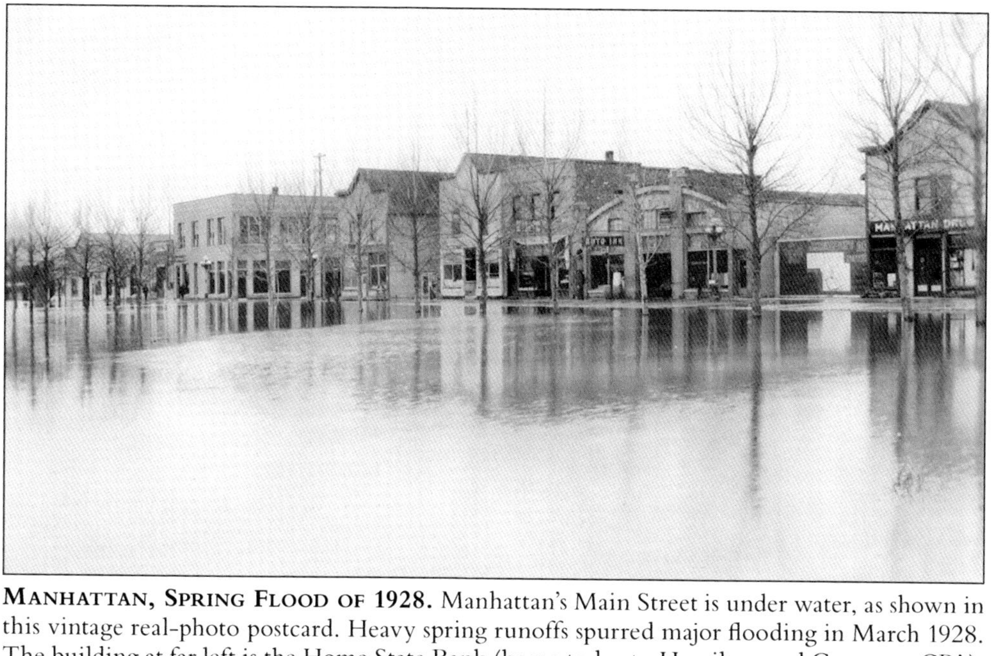

MANHATTAN, SPRING FLOOD OF 1928. Manhattan's Main Street is under water, as shown in this vintage real-photo postcard. Heavy spring runoffs spurred major flooding in March 1928. The building at far left is the Home State Bank (home today to Hamilton and Company CPA). The Manhattan Drug Company can be seen at the far right. The building with the curved roof is the Auto Inn Garage. Some of the writing on the back of this card states: "March 9, 1928 flood."

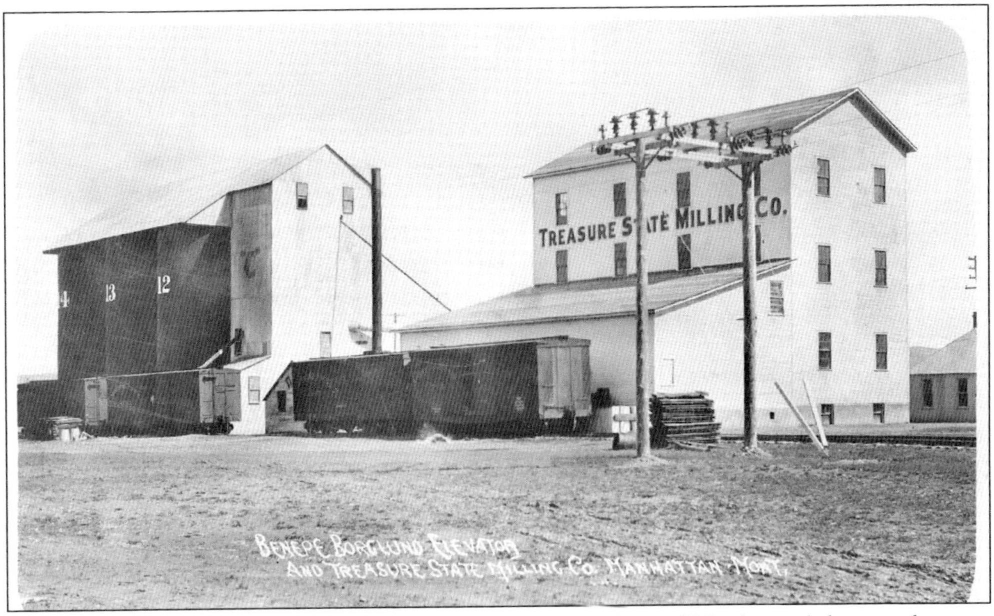

MANHATTAN, TREASURE STATE MILLING COMPANY. One of Manhattan's largest elevators and mills is shown here. At left is the Benepe-Borglund elevator, used to store wheat, and at right is the Treasure State Milling Company. Northern Pacific Railroad cars are stationed beside both buildings, as shown in this real-photo postcard, postmarked 1911. (Courtesy of Ken Hamlin.)

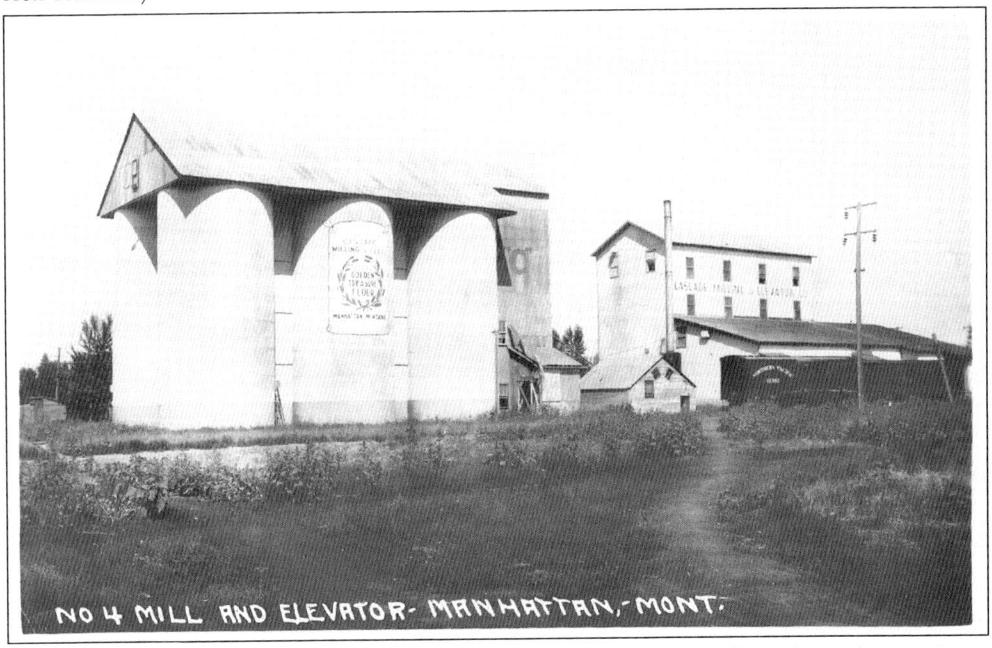

MANHATTAN, HOME OF GOLDEN TREASURE FLOUR. Another of Manhattan's prominent mills and elevators were those of the Cascade Milling and Elevator Company, seen in this *c.* 1920 real-photo postcard. Circular wheat shocks forming a garland served as the symbol for the company's product, Golden Treasure Flour, and can be seen on the center elevator bin at left. (Photograph by Wesley Andrews, Baker, Oregon.)

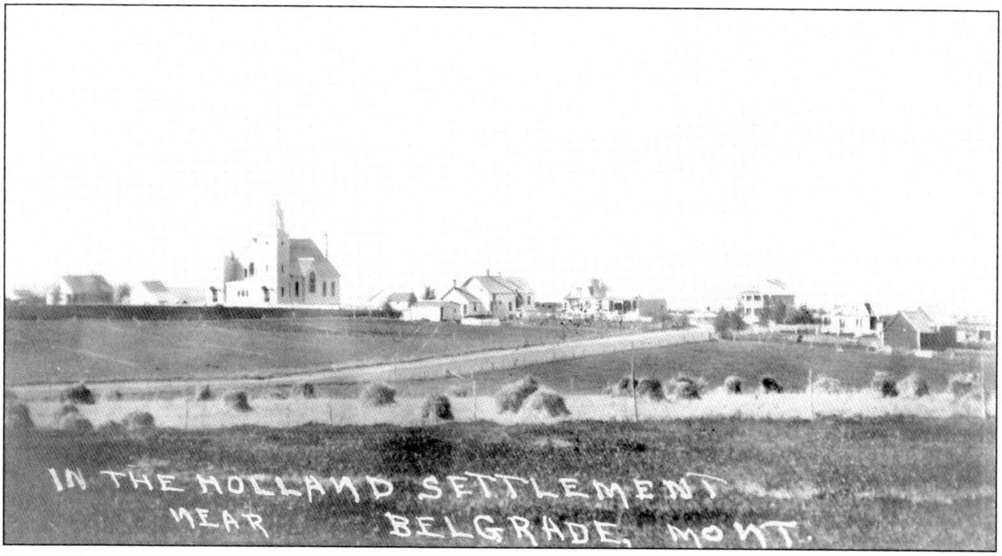

The Holland Settlement. Located south of Manhattan in the central Gallatin Valley are the communities of Amsterdam, Churchill, and Anceney, known as the Holland settlement. The name results from the influx of Dutch immigrants who were recruited by the Manhattan Malting Company to raise barley for the company. This real-photo postcard was postmarked from Manhattan, the nearest post office, in 1916. (Photographer is not identified; courtesy of the Pioneer Museum, Bozeman.)

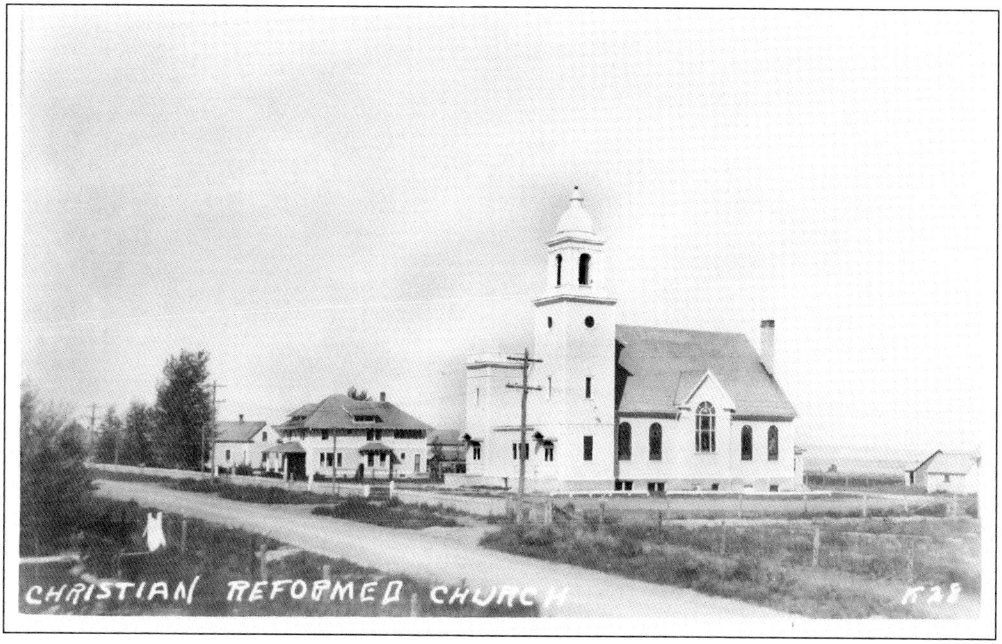

Churchill, Christian Reformed Church. This *c.* 1925 real-photo postcard shows the church that anchors the Holland settlement in Churchill, 7 miles south of Manhattan. The Dutch Reformed Church was organized in 1903, and this church was built in 1911, serving 40 families at the time. Children in the community have attended private school since 1911. The settlement's high school, called Manhattan Christian, is well known for its winning basketball tradition.

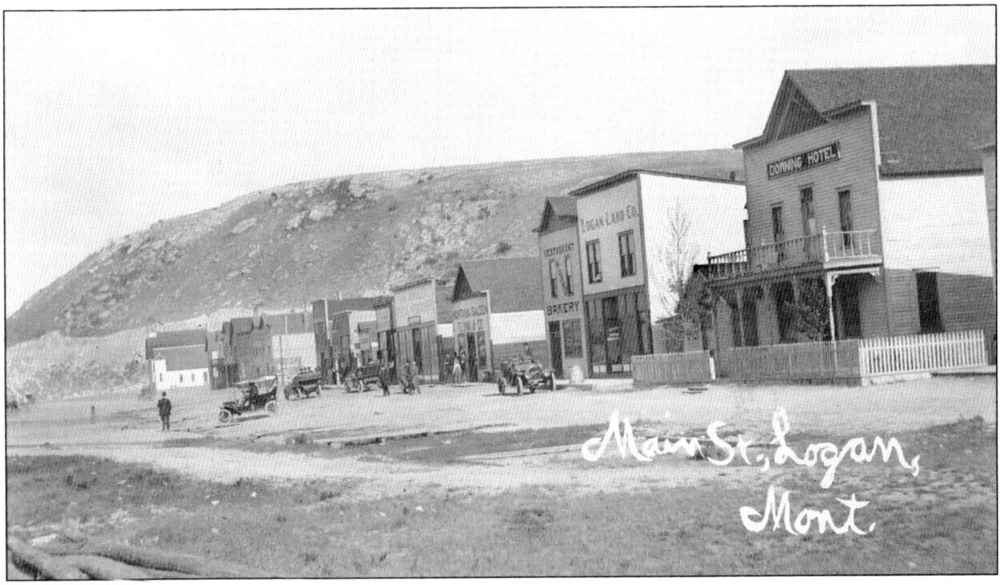

LOGAN, MAIN STREET VIEW. Just a few miles west of Manhattan, Logan was originally a stagecoach stop called Canyon House. When the Northern Pacific Railroad reached Logan in 1883, the town grew quickly. A small but vibrant Main Street is shown in this real-photo postcard, postmarked from Logan in 1910. At far right is the Downing Hotel. The Logan Land Company, a restaurant and bakery, and the Montana Saloon are visible farther down the street.

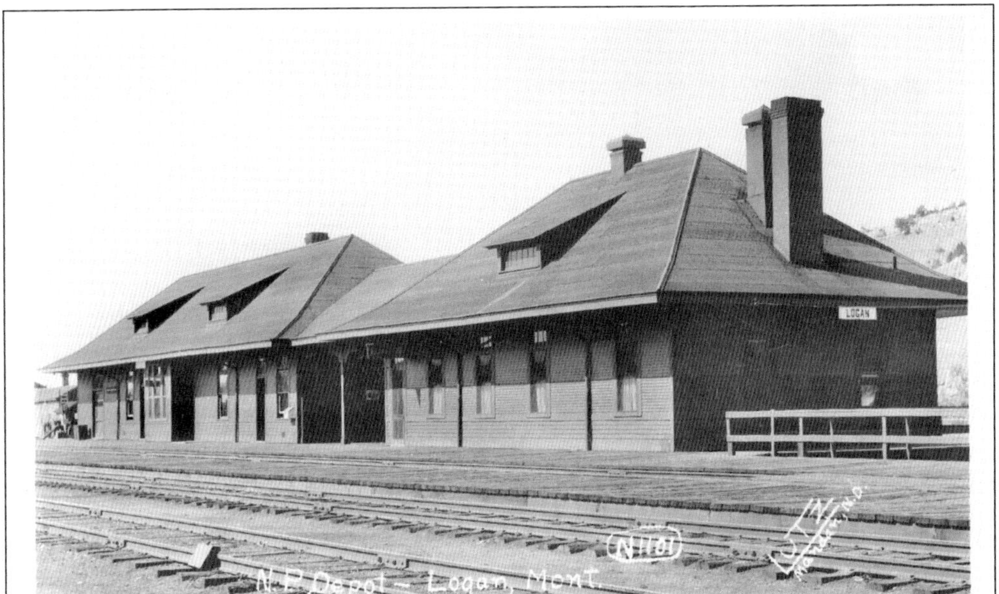

LOGAN, NORTHERN PACIFIC DEPOT. This *c.* 1920 real-photo postcard shows the handsome train depot at Logan. The Northern Pacific Railroad chose Logan as one of its key operating centers when it stretched through the Gallatin Valley in 1883. A roundhouse, section house, sand house, coal dock, and other structures were built to serve the railroad. This depot was torn down about 1975. (Photograph by Lutz, Mandan, North Dakota.)

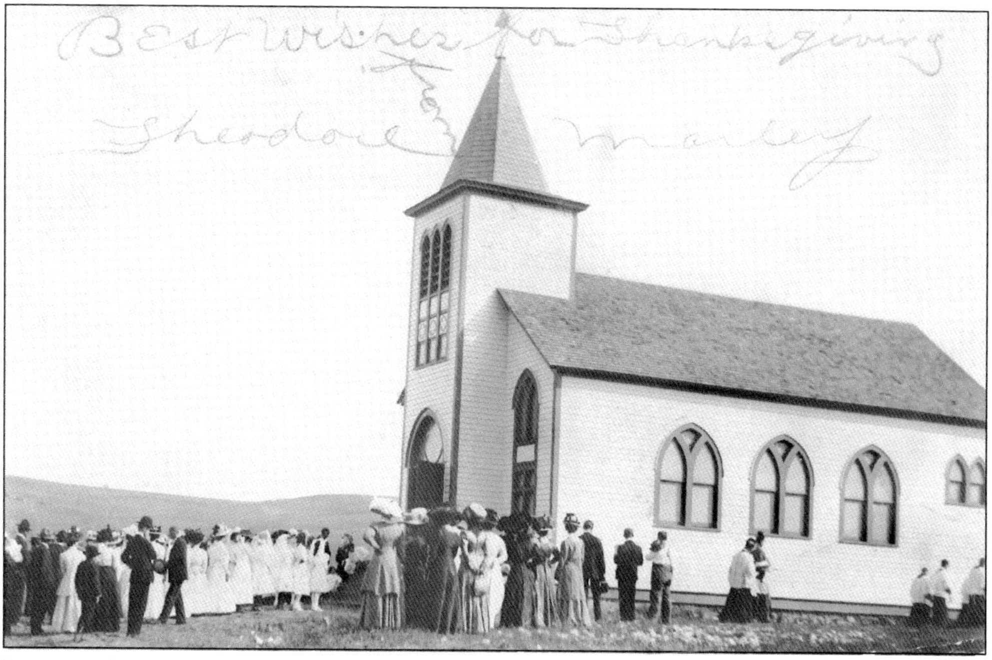

LOGAN, CATHOLIC CHURCH DEDICATION. On Sunday, October 3, 1909, Bishop Carroll of Helena dedicated the new Catholic church at Logan. Later that same day, the bishop conferred the sacrament of confirmation to young members. The bishop and several altar boys are seen walking along the right side of the church in this vintage real-photo postcard, postmarked from Logan in November 1909.

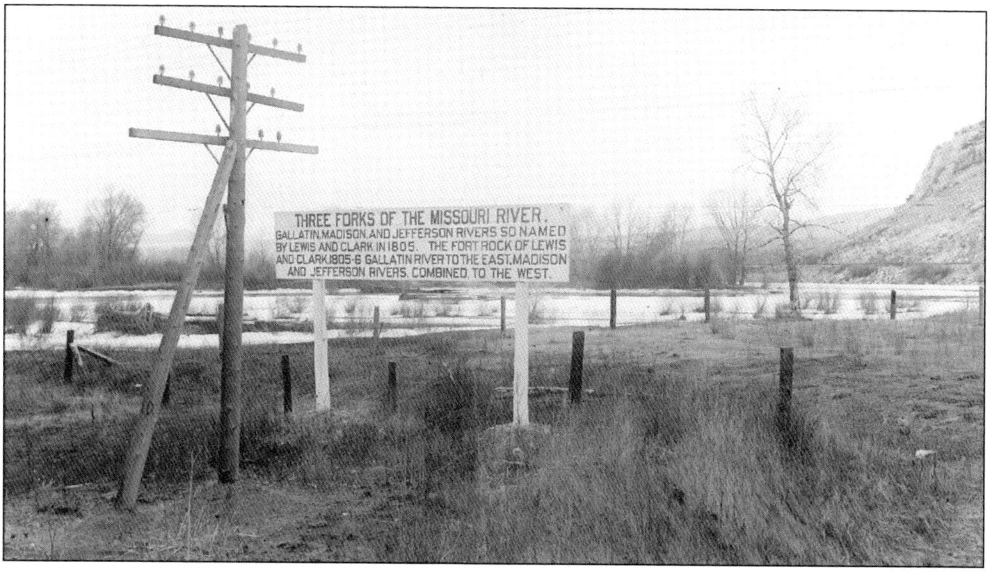

THREE FORKS OF THE MISSOURI RIVER. About 6 miles west of Logan, the headwaters of the Missouri Rivers are found. The confluence of the Jefferson, Madison, and Gallatin Rivers give birth to the Mighty Mo. The significance of this location was recognized early on, as noted by the historical sign shown on this *c.* 1909 real-photo postcard. Today this old sign is gone, but new signs are in place at nearby Missouri Headwaters State Park, located 4 miles northeast of the town of Three Forks.

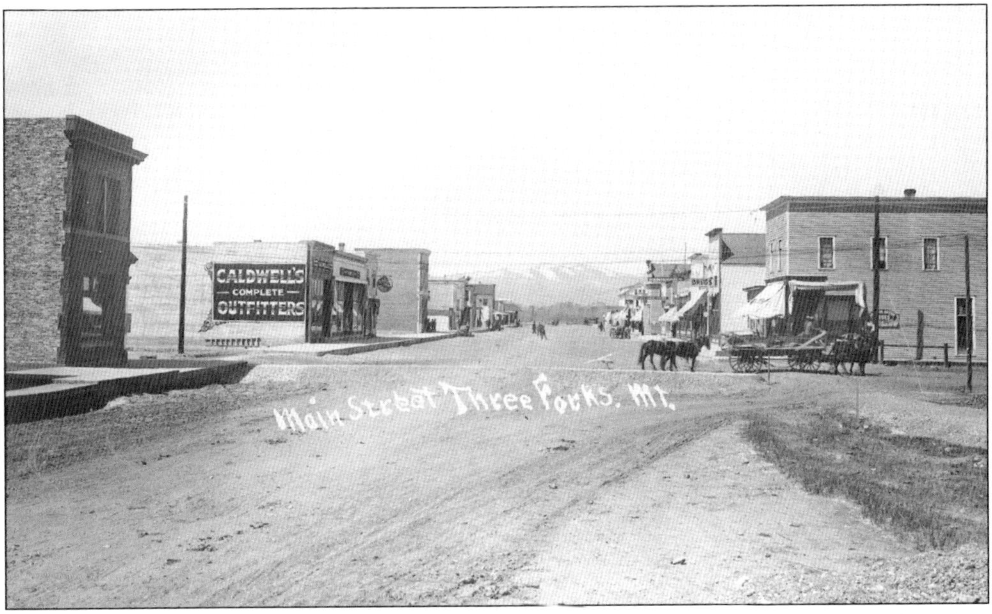

THREE FORKS, MAIN STREET IN 1912. The new town of Three Forks was less than four years old when this real-photo postcard, postmarked June 7, 1912, documented the main street looking north. The First National Bank is at far left. The two-story structure at the far right is Hamilton Grocery. The old town of Three Forks moved to its present site about 1 mile to the south in 1908 to be close to newly constructed railroad tracks. By 1909, the population was 800.

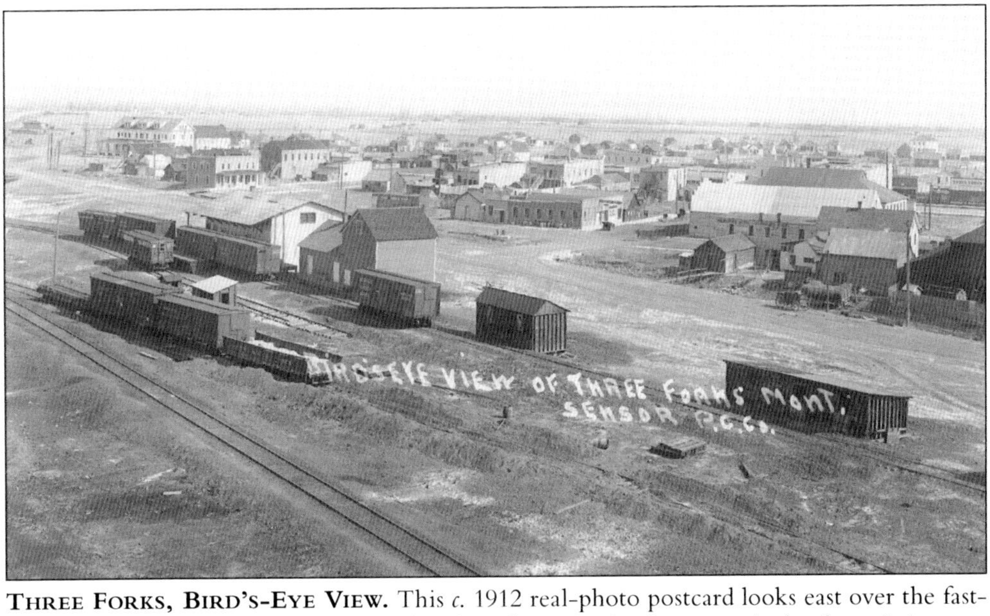

THREE FORKS, BIRD'S-EYE VIEW. This *c.* 1912 real-photo postcard looks east over the fast-developing town. The CMStP&P Railroad yards are in the foreground; the depot is just out of sight to the left. The Sacajawea Hotel, known also over the years as the Sacajawea Inn or Sacajawea Hotel Inn, is the large three-story building at far left, and the Henslee Auditorium and Livery, with its large white roof, is visible at center right. (Photograph by Sensor Post Card Company, Three Forks, Montana.)

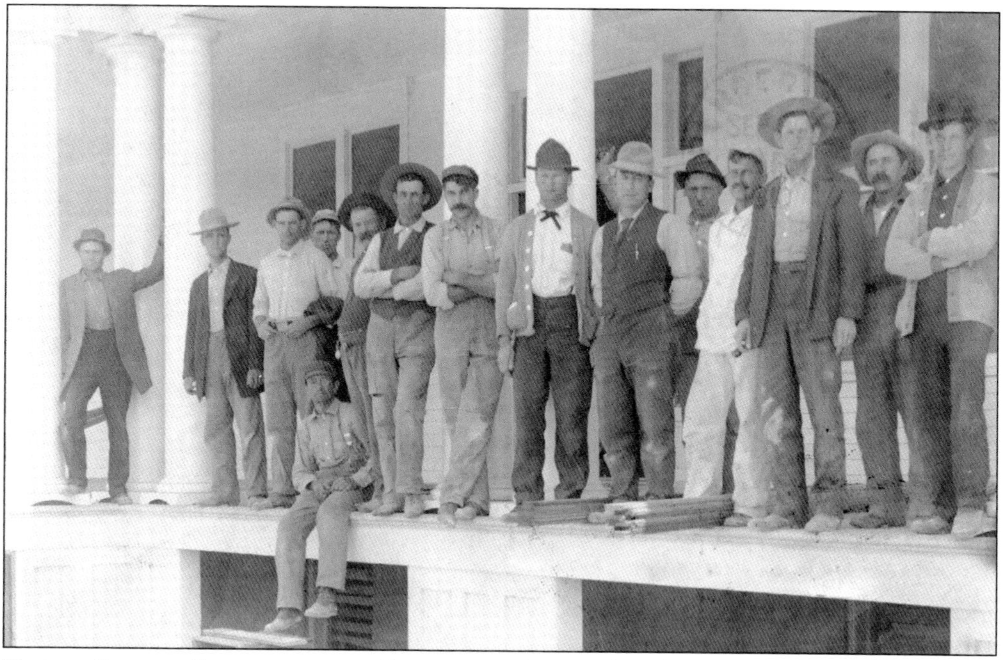

Three Forks, Carpenters at Sacajawea. Postmarked from Three Forks in September 1910, this real-photo postcard shows carpenters and other workers standing on the porch of the Sacajawea Hotel. The message on back includes, "What do you think of this Bunch of wood Butchers." Part of the hotel was moved a mile from the original Three Forks to its new venue on the north end of new Three Forks. A new addition to the hotel was being built at the time this image was taken. (Courtesy of Steve and Robin Hamilton.)

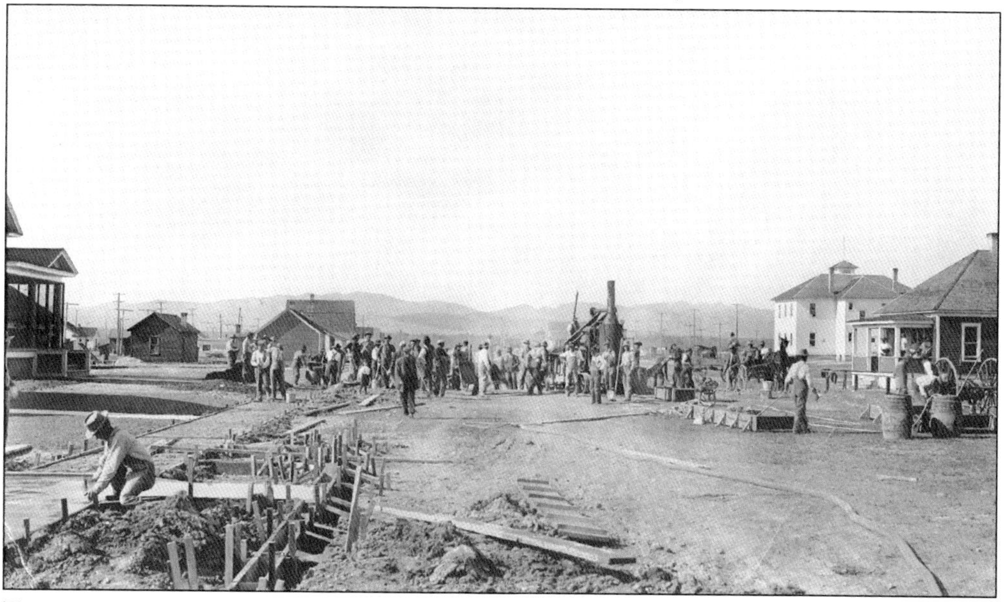

Three Forks, Sidewalk and Street Construction. Workers are busy staking out and pouring concrete sidewalks in this view looking north on Third Street. The white building at the right is a schoolhouse. Three Forks was about two years old when this *c.* 1910 real-photo postcard image was made. (Courtesy of Ken Hamlin.)

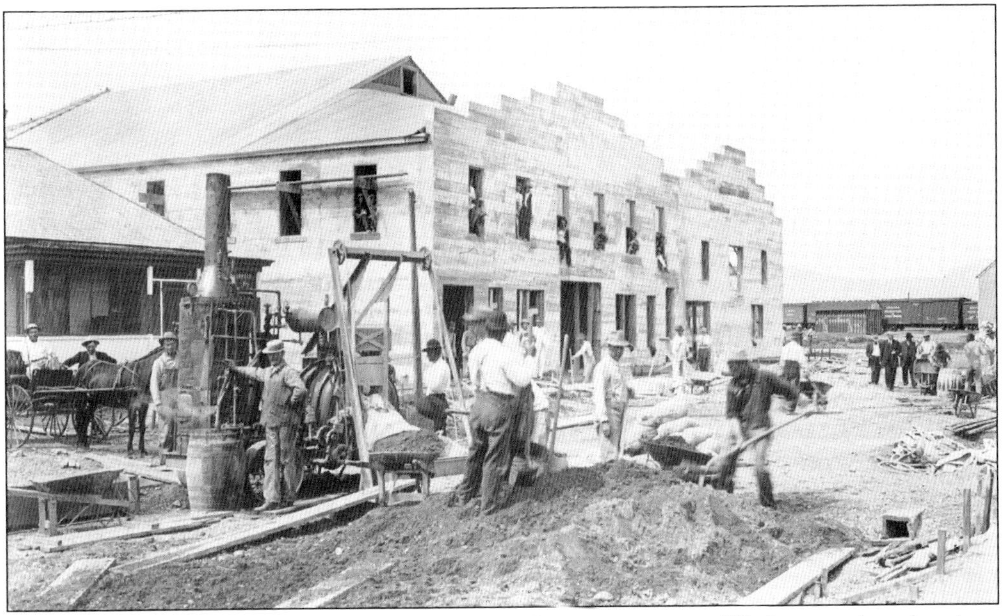

THREE FORKS, HENSLEE BUILDINGS UNDER CONSTRUCTION. Workmen take a break to peer out of open second-floor windows during the construction of the Henslee Auditorium, Garage, and Livery buildings. This *c.* 1909 real-photo postcard view looks west on Cedar Street, one half block from Main Street.

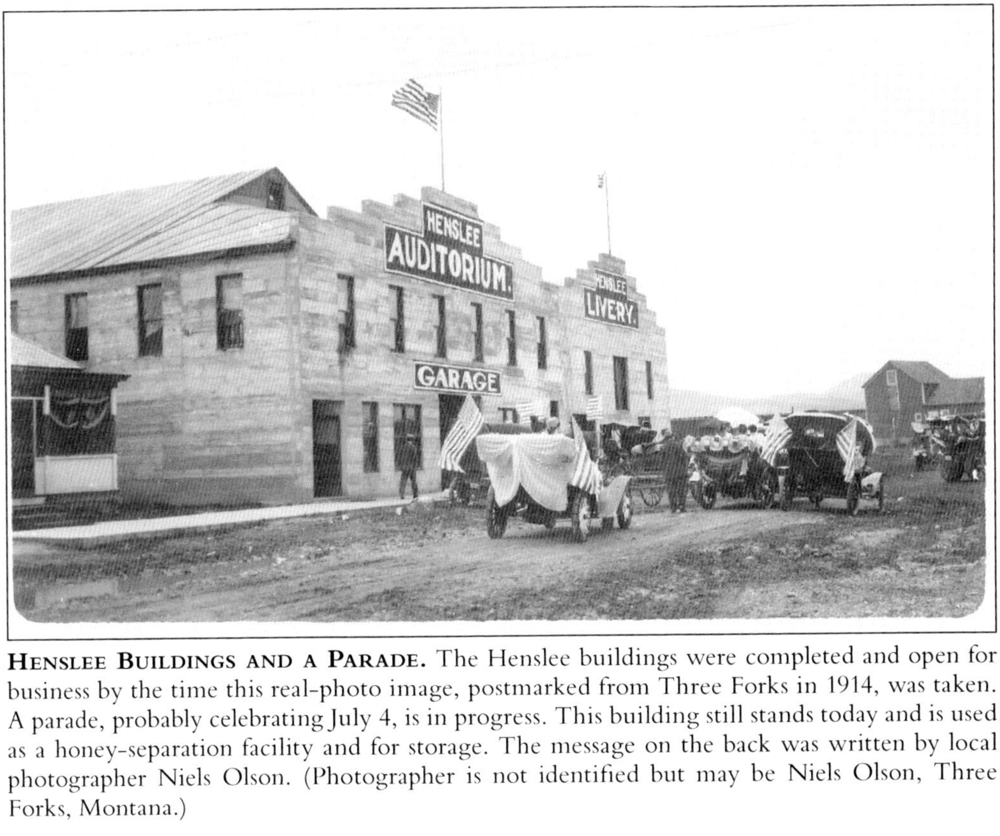

HENSLEE BUILDINGS AND A PARADE. The Henslee buildings were completed and open for business by the time this real-photo image, postmarked from Three Forks in 1914, was taken. A parade, probably celebrating July 4, is in progress. This building still stands today and is used as a honey-separation facility and for storage. The message on the back was written by local photographer Niels Olson. (Photographer is not identified but may be Niels Olson, Three Forks, Montana.)

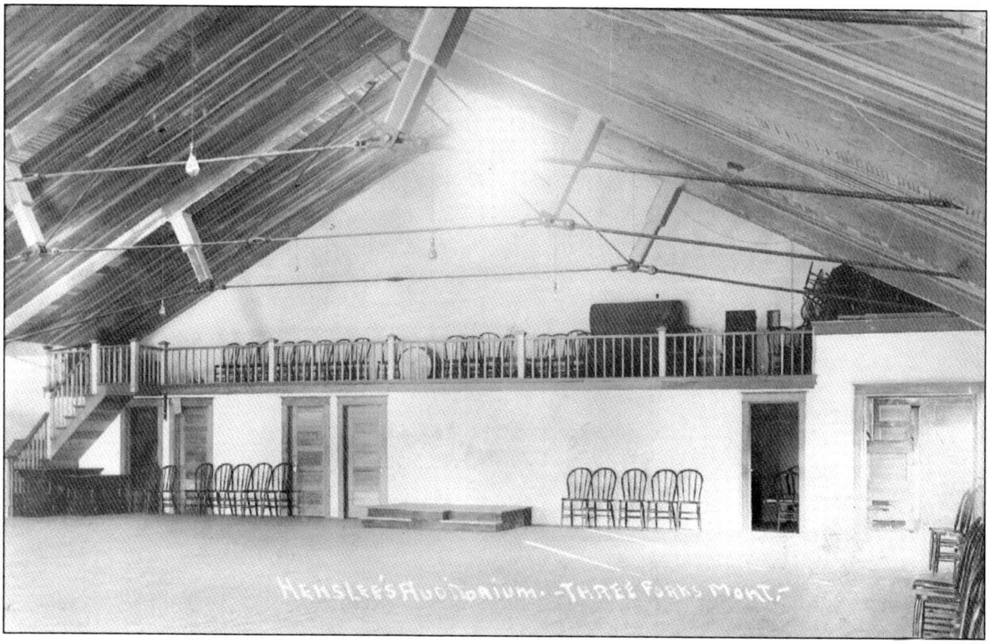

HENSLEE AUDITORIUM INTERIOR. The auditorium pictured in this *c.* 1912 real-photo postcard image served as a venue for dances and other events in early-day Three Forks. A spacious floor and lots of seating can also be seen in this interior view. A grant to refurbish the building is currently being sought by the present owners.

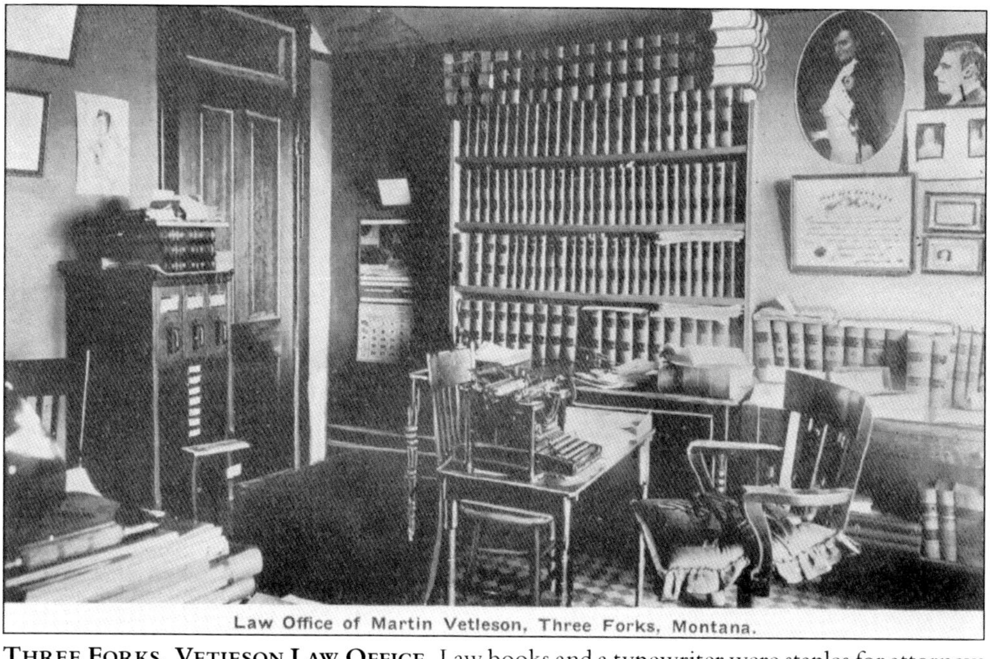

THREE FORKS, VETIESON LAW OFFICE. Law books and a typewriter were staples for attorneys a century ago. This printed postcard shows the interior view of Martin Vetieson's office. Note the picture of Napoleon on the wall. His office was in the Independence Telephone Building on Main Street. Vetieson sent this postcard to a well-known Helena attorney, Wellington Rankin, in 1918 with a short note regarding a legal matter.

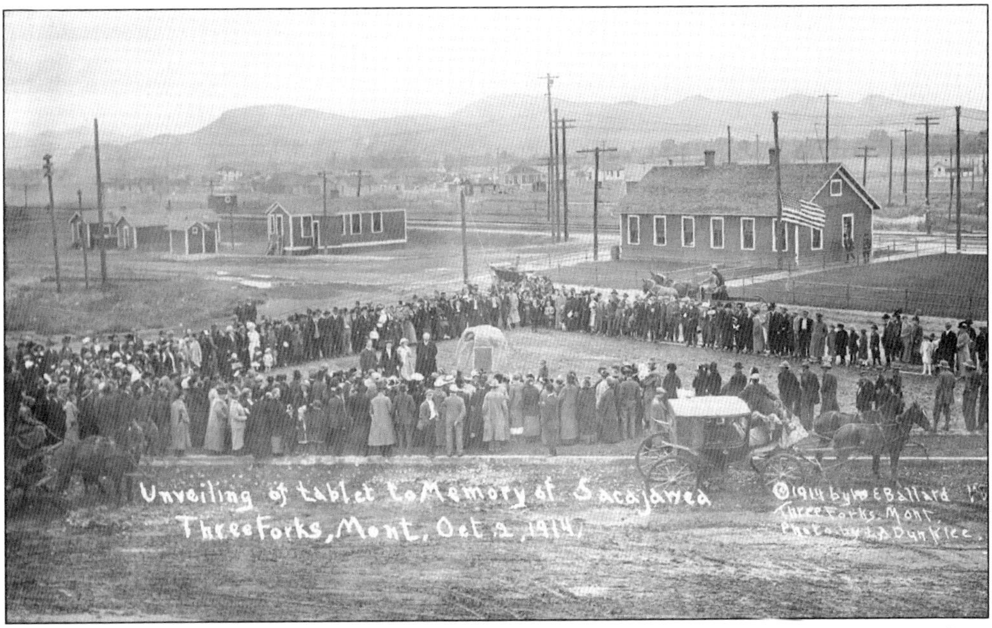

THREE FORKS, SACAJAWEA MEMORIAL DEDICATION. Dedicated to the Native American woman who served as a guide to Lewis and Clark, a stone tablet is unveiled before a large crowd in this *c.* 1914 real-photo postcard. Three blue spruce trees, representing the three forks of the Missouri River, were planted in the triangular-shaped park. This view was taken from an upper floor of the Sacajawea Inn, which has operated at the north end of Main Street for almost a century. (Photograph by L. A. Dunklee.)

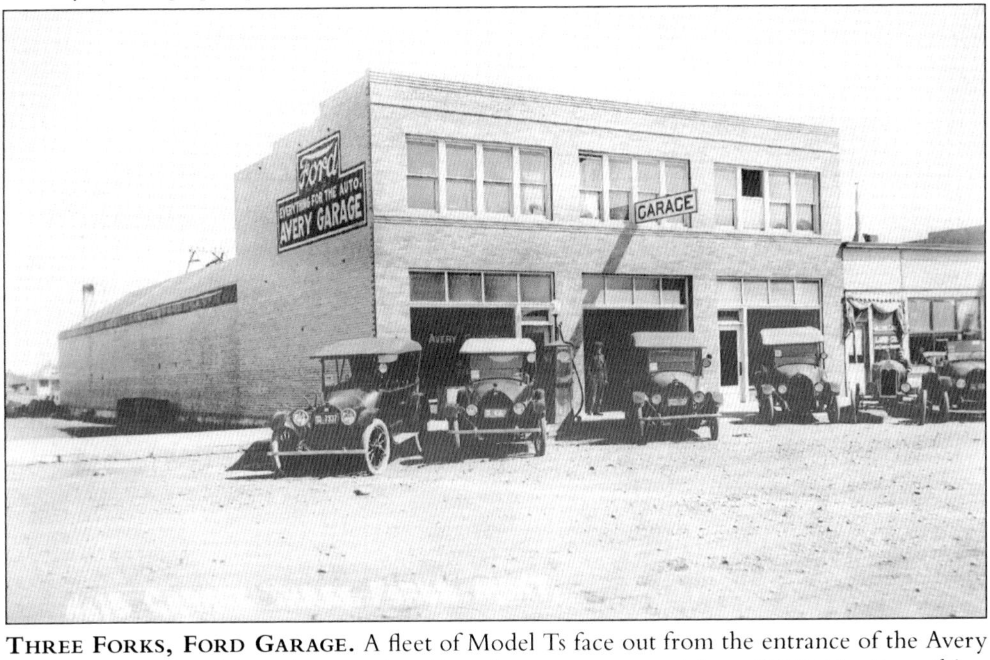

THREE FORKS, FORD GARAGE. A fleet of Model Ts face out from the entrance of the Avery Garage. The advertising sign on the side of the garage proclaims, "FORD—Everything for the Auto—Avery Garage." A single gas pump is visible on the sidewalk in this *c.* 1918 real-photo postcard.

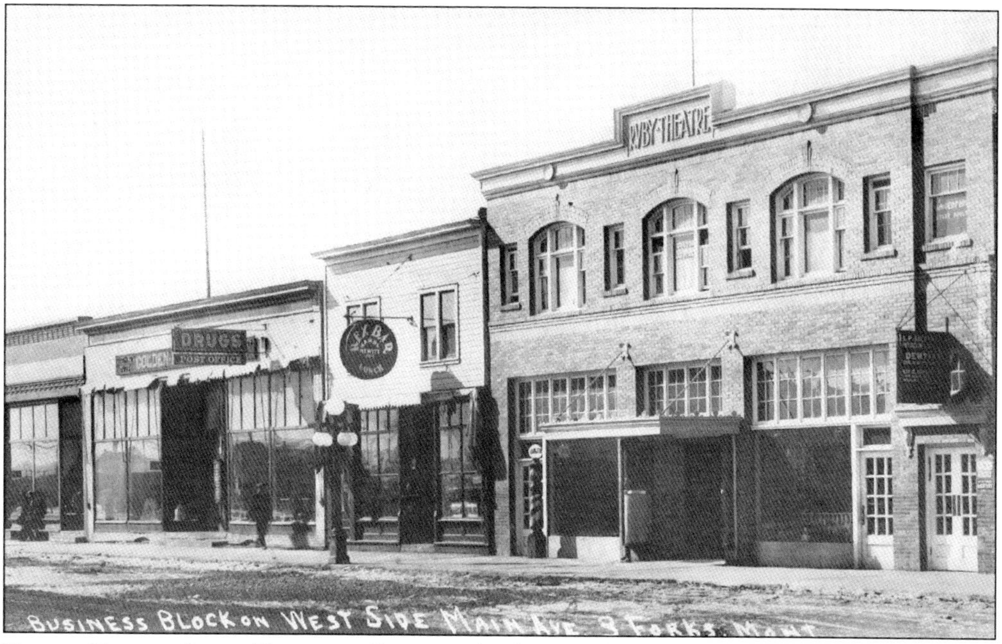

THREE FORKS, RUBY THEATER BLOCK. This business block on the west side of Main Street featured the Ruby Theater with its impressive brick facade at right. Seen in this *c.* 1919 real-photo postcard image are a sign for "Bath," visible at the top of a pole at the left edge of the theater building; the Rex Bar; a drugstore; the post office; and a dentist office at far right.

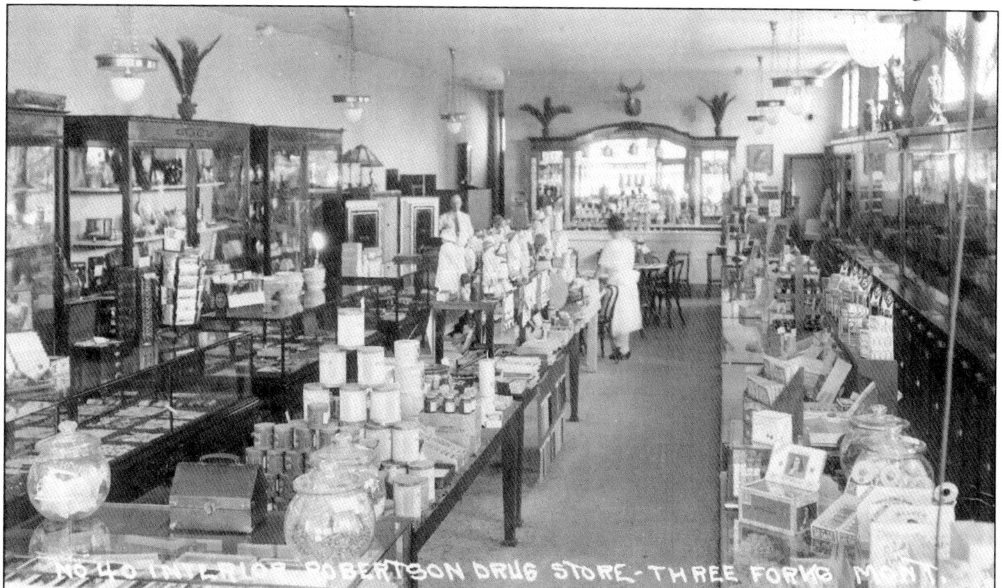

THREE FORKS, ROBERTSON DRUG STORE INTERIOR. This well-stocked drugstore was located on the corner of Main Street and Cedar Avenue. The building still stands and is now an architectural and engineering office. The large glass furnishings at left have been saved and now grace the interior of one of Three Fork's newest stores, the Montana Side Saddle. This real-photo postcard was postmarked from Three Forks in 1926. (Photograph by Wesley Andrews, Baker, Oregon.)

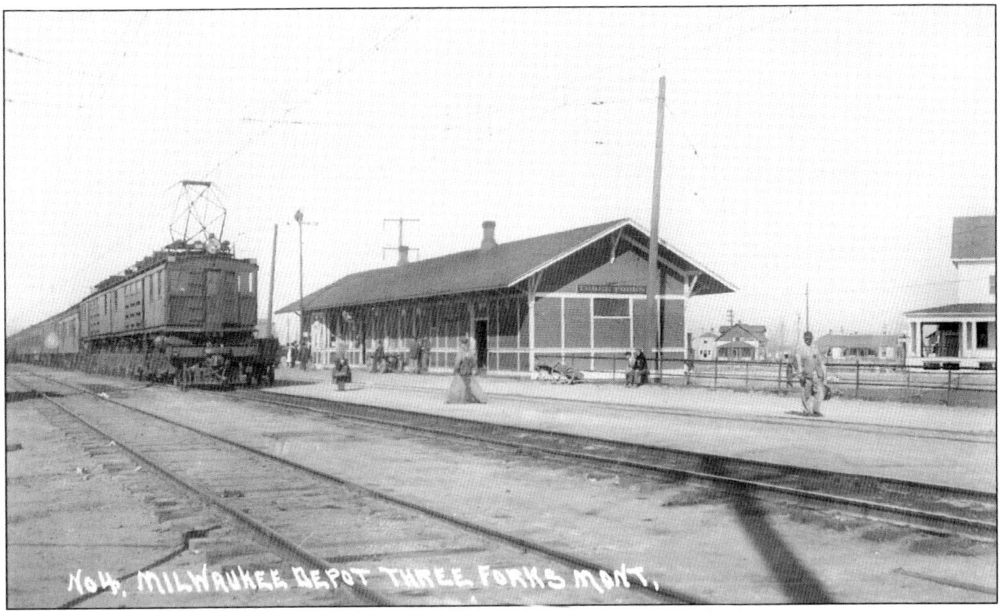

THREE FORKS, ELECTRIC TRAIN AT DEPOT. Postmarked from Three Forks in 1931, this real-photo postcard view shows an electric-powered engine at the Milwaukee Road (or CMStP&P Railroad) station, located in the northwestern section of Three Forks. The first electric train ran in 1915 between Three Forks and Deer Lodge, Montana. The system used a 3,000-volt DC overhead line. The Sacajawea Hotel can be seen at far right. (Photograph by Wesley Andrews, Baker, Oregon.)

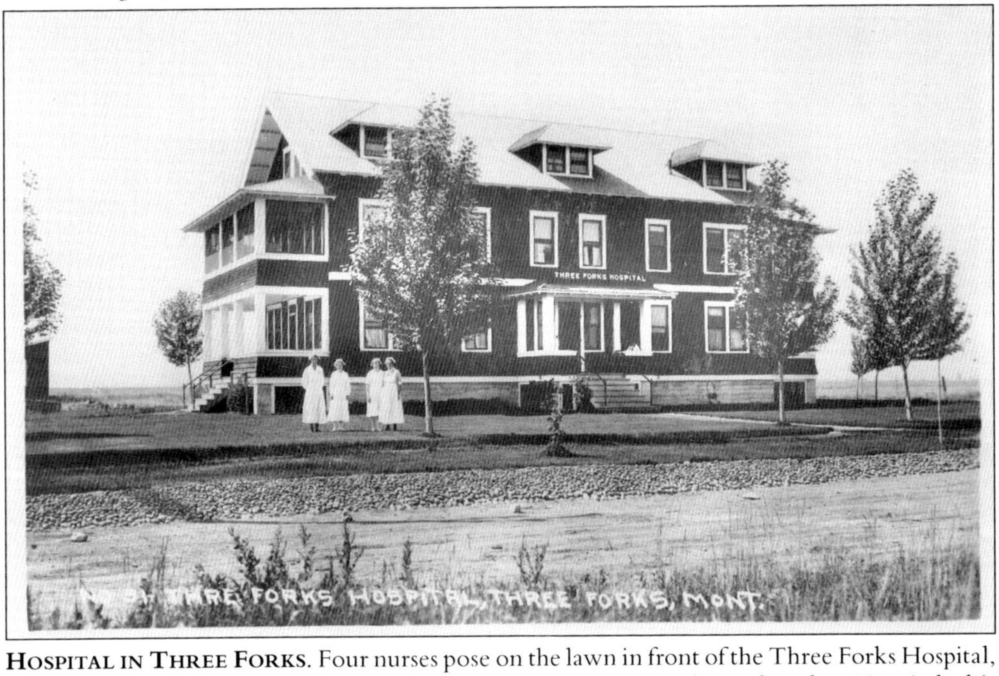

HOSPITAL IN THREE FORKS. Four nurses pose on the lawn in front of the Three Forks Hospital, which was built in 1914 and provided 20 beds. Also known as the Milwaukee Hospital, this building later became a nursing home. Today it is an apartment building. This image was taken from a *c.* 1925 real-photo postcard. (Photograph by Wesley Andrews, Baker, Oregon.)

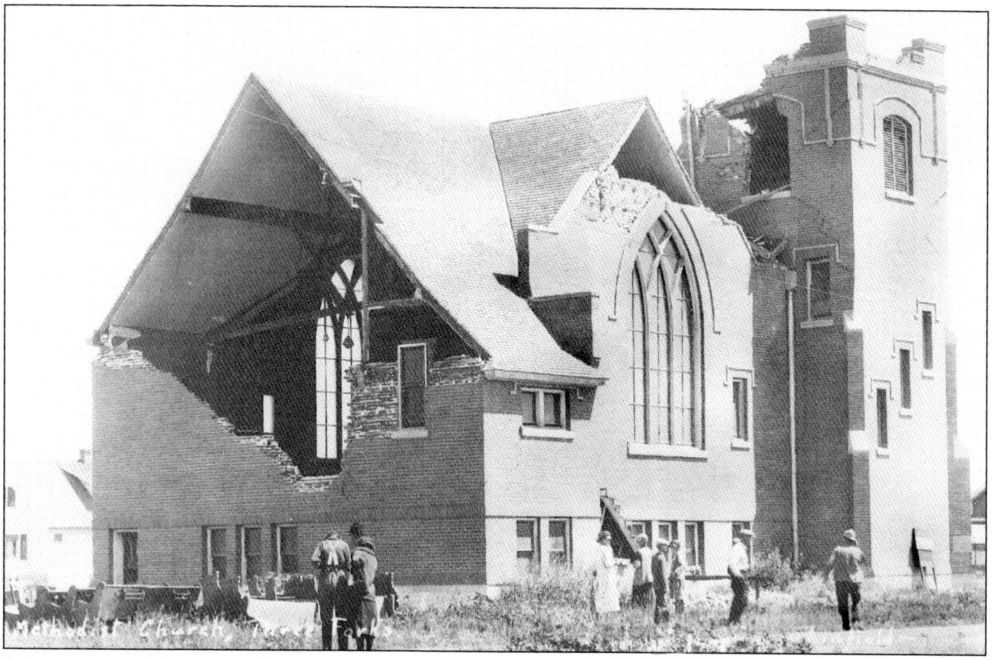

Methodist Church Earthquake Damage, Three Forks. Despite the heavy damage suffered by this church as a result of the June 1925 earthquake, it was repaired and continues to serve its Methodist congregation today, from the corner of Cedar Avenue and Second Street. The United Methodist Church of Three Forks stands across the street from the Montana Historical Research Library, Inc. This image was taken from a *c.* 1925 real-photo postcard. (Photograph by F. B. Linfield, Bozeman, Montana.)

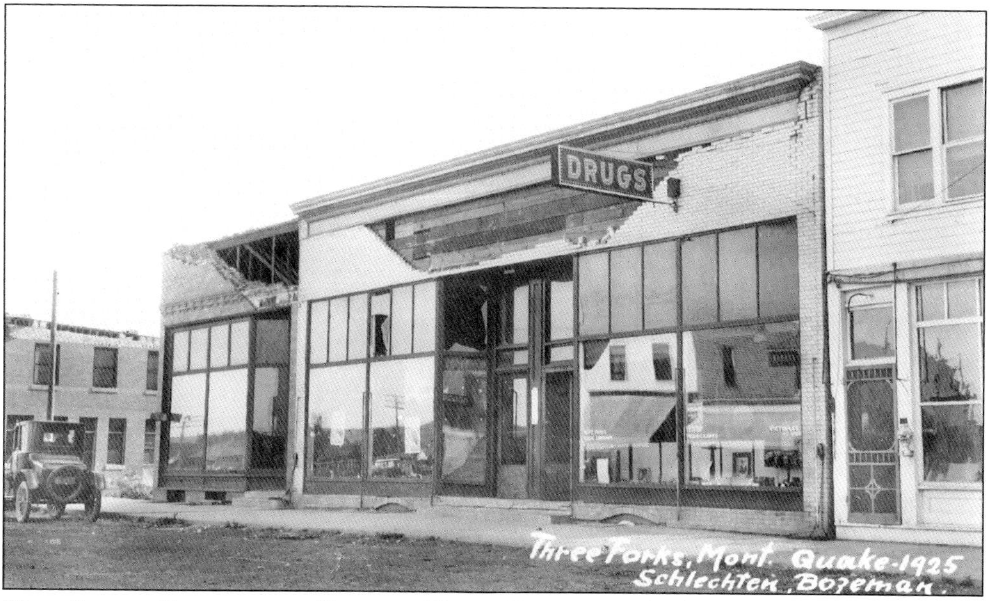

Main Street Earthquake Damage, Three Forks. Another look at the destruction caused by the 1925 earthquake is shown in this vintage real-photo postcard view. The drugstore on Main Street and the adjoining business were hard hit by the 6.7 quake, as was the Three Valleys State Bank building at far left. (Photograph by Schlechten Studio, Bozeman, Montana.)

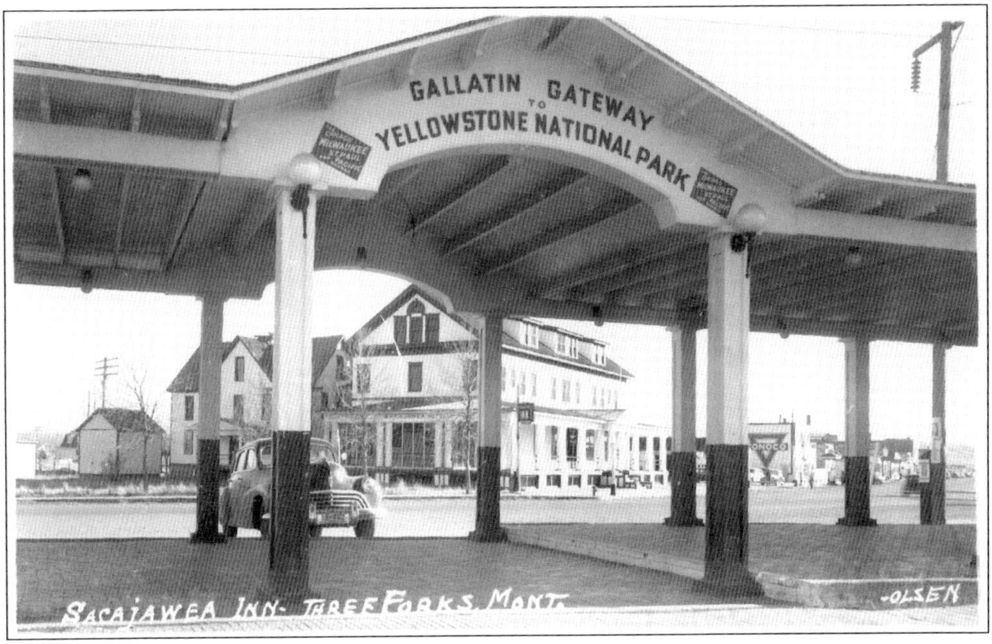

THREE FORKS, SACAJAWEA INN FROM TRAIN PORT. This *c.* 1945 real-photo postcard image shows the Milwaukee Road port advertising the Gallatin Gateway entrance to Yellowstone National Park. The railroad route from Three Forks to Gallatin Gateway was about 35 miles. The Sacajawea Inn is framed in the background. (Photograph by Niels Olsen, Three Forks, Montana.)

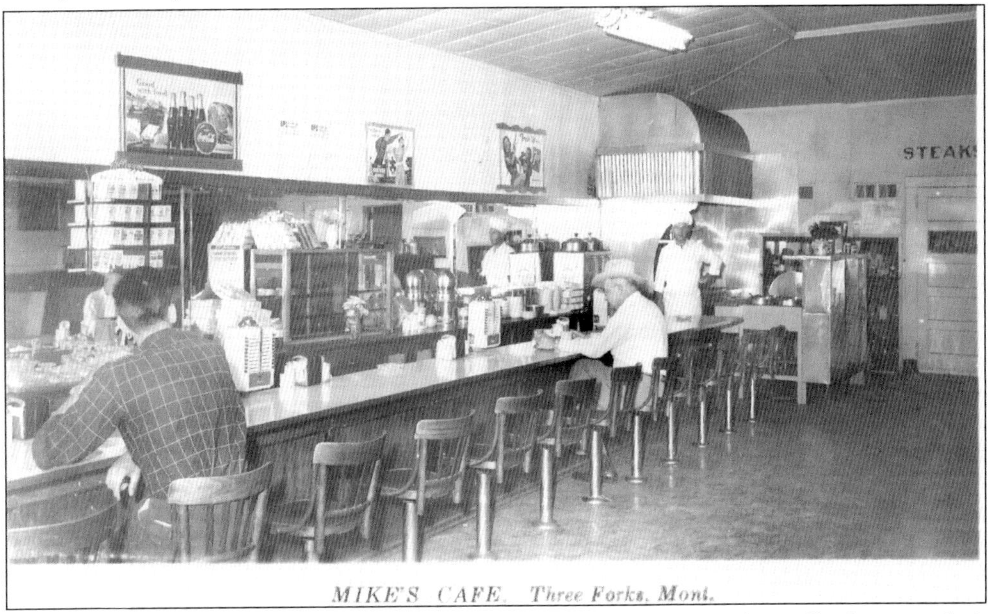

THREE FORKS, MIKE'S CAFÉ INTERIOR. The food was good and the coffee hot at Mike's Café. Advertising is visible on the upper back wall for Coca-Cola, Mission Orange, and 7-Up soft drinks. Two miniature jukeboxes sit on the counter. Located on Main Street, the café was later known as the Headquarters Club and operates today as the Three Forks Café. This real-photo postcard was taken around 1945.

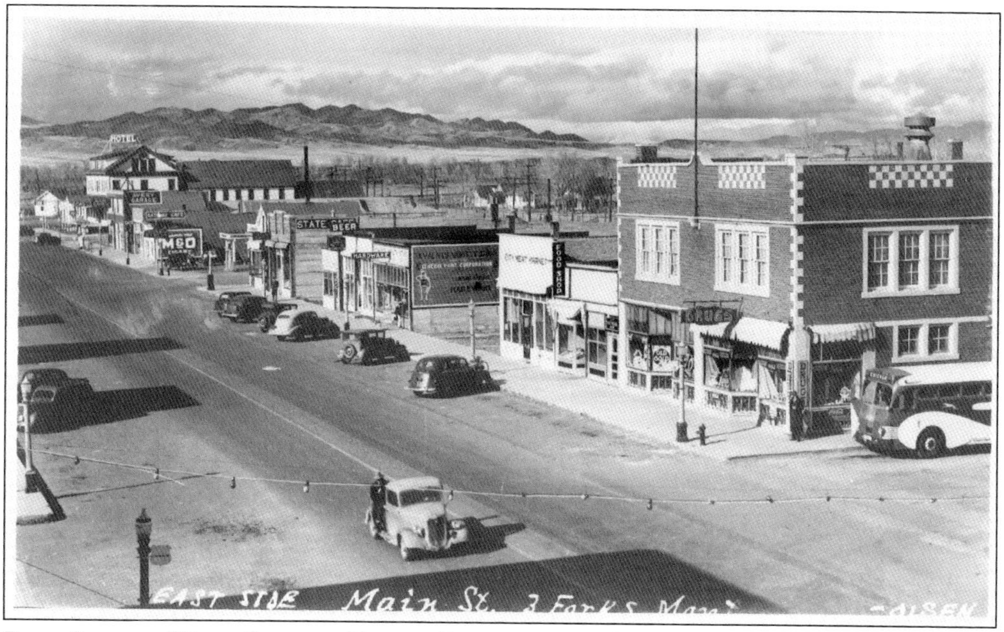

East Side of Main Street, Three Forks. Except for the fellow riding on the running board of the car in the center foreground, all seems normal in this *c.* 1945 real-photo view taken in downtown Three Forks. A Greyhound bus is parked at the corner drugstore at far right, and various businesses, including the City Meat Market, K. Valnes Variety Store and Hardware, Gateway Café, and Avery Garage, are visible. The Sacajawea Hotel Inn anchors the north end of Main Street. (Photograph by Niels Olsen, Three Forks, Montana.)

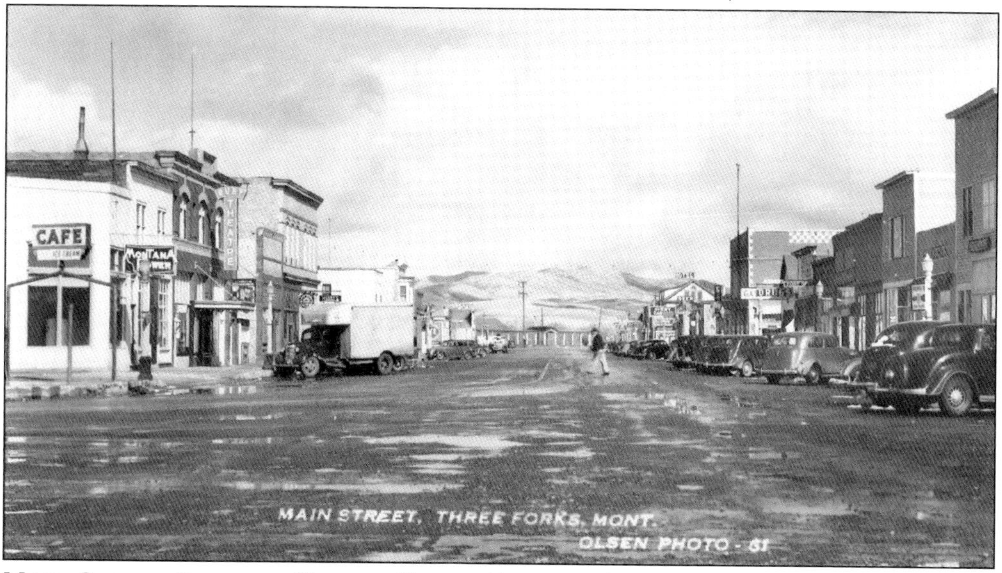

Main Street Looking North, Three Forks. After a good rain, photographer Niels Olsen took his camera to the center of Main Street to capture this image for a *c.* 1945 real-photo postcard. The Ruby Theater and the Montana Power office are seen at left. On the right side of puddled Main Street are the city post office, a drugstore, and a gas station. The Milwaukee Road depot is partially visible at the end of the street at left. (Photograph by Niels Olsen, Three Forks, Montana.)

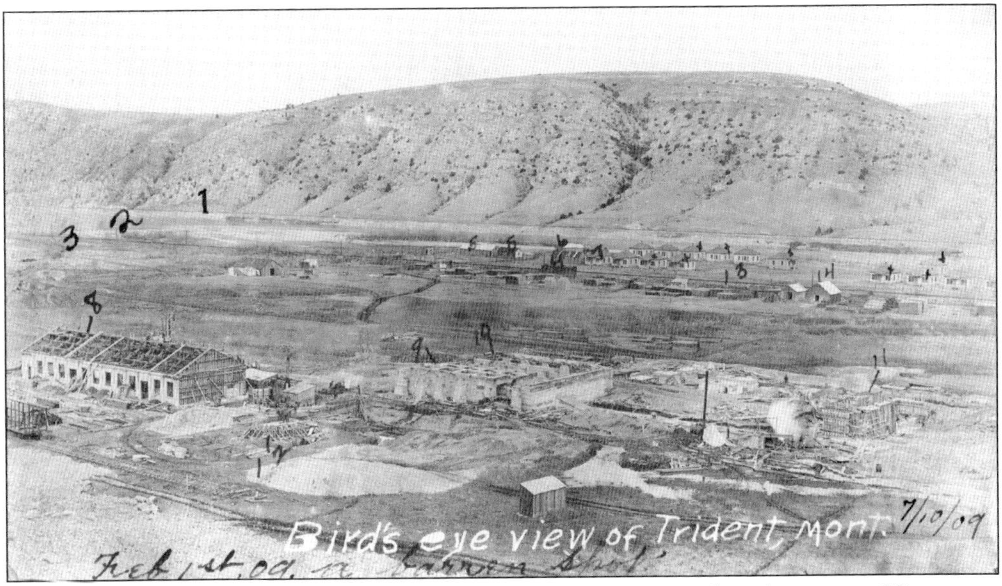

Cement Plant Under Construction in Trident. To take advantage of limestone deposits in northwestern Gallatin County, construction of a cement plant began in 1908. Buildings were well underway at the time this *c.* 1909 real-photo postcard, looking west to the Missouri River, was taken. The machine shop is yet to be roofed at lower left, and foundations are being put in place for many of the plant's structures. Trident is located about 5 miles north of Three Forks. (Courtesy of Ken Hamlin.)

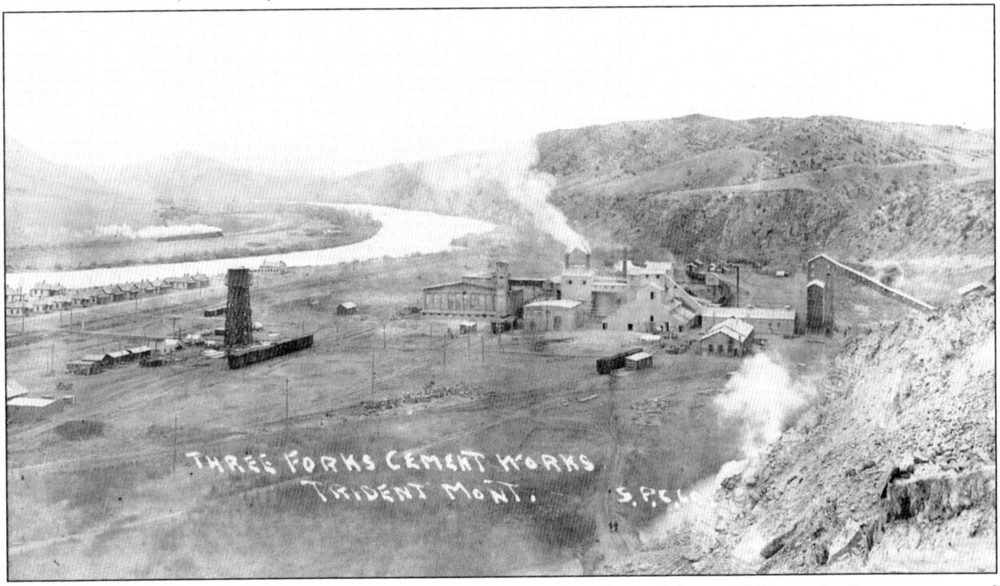

Cement Plant in Operation, Trident. By the time this *c.* 1912 real-photo postcard image was taken, the Three Forks Cement Works was very productive. This view looks to the northwest. A train steams away at the upper left, across the Missouri River. The company houses at far left near the river were reserved for American workers. Austrian and Italian workers were forced to live in separate housing north of the plant complex. Some of this segregated housing is visible in the center right background. (Photograph by Sensor Post Card Company, Three Forks, Montana.)

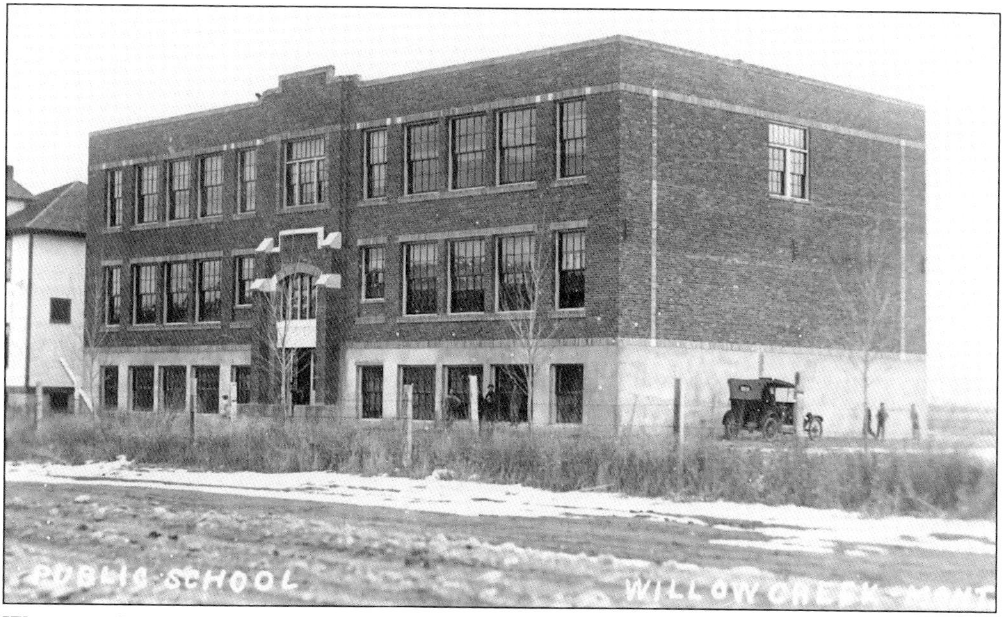

WILLOW CREEK PUBLIC SCHOOL. This *c.* 1918 real-photo postcard shows the new public school in the small homesteading community of Willow Creek, located about 7 miles southwest of Three Forks. Willow Creek was the site of one of the first church missions in the Gallatin Valley in 1865. The town's future was boosted by the arrival of the Northern Pacific Railroad in 1883 and further enhanced by the arrival of the Milwaukee Road in 1908. (Courtesy of Steve and Robin Hamilton.)

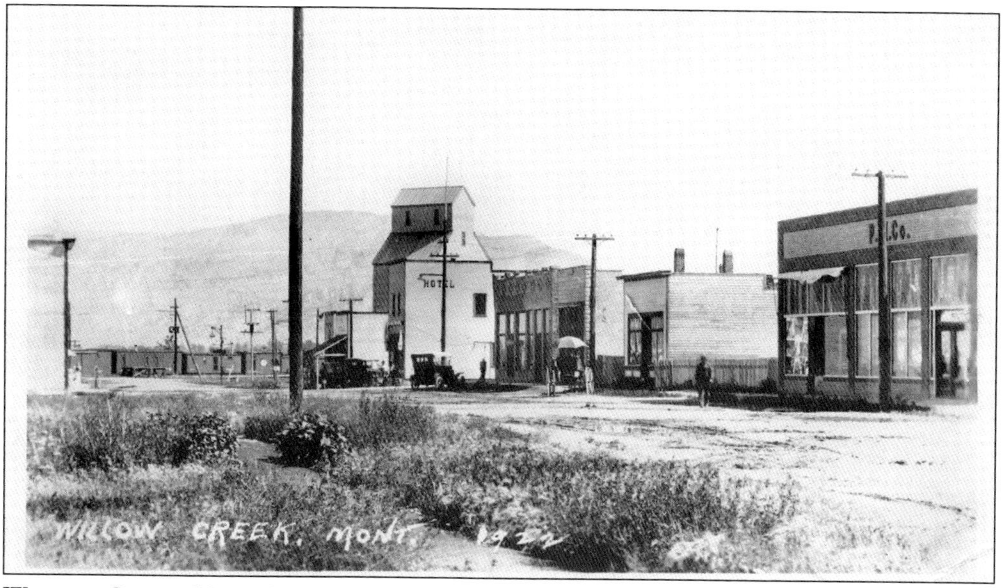

WILLOW CREEK MAIN STREET. Several businesses, including a hotel (center, in front of the grain elevator), made up most of the town's tiny Main Street, seen in this *c.* 1922 real-photo postcard view. Periods of drought adversely affected the marginal farming in the area and have kept this small town from growing much in population. It remains one of Montana's smaller towns today, with about 200 inhabitants. The town has taken pride over the years in its strong, winning prep basketball tradition.

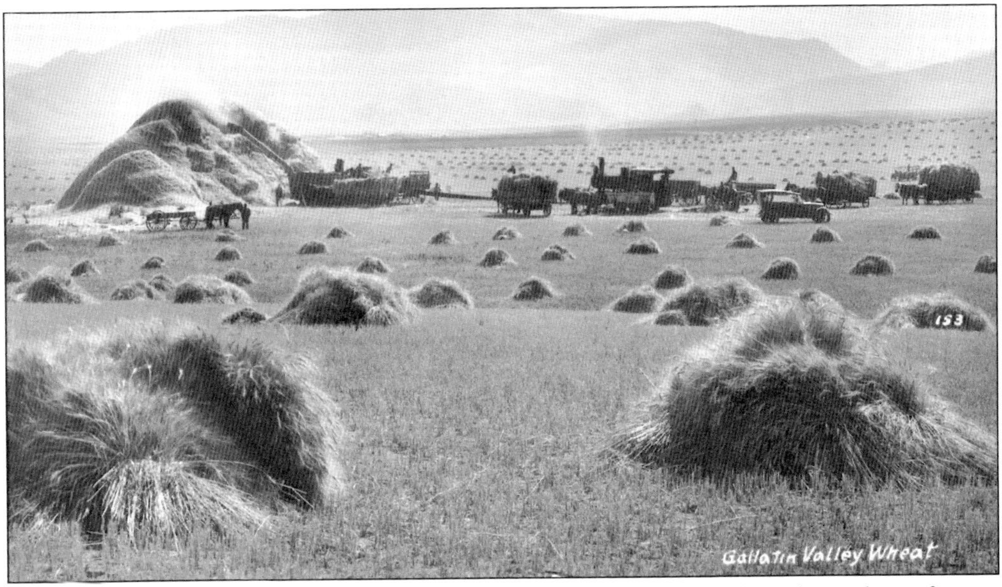

HARVESTING WHEAT AROUND 1925. The fertile Gallatin Valley has always been famous for its wheat, barley, potato, and sweet pea crops. This rather artistic image of a wheat-harvesting scene somewhere in the valley is taken from a vintage real-photo postcard. Wheat shocks in the foreground frame a pastoral harvesting operation, complete with horse-drawn wagons, a single auto, a thresher, and a big stack of wheat. (Photograph by Schlechten Studio, Bozeman, Montana.)

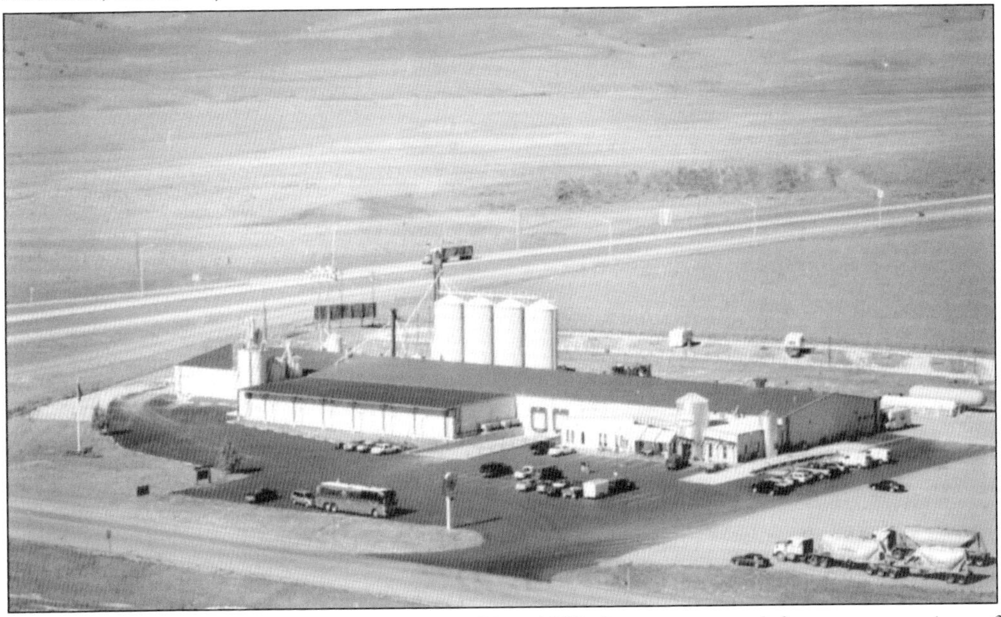

WHEAT MONTANA FARMS AND BAKERY. This *c.* 1997 chrome postcard shows an overview of the Wheat Montana Farms and Bakery facility. Located near the intersection of Highway 287 and Interstate 90 in northwestern Gallatin County, this company grows and processes its own wheat, and then markets fresh bread, bagels, buns, and more—a true start-to-finish operation. Operated by Dean Folkvord and his wife, Hope, this one-of-a-kind "wheat-plex" has been in business since 1993.

Ten

Gallatin Valley Miscellaneous Views

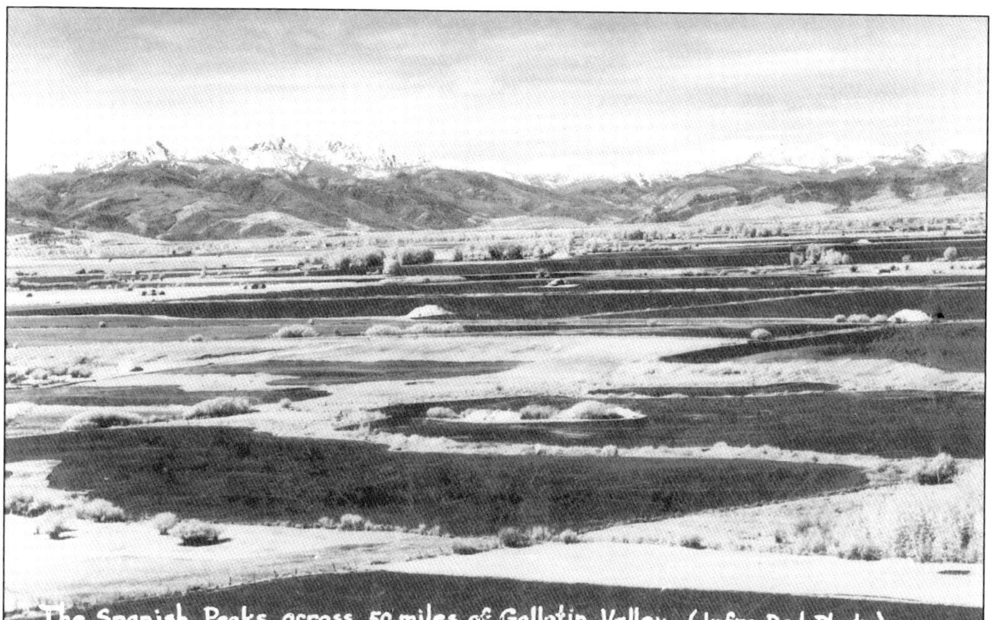

Across 50 Miles of Valley. This *c.* 1950 real-photo postcard looks southwest across the Gallatin Valley to the Spanish Peaks in the background. Despite a large increase in population in the past 10 years—the area has grown from under 70,000 to 90,000 since 2000—most of the valley is still used for farming and ranching. The smaller acreage mom-and-pop operations are becoming fewer and fewer, however.

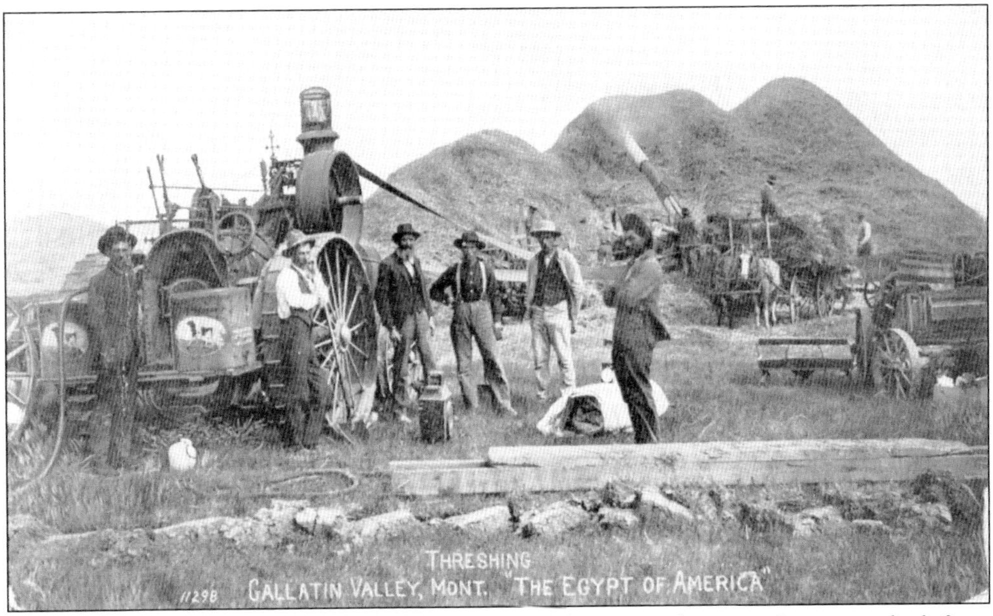

Threshing in "The Egypt of America." This printed postcard, postmarked from Bozeman in 1908, shows a threshing operation. Note that the large tractor at left is powering the thresher. The reference to the Gallatin Valley as "the Egypt of America" was used to promote the valley's rich, fertile soil, comparable to the lush gardens and vegetations for which Egypt's Nile Valley was famous. (Courtesy of R. Dale Beland.)

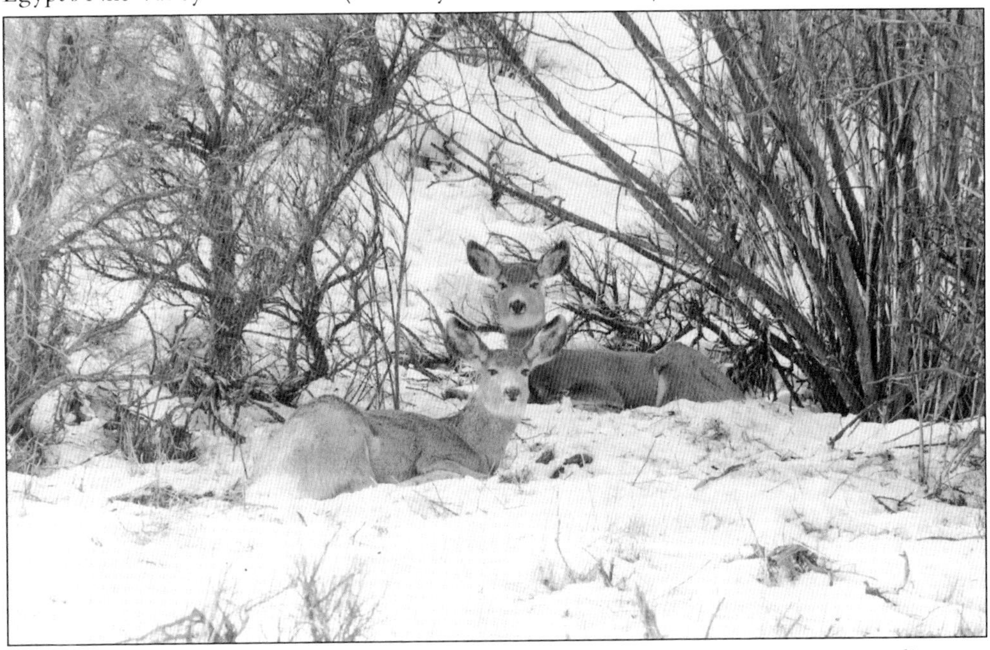

Valley Wildlife. Two deer are nicely camouflaged within their winter surroundings, as shown in this *c.* 1925 real-photo postcard image. The Gallatin Valley and the surrounding mountains and valleys are rich in wildlife and fishing habitat. Today locals and visitors alike enjoy the best in hiking, biking, fishing, and skiing, all amidst spectacular scenery. (Photograph by Schlechten Studio, Bozeman, Montana.)

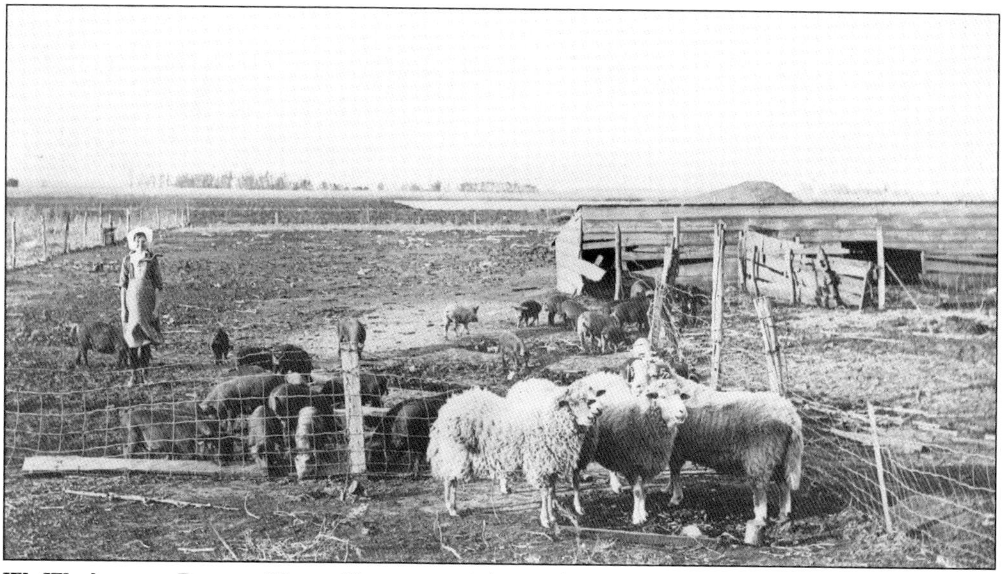

W. W. Atkins Ranch Near Bozeman. The smiling young girl at left was probably in the midst of her feeding chores in the pigpen when her father (or mother) decided to try out their new Kodak postcard camera. The three woolies in the foreground look a bit sheepish but try their best to smile. Written on the back of this *c.* 1910 real-photo postcard is "W. W. Atkins ranch at Bozeman, Montana—sheeps, pigs, few cattle, poultry."

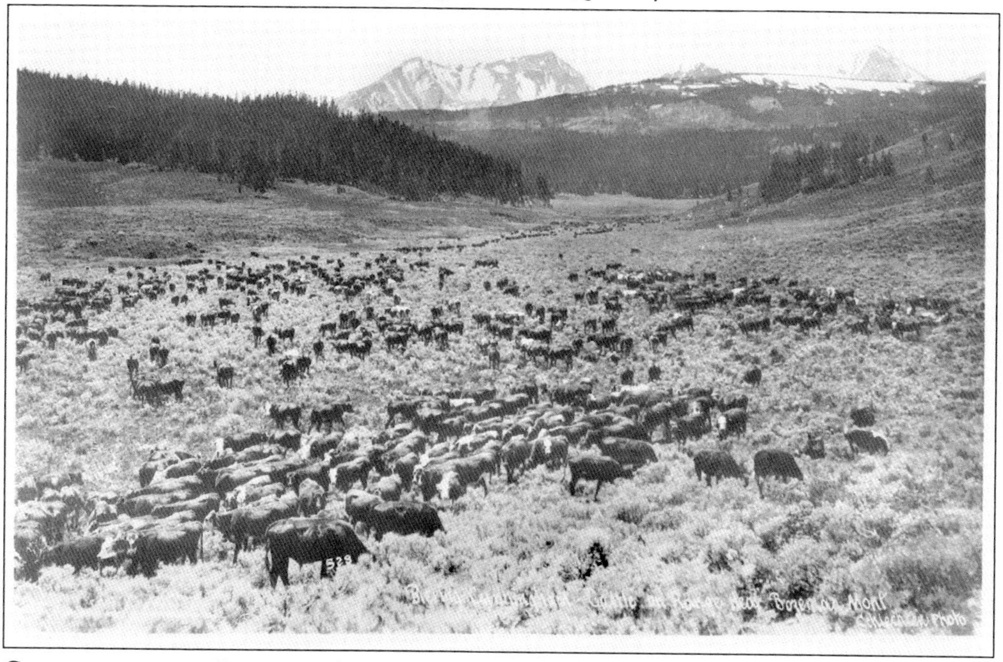

Cattle on the Range. This *c.* 1945 real-photo postcard shows part of the Biering-Cunningham herd. Cattle breeding has been an important and successful aspect of the cattle industry, prominent in the Gallatin Valley since the 1880s and throughout the 20th century. Registered Herefords and Angus cattle have been raised here. In 1968, the American Simmental Association established its headquarters in Bozeman. (Photograph by Schlechten Studio, Bozeman, Montana.)

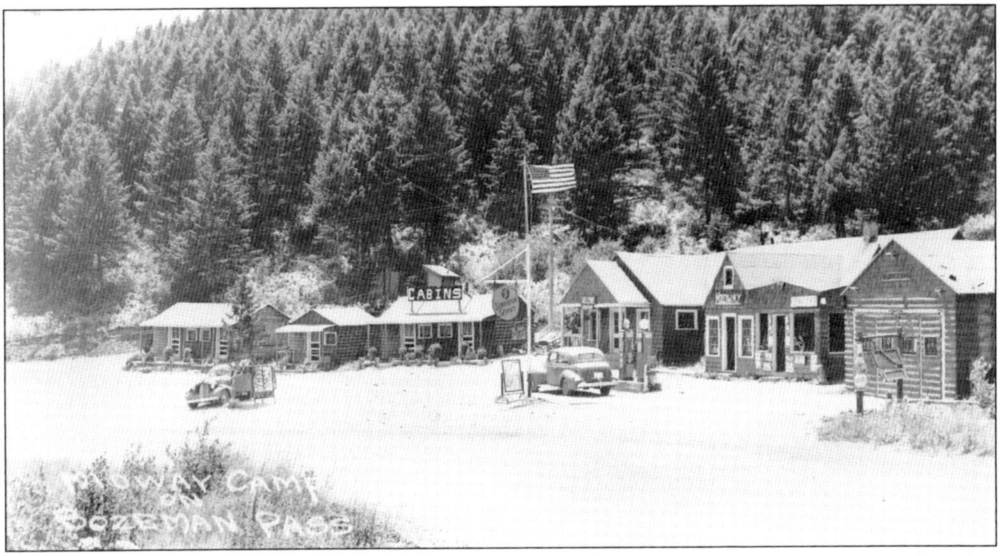

Midway Camp on Bozeman Pass. Old-timers and some baby boomers may remember this roadside stop on Bozeman Pass, which acts as the east slope of the Gallatin Valley drainage. This *c.* 1945 real-photo postcard image shows the Midway Camp with its cabins, gas station, and store. It was a charming and welcome stop on the old twisting two-lane highway over the pass between Bozeman and Livingston. Today the I-90 freeway has replaced the old highway, and the Midway Camp is just a memory. (Courtesy of Ken Hamlin.)

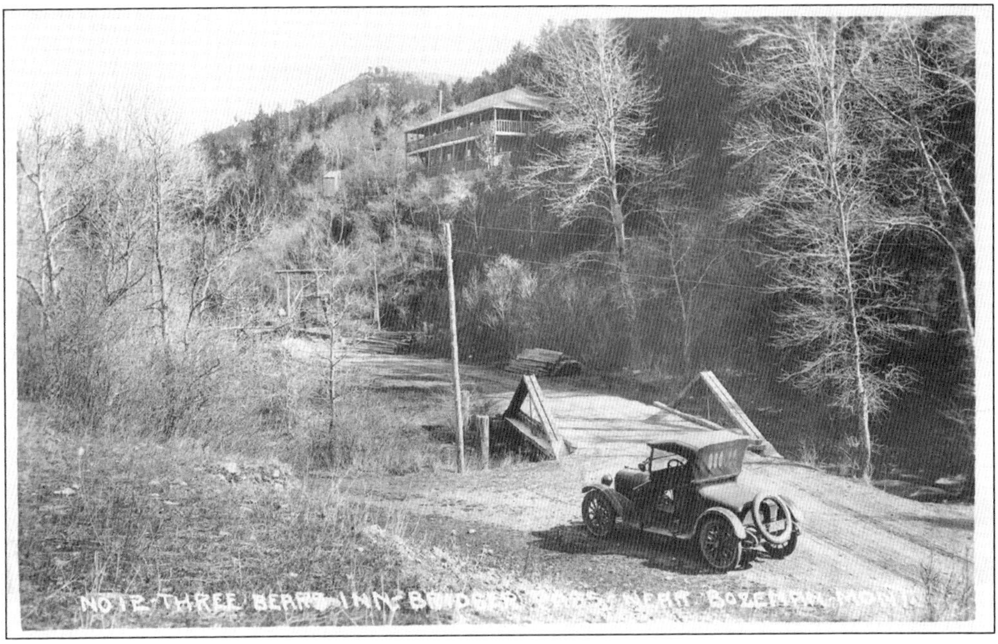

Three Bears Inn on Bridger Pass. Thomas Quaw, the founder of the town of Belgrade, built this fancy summer home in 1905. He named the home the Three Bears after his three daughters. It stood near the entrance to Bridger Canyon and was supported by stilt beams. The home was later converted into an inn by Eugene Quaw, Thomas's son. The structure, which is visible at upper center in this *c.* 1920 real-photo view, burned in 1932. (Photograph by Wesley Andrews, Baker, Oregon.)

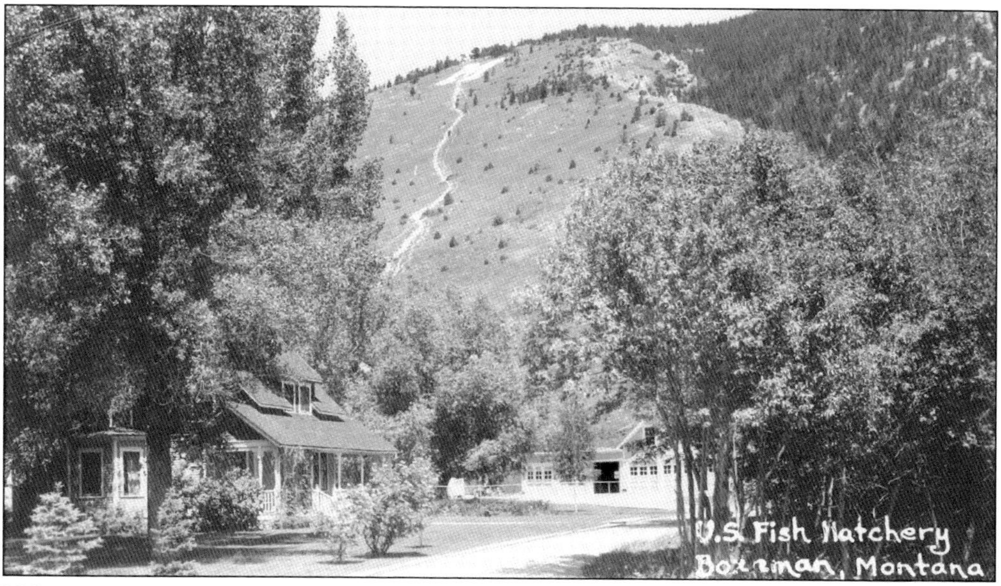

U.S. FISH HATCHERY, NORTHEAST OF BOZEMAN. This *c.* 1945 real-photo postcard shows two of the buildings at the hatchery, located about 4 miles northeast of Bozeman near the entrance to Bridger Canyon. Founded in 1897, the hatchery was used to raise and stock trout and grayling in waters in Montana and surrounding states. Today it is known as the Bozeman Fish Technology Center and has new roles, including fish-diet testing, study of fish diseases, and water-quality improvement.

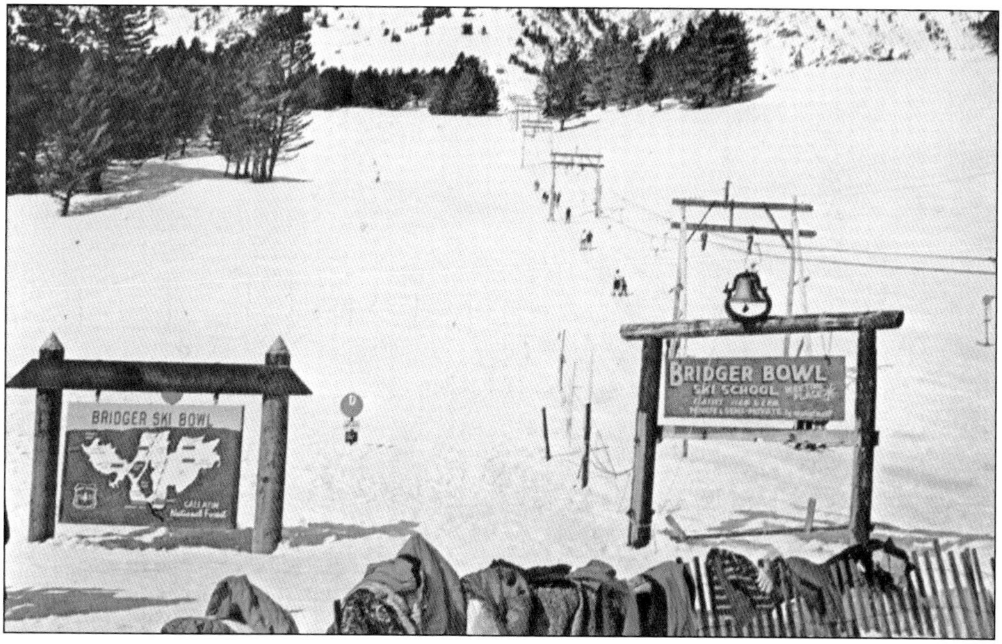

BRIDGER BOWL SKI AREA. This *c.* 1957 chrome postcard view provides a look at the recently opened Bridger Canyon Snow Bowl, as it was called back then. Skiers are shown climbing up the slope using a rope tow. The first chair lift began operation in 1964. A sign at right advertises the Bridger Bowl Ski School. Located about 16 miles northeast of Bozeman, this ski area is one of the few private, nonprofit ski areas in the United States.

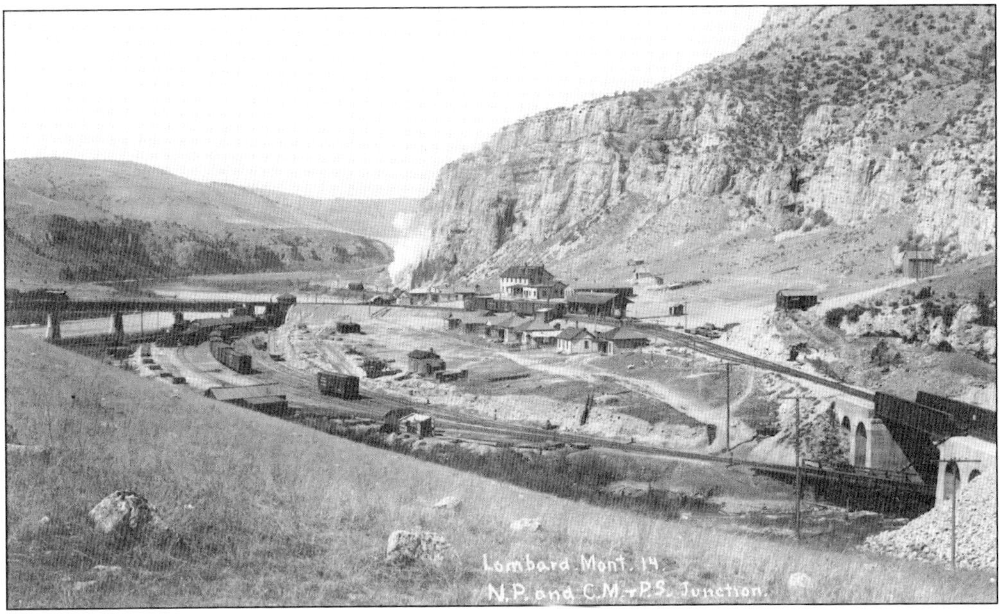

Lombard. In 1909, the Milwaukee Road purchased the Montana Railroad. This railroad was constructed to connect the silver mines of Castle (in Meagher County to the north) with the smelters of Butte via Three Forks. The station at Lombard, located near the northwest tip of Gallatin County, was an important link. Lombard, shown in this *c.* 1914 real-photo view, was a junction for both the Milwaukee Road and the Northern Pacific Railroad.

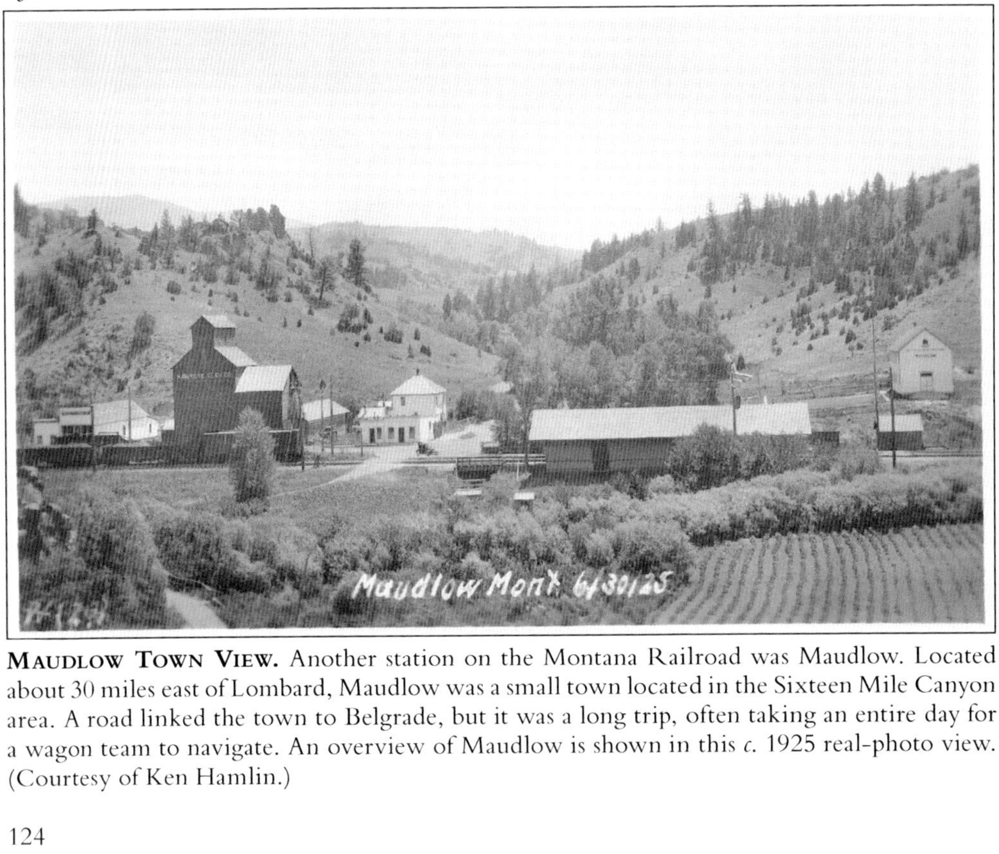

Maudlow Town View. Another station on the Montana Railroad was Maudlow. Located about 30 miles east of Lombard, Maudlow was a small town located in the Sixteen Mile Canyon area. A road linked the town to Belgrade, but it was a long trip, often taking an entire day for a wagon team to navigate. An overview of Maudlow is shown in this *c.* 1925 real-photo view. (Courtesy of Ken Hamlin.)

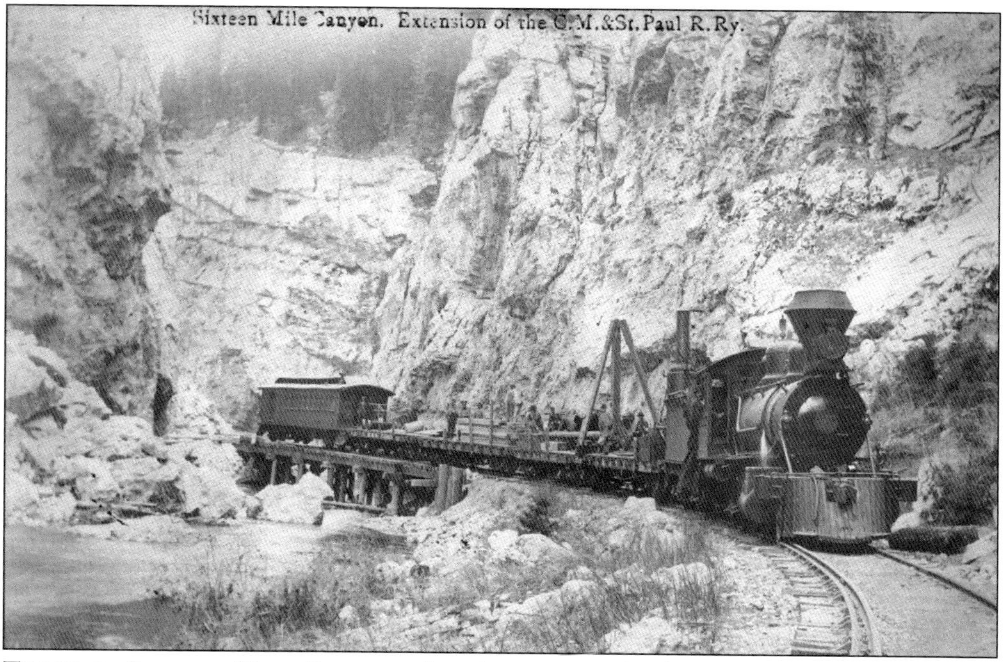

Train in Sixteen Mile Canyon. A maintenance train chugs through the Sixteen Mile Canyon near Maudlow in this real-photo postcard, postmarked 1908. The train appears to be transporting railroad ties and equipment used to repair the tracks.

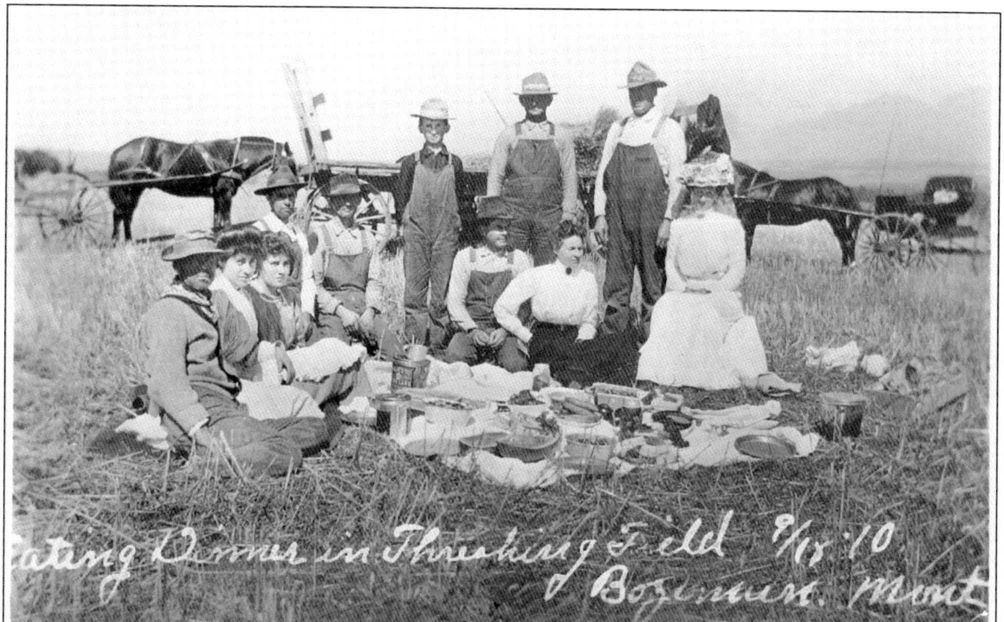

Dinner Break in the Gallatin Valley. Farmers, hired hands, and lady folk pause for a photograph before partaking of dinner in a threshing field. This scene was taken in the Gallatin Valley near Bozeman during the September harvest in 1910. A hay wagon and two horse-drawn buggies are partially visible in the background of this real-photo postcard.

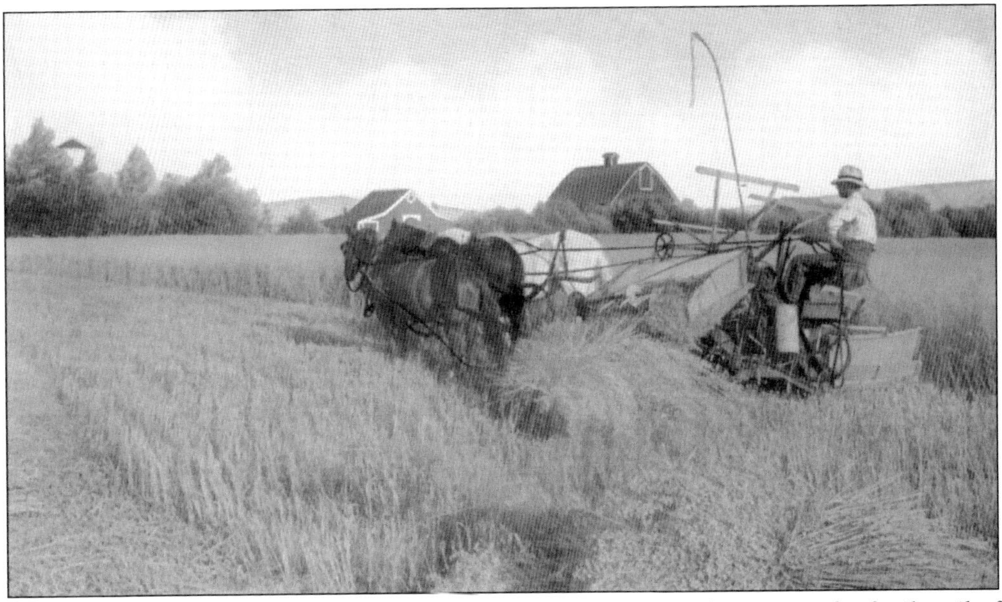

Valley Oats Win Grand Prize. This *c.* 1920 printed postcard promotes the fertile soil of the Gallatin Valley. Part of the caption reads, "The Oats from the Gallatin Valley, Montana, won Grand Prize at New York Land Show." More text is printed on the back, including "Gallatin Valley is called the 'Granary of Montana' and yields enormous crops of small grain." This card was published by the CMStP&P Railroad to entice potential homesteaders to travel by rail to the Gallatin Valley.

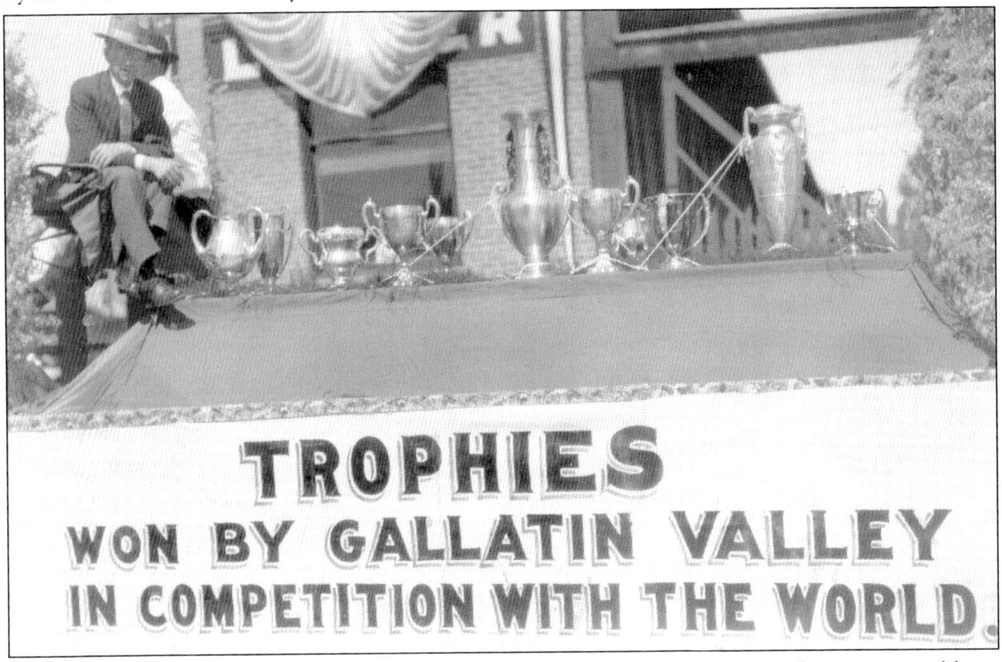

Best Crops in the World! This *c.* 1910 real-photo postcard shows a float, presumably at the Bozeman Sweet Pea Carnival parade. Displayed are trophies awarded to the Gallatin Valley for superior crops and grains in open competition with all-comers from everywhere. (Courtesy of the Pioneer Museum, Bozeman.)

Bibliography

Bates, Grace. *Gallatin County Places and Things Present and Past.* Manhattan, MT: self-published, 1994.

Burlingame, Merrill G. *Gallatin County's Heritage—A Report of Progress 1805–1976.* Bozeman, MT: Gallatin County Bicentennial Publication, 1976.

Jenks, Jim. *A Guide to Historic Bozeman.* Helena, MT: Montana Historical Society Press, 2007.

Iverson, Ron. *The Princess of the Prairie.* Bozeman, MT: Montana State University, McGill Museum, 1965.

Malloy, Denise Glaser, and the Pioneer Museum of Bozeman. *Bozeman.* Charleston, SC: Arcadia Publishing, 2008.

Robinson, Jeff, Nick Ehli, and the *Bozeman Daily Chronicle.* "The Gallatin Collection, Vol. 1." Bozeman, MT: *Bozeman Daily Chronicle*, 2001.

Smith, Phyllis. *Bozeman and the Gallatin Valley a History.* Helena, MT: Twodot, Globe Pequot Press, 1996.